Letters from A Wondrous Empire

MW00659231

Letters from A Wondrous Empire
An Epistolary Memoir

A Peace Corps Writers Book - an imprint of Peace Corps Worldwide

Copyright © 2021 by Cynthia Nelson Mosca
All rights reserved

Printed in the United States of America
By Peace Corps Writers of Oakland, California.

No part of this book may be used or reproduced in any manner
Whatsoever without written permission except in the case of
Brief quotations contained in critical articles or reviews.

For more information, contact peacecorpsworldwide@gmail.com.

Peace Corps Writers and the Peace Corps Writers colophon
are trademarks of PeaceCorpsWorldwide.org.

Book design and cover creation by Dania Zafar.

ISBN-13: 978-1-950444-34-2
Library of Congress Control Number: 2021913514

First Peace Corps Writers Edition, July 2021

Letters from A Wondrous Empire

AN EPISTOLARY MEMOIR

CYNTHIA NELSON MOSCA

A PEACE CORPS WRITERS BOOK

In memory of my grandmother, Clara Nagel Linton, "Ma," who started my travels into the world, and for Dennis Schulz, who has shared so many of my journeys.

CONTENTS

WOLDIA: 1967-1969

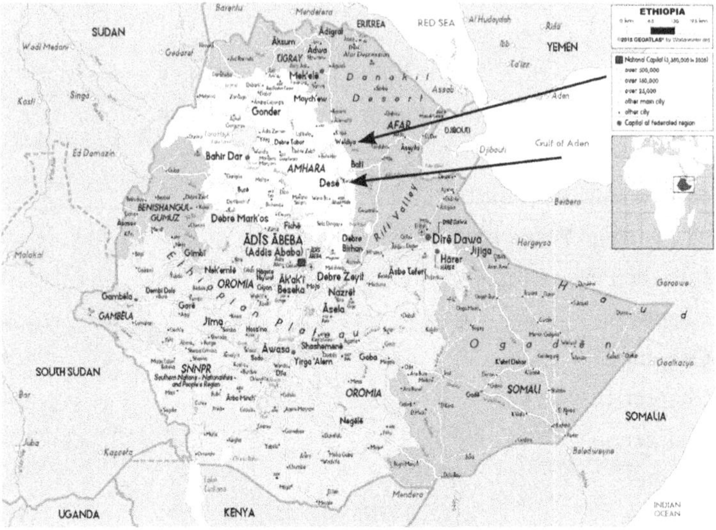

September, 1968: From Ethiopia to Kenya to Uganda to Kenya to Tanzania to Kenya and back to Ethiopia

LETTERS FROM A WONDROUS EMPIRE: AN INTRODUCTION

SOME OF THIS STORY MAY SEEM TO BE A SAD AND BRUTAL TALE, BUT IT was this adventure that shaped who I have become. The years have softened it all.

After some of the letters, I added a 76-year-old woman's hindsight or observation.

The letters to Barb are from the young woman, Cindy, at 23 and 24 years of age.

Camelot references are to the idealism of the sixties and the presidency of John F. Kennedy who established the Peace Corps in 1961.

Girl at an Open Half-Door, 1645 by Rembrandt van Rijn

Letters from a Wondrous Empire: An Introduction

The painting, *Girl at an Open Half-Door,* is on the teal wall in my living room. It is a tiny (4 inches x 4 ½ inches), sturdy reproduction of Rembrandt's painting. It has traveled everywhere with me for what seems like forever. This "girl at the open half-door" has looked away from me for more than fifty years. I know that one day she will glance up at me, smile, and say (I hope in English and not Dutch), "Out with it. Tell what really happened."

Rembrandt was a master at painting light and also using it in his etchings. In both mediums, light and shadow are apparent. It is because of his use of shadow that we see the light. Examine his paintings and you will see how the light emerges from the dark.

The light in this painting, *Girl at an Open Half-Door,* was an epiphany moment for me. I was twenty years old and had never seen a painting done by a master, and this was the master of light — Rembrandt Van Rijn. I paid a price for this tiny reproduction, but as you will come to know, she has helped me to not only see the light but to find the light and to be grateful for it.

Before my mother and aunt died, they gave me all of the letters that I had sent to them while I was in the Peace Corps in Ethiopia. These letters are now loosely filed in a purple plastic expandable file in my studio. I carried the letters with me for years. At one point, I sorted them chronologically. Yet, I never sat down and read them. Then came Covid-19. Dennis, my significant other, and I returned from Portugal on March 15, 2020 to self-quarantine. Like so many others, we began to sort, organize, and purge unnecessary items from our home. At last, I began to read what my family had saved for me so many years ago. The painting and my letters form the basis of my story.

I have often heard people say that they have few regrets and that even if they could change something about their lives, they wouldn't change a thing. I have never felt that way. I would change quite a bit:

I would be freer, more honest, and live more openly and without secrets. I come by secrets naturally through my mother, but that's another story. However, when asked to speak about my experiences in Ethiopia, I have always said it was transformative. It was. Now, many years later and using these letters, I begin a new journey of finding the truth of this experience, of shining a light on it.

PROLOGUE

At 75, I sit on the deck, sun warming my back, surrounded by flowers, shaded by the small grove of trees, and reminiscing about how I came to be here, in this place, at this moment. When asked (without much prompting), I've always said that Ethiopia changed my life.

My grandmother, Ma, proved to be the impetus for much of what I've done because it was she who wouldn't give me up. I was born in 1944 in the Home for Infants and Mothers in Green Bay, Wisconsin. My mother was there to give birth and then put me up for adoption. When Ma found out, she collected money from her adult children to buy a bus ticket for herself and her youngest child, Barb. They got on the bus and went to Green Bay. She told my mother not to come home without her grandchild. The trip from Green Bay to Shell Lake, Wisconsin was my first adventure.

I remember Ma was sitting at the kitchen table when she called me over to fan her. I picked up a newspaper and began to fan Ma. Her color was gray. I was frightened by the ashy hue of Ma's face and called out for my mother. Hazel put her arm around Ma and brought her into the next room where there was a daybed. She helped her to lay down and then started calling doctors. None could be reached. No one was home. It was a Sunday. Aunts, uncles, and children who had come for Sunday dinner crowded the room. The adults forgot about any little ones in the room. Ma closed her eyes. Finally, one of the doctors came, but Ma had died. At five years of age, I had watched it all. This picture never left me. Nor did my version of Ma. I have carried her with me everywhere, this woman who forbade my mother to give me away, who couldn't stand to see me disciplined even when I deserved it, for years she visited my dreams.

My life has been an ordinary one, a pinprick in the universe. I was born, grew up, and ended up in the Midwest. How much more run-of-the-mill could one be? And in this tiny life, I have been so fortunate. There has been sadness, of course, but also so much happiness. I entered the wondrous empire of Ethiopia in a perplexed state. I left Ethiopia, not with all of my problems solved, but knowing I had had the adventure of my life. I had no idea then that the joy I found there would stay with me my entire life.

The journey with its twists and turns to 75 began when I was young in the kitchen of an old shingled house in Shell Lake, Wisconsin. I wanted to see the world. The voyage began with books. "Where is she?" someone would ask.

My mother's response was always the same, "Somewhere with her nose in a book."

My first answer to the question, "What do you want to be when you grow up?" was a stewardess (this was before the invention of the non-gender flight attendant label). Later, I wanted to join the Navy and see the world. At the end of 8th grade, my parents sat me down and told me that when I graduated from high school I could no longer live at home. I had to figure out what I was going to do. I could not stay in Shell Lake. There was no future for me there.

I thought about that. Consequently, as a freshman in high school, without any resources, I selected the courses in the college track. I loved drawing and painting, and I spent almost as much time doing that as I did reading. I decided to become an art teacher. My parents didn't say "no," though they didn't have the money to put me through, even a state school. They were of a generation when my working mother should have been at home tending to her four stepping-stone daughters. Instead, my mother told me if my grades were good enough to get me admitted to college, she would go with me to the bank and help me get a loan. At fourteen, my path into the much larger world began.

That road from a small town to this garden was circuitous and meandering. It didn't go through the magic forest; it was sometimes dark. There were adventures and misadventures. Some escapades happened from choices, good and bad, some burst upon me. When I had a choice, I rarely used my head and said "no." It was either a tepid "okay" or a running jump into the water over my head. My motto seems to be, "Well, I haven't tried that yet."

My mother's concern was always, "what will the neighbors think?" She would hate this story. She would never have given me the letters that I wrote to her and Aunt Barb if she thought that I might put pen to paper and write it all down one day. For years these letters lay in the dark. I began chronicling them so that I might remember those long-ago years and reflect on them. One wouldn't think it would take fifty years to reflect, but apparently, it has.

The big adventure began in 1967. The question now is what did I learn in the Peace Corps? The first thing I learned was how to swear in both English and Amharic. The second thing was how to light a Coleman lantern. The third lesson was that the accident of where you're born has overwhelming effects. Many of us ought to be very humble about our achievements. They often have more to do with birthplace than cleverness. The most important lesson has been to take the time to stay in touch with people, to value each person who comes along. Letting go is easy. Staying connected takes work.

We saw Woldia as Camelot. How was this so? Ethiopia has

suffered revolution, famine, a dictator, diversity that is boiling over to be free of those who are different, and a fair amount of corruption. And now, with Prime Minister Abiy Ahmed aligned with Isaias Afwerki, the future looks uncertain. So, how could this have been Camelot? For me, at least, it was because of the kind and generous people I met there and worked with and got to know. It was the dedication and determination of the students; it was the hope I saw in so many that they could make a positive contribution.

Isn't that Camelot – a brief moment when there is harmony in a world full of sadness?

My first trip traveling from Green Bay, Wisconsin to Shell Lake set the stage for many trips in my life, somewhat chaotic and a bit stressful, but always an adventure.

Adventure filled my life in Shell Lake — fishing for catfish in the lake, cooking the fish over a fire in my friend Ruth Ann's backyard, exploring an old house that was down in the hollow which my mother had specifically forbidden, riding bikes out into the countryside to steal apples hanging over fences. Summer was the time for the lake, bare feet, and bikes. It was a time when your mother sent you to the lake with a bar of soap. In Winter, Dad plowed a circle on the frozen lake, and we had a skating rink. It was a time of light and innocence.

When I was in seventh grade, an older boy Howard liked me. Whenever he would come near me, he would start to sing, "I wish I was an apple, a hanging on a tree, and every time my Cindy came, she'd take a bite of me." I was delighted and totally mortified.

Every afternoon the big yellow buses lined up in front of the school to collect the kids and take them back to their farms or trailer homes. One golden autumn day, Mark, Howard's younger brother, leaned out of the bus window, yelled at me, and gave me the finger. The kids on the bus howled with laughter. I kept on walking.

That night at supper, I stuck up my index finger and asked my mom and dad what that meant. They were flabbergasted. Both of them talking at once— "where did you see that? Who did that? don't ever ever do that. It's disgusting!"

"Why?" I wanted to know. "What does it mean?"

"Never mind," my mother said, "just know that it is not something you should ever do!"

The next day walking home from school with a worldlier friend, I told her what happened at the supper table. She laughed and said, "Oh, that means, fuck you!"

I gave a little chuckle to indicate understanding and walked on thinking, "And what does that mean?"

SENIOR YEAR: MAY, 1962

In high school, until he started to drive, Dale rode the bus to school every day, and I walked the block from my house to the school. We became friends when he began dating one of my good friends, Patty. I loved talking to him about what he wanted out of life, would he take over his father's farm, where did he see himself after graduation?

One day, the faculty had arranged three rows of chairs in a semicircle on the high school gym floor. In the center sat a blue-jeaned young man in his early twenties. He nervously looked down at his notes and then up at the small audience. The forty-two juniors sat mumbling to each other, waiting for Mr. Rundle, the principal, to introduce the speaker. We were ready to listen to anyone who got us out of class.

The young man began to talk. He explained the goals of the Peace Corps:

1. To help the people of interested countries in meeting their needs for trained men and women.
2. To help promote a better understanding of Americans on the part of the peoples served.
3. To help promote a better understanding of other peoples on the part of Americans.

Two of the teenagers in the audience were profoundly affected by what this young man had to say. He never knew what an impact he had on our lives.

Dale was one of these kids. I was the other.

THE COLLEGE YEARS: 1962-1966

DALE GREW UP WORKING ON HIS DAD'S FARM AND THEN HAD A YEAR or two of coursework at Kendall College in Chicago. He left one of the smallest towns in America to attend school in the third-largest city in the USA. Kendall was a small private junior college started by two Methodists. Like many of our classmates, he had a strong religious foundation. He thought this would be an excellent place to begin venturing out. And venture out, he did. In 1964 he was the first of us to join the Peace Corps. Leaving Wisconsin behind, he flew over 6,000 miles to Okitipupa, Nigeria. He completed his two years working with farmers in the countryside.

June 6, 1965
Ministry of Agriculture
Okitipupa, Nigeria

Dear Cindy,

It's a lazy Sunday afternoon, and I have found myself with nothing to do, so I thought I would drop you a line or two. Okitipupa is the TV type of Africa. It's hot and humid. It is impossible to go through the jungle unless you cut your way through. The Nigerians travel on the river with dugout canoes, fish with spears, wear little clothing, if any, and fear the Gods. It is the type of place I expected to find when I came over here. There are two clubs 3 miles down the river. We spend time there too, always interesting.

Did I tell you about the trip to East Africa? I guess not. Seventy-five of us are taking a chartered flight to East Africa in August. We will spend three weeks over there visiting Kenya, Uganda, and Ethiopia. I'm really looking forward to it.

As of this month, I have one year left in the P.C., unless I extend a year. Ha. Ha. I can't remember when I last wrote to you, so if I have repeated myself, please overlook it.

How is school coming along? I would guess that it will soon be over for the year. God, how the time sometimes flies. The days can get very slow over here, but still, the time is going fast. As long as I'm busy, time goes alright, but it's when things slowdown that the world looks pretty bad.

I know I have written to you more times than you've written to me, but don't sweat it. I often have nothing to do, and you are busy with school and drinking beer.

Dale

PS You have helped me fill a very dull afternoon.

June 23, 1965
Ministry of Agriculture
Okitipupa, Nigeria

Dear Cindy,

It was very good to hear from you. The pictures are really great. When I saw that snow, I almost went out of my mind. I have never seen anything that looked so good. It was good to see you, Ruthann, and Mick. Believe me; the pictures made me a bit homesick. I would give anything for a week or two stateside. There are three ways I could get home: 1) Leave the Peace Corps 2) Death in family 3) Serious accident or sickness. None of them are to my liking, so I guess I will have to stick it out for another 12 months. We use months instead of years. It sounds better.

It's been raining for nine hours and looks like it isn't about to stop, so all I can do is sit around the house. I'll be damned if I'm going to get wet, the rain is like ice over here; believe it or not.

Work is going slow, but that's to be expected. Last night USIS (United States Information Services) came down and showed three movies. It was really something. There were around a thousand people who showed up. We showed it outside. We had to keep beating (literally) the kids away from the projector. For most of them, it was the first time they had seen anything like this. It was worth all the trouble I went to in making the arrangements. I'm now a big man in town. Ha. Ha.

When I get some good pictures, I'll send them to you. I've sent all of mine home but will have some more in a week or two. You gave me snow; I'll give you palm trees and jungle.

Glad to hear that you are thinking about the Peace Corps. I don't think you would ever regret it. I know I wouldn't change these two years for anything. Sometimes I wish I had finished college before joining, but I think school will have more meaning to me when I return. If nothing else, it is worth it just to see the world. If I can round up the money, I'm going to travel home by way of the East. I want to see India and Japan. It's too early to worry about my trip home. We're only young once, and I plan on seeing as much of this world as possible. Anyway, keep thinking about the Peace Corps. It's a great organization. With guys like me in it, it has to be good. Conceit, conceit.

I would like to see some of your paintings sometime. I think you have good ideas. When I was at Kendall College, we spent a semester studying art. We spent one week in the Art Institute of Chicago. Believe it or not, I found it interesting.

Say, if you see Ron, Tom, or Mick around, tell them to drop me a line. I'm tired of writing to them and getting no answer.

Thanks for the pics,
Dale

September 21, 1965
Okitipupa, Nigeria

Dear Teacher,

It must be great to be in your last year of college. The only sad part about coming home is going back to college. It's a funny thing, but this traveling gets in a person's blood; at least it has gotten to me. I don't think I will ever be able to settle down to dull everyday living in the States. This world is too big, and I have not seen enough of it. Every time I think of the U.S., I think of the song about little boxes and the people who live in them.

[Dale is referring to Pete Seeger's song, "Little Boxes"—
Little boxes on the hillside
Little boxes made of ticky tacky... And they all look just the same...
And the people in the houses all went to the university
Where they all were put in boxes...And they all look just the same...

Maybe I will change when I get back home for a year or two, but right now, I want nothing more than an education in the States and then to leave. I think everyone should get out of the States and see how others live. I realize that I have been very lucky, but there are so many ways of getting out. Enough on that; maybe I have been over here too long.

I just returned from East Africa. It was the best trip I have ever had. I did nothing but relax, eat good food, dance, and drink. I visited many of the "sites," but only when I felt like it. Swimming in the Indian Ocean, dancing in Nairobi, living in a beach house, going to game parks, etc. ... What a life. Now I'm out of money and back at work. How dull, but I'm over here to work, not run around the continent.

You said something in your last letter about a rainbow. Maybe I should not say this, but we flew over a rainbow on our way to Ethiopia. We flew over the Blue Nile Falls (Tis Abay), and the mist and the sun formed a rainbow. I'm not bragging, but I couldn't help but tell you. I think this country is the place for you. I couldn't believe how beautiful the people are and the churches are filled with artwork which I'm sure you could appreciate more than me. Think about it.

I'm still waiting for the rains to let up. My work is almost nothing as long as it rains. We should be getting a dry season along about the end of October. I sure hope so. Must get to work now—Dale

Dale wrote this letter in 1965 after he vacationed in Ethiopia. He came home before I left for the Peace Corps, and we talked. He assured me that I would love the artwork, the handsome people, the history, and the variety of architecture.

In 1965, I was finishing my junior year at the University of Wisconsin, Eau Claire. I loved art, but throughout high school and most of college, I knew about painting and sculpture only through books. I read about the light in paintings but never understood what the descriptions were all about. In my junior year of college, I visited the Art Institute of Chicago and stood in front of Rembrandt's *Girl at the Open Half-Door*. Everything I had read became instantly clear. It was magic. This was light!

In April, I bought the *National Geographic* magazine that described Ethiopia as "Haile Selassie's Wondrous Empire." Nathaniel T. Kenny ends his article with these words: "At Jimma, however, hearing that a popular coffee planter Tekka Eganno, planned a picnic, the rain gods stayed their hands, sending only a glorious double rainbow...it is still a land of mystery...Tekka says somebody must one day climb the mountain at the end of the rainbow to see what is at the top. I wonder what is up there. I said nothing, but I knew the answer. The one who climbs it will find the same prize that is hidden in every corner of this exotic empire—adventure."

With this article and Dale's letter, I was hooked.

I graduated from college in 1966 as an art major in education with a minor in political science. I taught for a year in Wisconsin to appease my mother, who didn't want me to go, especially not to Africa. She kept saying, "If you love teaching, teach here. These kids need teachers too."

INTO THE PEACE CORPS 1967

I GOT A PHONE CALL IN THE OFFICE OF LOYAL HIGH SCHOOL, WHERE I was near the end of my first year of teaching. I squealed with excitement. I was almost hysterical, the secretary thought something terrible had happened, and she burst into tears. Peace Corps had accepted me into the Training Program for Ethiopia.

In June of 1967, I flew out of the airport in Eau Claire, Wisconsin. It was my first flight. I navigated the airport in Minneapolis and ended up on the correct flight to Salt Lake City, Utah, where I was to begin training for my assignment as a Volunteer to Ethiopia. It was a long day. I was almost silent by the time I arrived at registration in the cafeteria of the University. Lynne Moore and Rick Haas, two fellow volunteers who had both registered before me, took me to the dormitory to room with Lynne. As we walked toward the dormitory, the Rocky Mountains' dark foothills hid the rolling green of campus. Later, Lynne told me she was a bit intimidated by me as I seemed so confident. I was actually in shock. My silence was not confidence but fear.

I had no way of knowing that I was about to enter a very stressful training program. Amharic is a difficult language, much more so than the French I struggled with in high school. There would be many language tests and multiple psychological tests scattered throughout the coming weeks. Staff whisked those who were deemed unfit out in the middle of the night. In the morning, you would leave the dorm, go down for breakfast, and someone would be missing. They told the roommate not to speak of it.

Though not as frequently, this continued to happen in Blanding, Utah, where we did our practice teaching in an elementary school for Navaho children in summer school. The Peace Corps housed us four to a tent on a lot across the street from the school on the Navajo reservation. The rationale was to see how well we did in another culture.

The training was unremittingly tense. It was filled with cultural and language lessons. We were also videotaped teaching a class. Once back in Salt Lake City, we were given repeated inoculations, dental checkups complete with pulled teeth, and precise instructions on what we could and could not pack into elephantine trunks. The item that caused me no end of confusion was the directive that we could not pack Kotex pads. They were too bulky and too difficult to dispose of. I had once brought home a box of Tampax from the store, and my mother told me you had to be married to use those. What?! So now I had to figure out how to use them. When I told Lynne what my mother said, she burst into laughter. A half of a box later, I figured it out.

There were brief periods of relief when we might go to an R & B (rhythm and blues) club to dance. In Salt Lake City, one of the instructors who was married to an Ethiopian had us over for an evening of conversation, injera, and wat. And one free weekend in Blanding, a group of us went to the Grand Canyon. We removed the seats of a small VW (Volkswagen) Beetle. Eight of us piled in for the three-and-a-half-hour trip south through the Navajo reservation.

In a time of sexual freedom and experimentation, I was one of the few remaining twenty-two-year-old virgins left in the wild and wonderful and puzzling sixties. Near the end of our training, I found myself across from my room, sitting on the bathroom floor, bleeding and bewildered. The man responsible was one of my instructors. What happened to me in the dormitory of the university would now be called "date rape," but at that time, we had no labels. Trainees had only a few days before we left for a short visit home and then on to Addis Ababa, Ethiopia's capital. I refused to see him and was able to avoid him most of the time. I couldn't speak. I told no one.

Nothing was going to stop me from going to Ethiopia. Did this have an impact on my life? Absolutely. However, even at twenty-two, I was extremely tenacious, much like a dog tugging on a rope. Before this experience, I knew what my values were, and it was easy to live my life by them. I looked at life as right or wrong, just or unjust. After the rape, I wasn't sure how to act, what to think, what to hold onto. But one thing I knew for sure was that if I made it through all of the training (and by the time this happened to me, I had), I knew that I would go.

I began teaching at a school in Woldia, a small town in northern Ethiopia, in late September. On my twenty-third birthday, I received a package from the instructor who had assaulted me. He sent me the reproduction of the Rembrandt painting. What on earth has possessed me to cart this painting, small though it is, around with me for all of these years? Is it the magic of Rembrandt's light shining through? Or is it my need to carry a secret outside of myself? Or perhaps when I met her, I recognized her. She looks away. She's charming. She keeps her silence. I cannot bring myself to throw her away.

Both Ma and Aunt Barb were Catholic. While in college, I converted to Catholicism. When the rape occurred, it left me feeling very confused. I believed that sex was not to take place until I married. Where did that leave me? Was I now free to do as I pleased? The experience had been so traumatic and painful emotionally and physically that I was left unanchored. Afterward, I didn't understand the attraction of sex and, for some time, found it unappealing. My religious background first as a Methodist and then Catholic only served to emphasize the trauma. At a time when rock and roll, getting high, and having sex symbolized high spirits, good will, and free love, I found no joy in the experience. Nevertheless, not even date rape by an instructor could change my mind about going to Ethiopia. I didn't know what was ahead, but I buried my fears and continued forward.

What follows are the letters I sent home to Aunt Barb, my mother, and my sisters. I've incorporated all the letters I wrote into the ones I sent to Barb for narrative's sake. Barb was only eleven years older than me. She was more than an aunt; she was a lifelong friend. Following some of the letters are observations and additional comments from the older woman I have become.

CHAPTER 1

"Never forget what you have learned in the light when you are in the dark"
BRYAN DAVIS, EYE OF THE ORACLE

New York City
August, 1967

Dear Barb,

We are in New York for an overnight before leaving for Ethiopia. We will spend the day here and fly out tomorrow night. Here's what's happening:

1. Our hotel room is filled with six of us. A porter put all of our luggage in the room. All of a sudden, everyone was busy unpacking what they needed for tonight and tomorrow. He put his hand out. I gave him what I had. He exploded. I yelled for the others to come up with more. He took it and left in a huff.
2. The next morning, Lynne and I went to the Guggenheim Museum. Again, I was treated to New York hospitality. The doorman yelled at me to go in or get out. I was blocking the entrance even though there wasn't another soul in sight. My San Francisco not-to-be-bullied friend told him off, "There are some people in this world who need to be thought of as a pimple on an alligator's ass. You're one of them!" Doesn't that just say it all? We went into the museum giggling as he stood with his mouth open.

Lynne can be tough, but she is also so funny. She has a foul mouth, but she looks innocent when these words come spewing out from between her smiling lips, and her eyes start to twinkle. She starts to laugh and punches me in the arm, "Huh, huh?" she says.

Growing up in San Francisco, she comes from a much different background. Her mom and dad divorced, and her mom remarried Elmer. She also has a brother, Denny. She talks a lot about her grandmother, Babbi, who grew up on one of the Farallon Islands, where her father was a lighthouse keeper. Lynne is very proud of being a 4th generation San Franciscan.

After the Guggenheim, we met our friend Carole (she was our neighbor in the dorm), her mother, and aunt for lunch at Tavern on the Green in Central Park. They had already ordered. Their food was being delivered as we arrived. Carole had ordered steak tartare. She made a scene—it was raw. The waiter (surely a native New Yorker) was not about to return it to the kitchen. I offered to take it, though never in my life had I eaten raw meat.

"It's fine; I'm sure it's good."

Ethiopia will be a relief. We leave late this afternoon.

Xoxo, Cindy

I knew that raw meat was a delicacy in Ethiopia. The Peace Corps had warned us not to eat it, but how can you refuse hospitality? Truthfully, I don't remember if it was good or not. Now, I can respond to rudeness if I need to, and sometimes I do even when I should not.

As a young woman, after the rigorous training program, the date rape, the anxiety about going to a country so different from my own, I was incapable of speech. The incident with the porter was as unexpected as the incident with the instructor. The doorman was the icing on the cake. I was so grateful for Lynne's intervention.

As soon as I knew we would be in New York overnight, I knew I wanted to see the Guggenheim. When I explained that to Lynne, she said she would find a way for us to see it. In college, I had studied Wright, his philosophy, and many of his buildings. One of his principles was that a building should fit in with its environment. It should be humane, functional, and have a relationship with its surroundings. The Guggenheim is so different from everything around it; it's a huge surprise. It's almost as much of a surprise as the La Sagrada Familia by Gaudi in Barcelona, Spain. Almost as much of a surprise as the many rude New Yorkers we encountered.

I just knew I had had enough of New York. I swore then I would never go back. I was in my fifties before I returned.

August, 1967
Addis Ababa

Dear Barb,

We've arrived in Addis Ababa. We got here at about 6:30 in the evening a few days ago. The Ethiopia Peace Corps met us at the airport with a bus and brought us into the city. We arrived at the D'Afrique Hotel very late. We are staying at a number of hotels just as we did in New York, so there were several stops along the way before we got to ours. The bus stopped at each hotel to let out the volunteers who were going to be staying there and to collect the luggage that was pulled from under the bus and put on the sidewalk.

It was getting dark as we stopped at one more hotel. Susan stepped down from the bus to point out her suitcases. Out of the dusk came a taxicab. It jumped the curb, plowing into her and the pile of luggage. It was a mess. We were ordered to stay seated. There was a Peace Corps doctor with us who immediately went out to help. An ambulance was called. It arrived quickly but without a stretcher. It went back to retrieve one, and, in the meantime, the doctor continued to administer first aid. Susan's husband and the doctor both traveled with her in the ambulance. It wasn't until the next day that we learned what had happened.

Susan died. In the time it took the ambulance to go back and return, she drowned from fluid in her lungs. Everyone is in shock. She and her husband came right from their honeymoon to Salt Lake City for training. He had lots of trouble learning Amharic, but Susan was determined that they would get to Ethiopia. She found an instructor who was willing to tutor him, and they were both able to pass the language tests. We were told he and the doctor left yesterday to fly home with her body. How awful is that?

We have orientation classes, but tomorrow we have the day off to see Addis Ababa and to do some shopping for things we will be taking to our town. Lynne and I will be in Woldia, which is a small town about 300 miles north of here. It has a secondary school with grades 7 - 12. We met the married couple who are there now, Don and Jackie Schlenger. He is a tall red-haired guy with a great smile. She is pretty, elegant, and very assured. We're having dinner with them tomorrow night. I'm a little nervous.

Everything has been thrown at us — Ethiopian money (birr), a checking account, health regulations, maps, schedules; it's a whirlwind. I am having trouble getting used to the smells; it's a mixture of urine, eucalyptus, odors from cooking, and something that smells like sewer. Addis has many beautiful buildings but not much in the way of sanitation. People go to the bathroom wherever they happen to be standing. There is a remarkable black statue of a lion with a gorgeous stylized mane, the Lion of Judah. It happens to be a favorite urinal, and it just reeks. I'm also having trouble getting used to the lepers begging in the streets with their stumps wrapped up in rags. I don't know if I should look away, but I do. If I look into their eyes, what will I see? I'm afraid to touch them. How do you give a coin without contact? Some hold a cup if they have a hand or part of one, some have a can on the ground, but what of those who don't? I am ashamed of myself.

We stepped around the lepers to enter the building where a reception was being given for us, complete with fancy Italian cookies and entertainment. The volunteer from our town, Don Schlenger, played guitar and sang a song he had written (I think), "Almaz mini die no." The experienced volunteers loved it and couldn't stop laughing. We didn't get it. Soon we were back outside to face the city. I am excited and disheartened at the same time. I will be glad to start working. I think we leave next Wednesday. Lynne and I will share a house.

They gave us a list of things we need to buy, including toilet paper, sheets, and a pressure cooker, which I remember Ma using. A friend of Carole's took us for lunch in the Mercado and then helped us shop. What an experience! First, the lunch, which he loved but which the three of us couldn't quite get the hang of. The injera (a very large pancake cooked only on one side) was so sour that it was like eating solidified sour cream. You're supposed to take a piece of the injera, which is made of tef, a grain unique to Ethiopia, and use that as a spoon to scoop up the food you want to eat. In this case, we had doro wat (a spicy chicken stew). Lynne, Carole, and I all reused our pieces of injera because it was so sour. Her friend told us this was rude. Then the shopping — bargaining for a pressure cooker; just tell me the price!

I promise the letters will get better. I think I am having a bit of culture shock, at least that's what they told us to be aware of in training,

More to come.

Xoxo, Cindy

Chapter 1

I remember the Hotel D'Afrique as being very modern. Lynne and I shared a room. Entering the room that night, we were unusually quiet. The hotel, with its new architecture, white and gold rooms, and brand-new furniture, contrasted sharply to the smell of sewer coming from our bathroom.

The next morning, we showered, dressed, and headed silently down to the dining room. A handsome waiter in a white jacket, black pants, and tie greeted us and took us to a table. When the order came, I looked down at the bright orange yolk swimming in the undercooked white and found I couldn't take a bite. I picked up a piece of toast and stabbed it into the egg, pretending that I was eating. The horrifying events of the previous night were beginning to take effect. When I look back, all I remember is the startling orange of that egg and the smell of sewer coming from the bathroom in our room. I have often wondered about Susan's husband and what happened to his life. I don't remember his name, but I do remember how his life was so abruptly changed.

When we ventured out of the hotel, the day was full of sunshine. It was difficult to reconcile that with the events of our first hours in Ethiopia. Our first encounter with lepers on our way to the Peace Corps reception added to the nightmare we had just entered. Every time we were on a bus and it pulled into a town, we would once again find these impoverished, disfigured men, women, and children pushing into the openings of the windows or the door as passengers got on or off begging for help. We never became used to it. Our first impressions of Ethiopia were surreal, first painted in grim dark colors and then overflowing with the harsh light of day. It was more Hieronymus Bosch than Rembrandt.

CHAPTER 2

"Like the Arthurian years at Camelot, the sixties constituted a breakthrough, a fleeting moment of glory, a time when a significant little chunk of humanity briefly realized its moral potential and flirted with its neurological destiny, a collective spiritual awakening that flared brilliantly until the barbaric and mediocre impulses of the species drew tight once more the curtains of darkness."

~ Tom Robbins, author of Jitterbug Perfume

September 23, 1967

Dear Barb,

Woldia at last!

We began our journey north to Woldia in a large Land Rover with several other volunteers who would be dropped off along the way. We were the last stop. Harry Bingham, our area rep, was with us. In late afternoon, we stopped in Dessie, the capital of our province. It is the third largest city in Ethiopia and is a journey back in time. There are horses and carts all over, but it is not for romantic rides around Central Park. The droppings from the horses add yet another smell and draw flies in the thousands. Lynne stepped down from the Land Rover and immediately the back of her stylish, cream-colored trench coat was covered in hundreds of flies! Instantly black! My own practical shit-brown coat was left alone. I was neglected, odd given the color. Though Addis Ababa had been very cold, it had neither horses nor many flies. You aren't allowed to drive once it is dark, so we spent the night in Dessie.

Chapter 2

There are three other volunteers living in Woldia. They are in their second years so will be leaving at the end of the school term this June. The married couple, Don and Jackie, live down the street. They appear to be happy with each other, and they know how things work in Woldia. Their house has larger rooms and is very nice. Andy lives behind them beside the river in a very small house, but he seems to like it. He was originally in Nigeria but was given the choice of going home or coming here when the civil war in Nigeria began. He doesn't speak Amharic and doesn't seem to care much for Ethiopia. It never meets with his approval when he compares it to Nigeria. I'm surprised Nigeria needed Peace Corps volunteers.

Lynne and I made it, and we are sharing a nice house made of chicka (straw and mud with a few surprises). It is whitewashed and looks very much like plaster. The house is situated right at the bottom of a bend on the ridge where the main road comes into town. Consequently, every time the daily bus announces its arrival with its horn, we know it. Out our back door, in our compound and below us, is Ato Fantew's house, so we don't have to worry about wild or wandering animals. He is our landlord. He is also a dresser (a nurse at Itegue Taitu Bitul Secondary School).

We have six rooms: a dining room, living room, kitchen, and three smaller rooms. We are sharing a bedroom with two twin beds (it's a little scary at night), a dressing room with our clothes, and a room where we can set up the wash tub for a bath and a large margarine can for a squat if needed during the night. The walk to the "detached" shintabet is really dark and creepy. Isn't that a great word? Shintabet, no need to translate that.

We have inherited some furniture from the last volunteers who were here, so we have a round dining room table with chairs and a cabinet for dishes. We have a wood-framed sofa with straw stuffed cushions on the seat. We have lots of book lockers gratis the Peace Corps. Each time a new volunteer is sent into a town, they receive a book locker with about a hundred paperback books. The "locker" is a thick black cardboard box with dividers for shelves like a bookcase. You can just set it up and start reading. Heaven! We bought new mattresses for the twin beds. The mattresses are stuffed with straw, so they are a bit poky.

We also inherited people. Asmama is amazing. He is a man who lives in the village and worked for the volunteers who lived here before us. He goes to the weekly market for us as we are in school. He can buy coffee, some vegetables, eggs, and spices there. He also cleans, makes sure we have water, washes our clothes, makes repairs, and goes to the shops as needed. He makes our lives much easier, and he is able to earn a living too.

The water lady is someone else we inherited. For 5¢ a jar, Dinka brings water to our house from the river in a huge pottery jug. She carries it on a sling on her back. I can't lift it off the ground even when it is empty.

Our final inheritance is Molla. He is in eleventh grade and was living here and running errands and generally helping last year. We have to continue to take lessons in Amharic, so he will be our teacher. Don and Jackie asked if he could stay for this year, and we agreed.

Last weekend, we had a surprise from USAID (US Aid for International Development). They sent us a crate of baby chicks, about fifty. They arrived with a note that said we should build a coop, buy corn to feed them, and when they became adults, we are to let them mingle with the local population of chickens. This is supposed to make the native chickens better, I think. Why would an agency send the NEW volunteers a present like this??

Can you imagine getting a crate full of baby chicks? Do you recall when Dad got us colored chicks for Easter one year? In a month we had 4 dead purple, green, blue, and pink chickees because none of us remembered to feed and water them! My mother warned us and Dad that she wasn't going to do it, and boy! She meant it. Say a prayer that with age I've become more responsible and will feed and water these little guys every day. Luckily for them, we have Asmama.

Chapter 2

We didn't know how to build a coop. It was Saturday afternoon, and Asmama had already gone home. We brought out saucers of water and sent Molla to the store to buy corn. We covered the floor of the living room with newspaper and blocked the door to the dining room by turning a chair on its side. There were several dead chicks in the crate, so we disposed of those first. Then we let the rest out so that they could stretch their little legs and eat and drink a bit. You should have seen the living room full of peeping, pooping, tiny yellow chicks. It probably wasn't the smartest idea. Here a chick, there a chick, everywhere a chick-chick. My San Francisco city friend, Lynne, had even fewer ideas than I did about how to take care of them. Ato Fantew heard about all of this from the driver who delivered them. He offered to help us build a coop. He and Molla started Sunday afternoon but couldn't get it done before dark. Peeping, scratching, pecking, and pooping continued for the rest of the weekend. It was Monday after school when we finally got them out of the living room. What a mess! Asmama earned his salary this week.

From what we've seen so far, Ethiopia is green and beautiful. Woldia lies on the edge of a high escarpment above the Great Rift Valley. We've been told that the part of the country where we live is like spring year-round. We are surrounded by mountains, which swoop down into valleys filled with the fields of small farms. The countryside is dotted with eucalyptus, cactus, poinsettias, and yellow wild flowers.

Nights are cool, and I've been wearing my long pajamas. We received a list of clothing to bring with us and the requirement for pajamas was very specific. They were to have long sleeves with snug cuffs and long pants with snug cuffs to protect the body from various kinds of insect bites. My mother could only find men's, but she bought several pairs. I split mine with Lynne because hers didn't have cuffs. We giggled over the slot for the penis. Everything is so confused right now, but we're doing fine.

So, here we are in Woldia. It is much nicer than either of the two bigger cities. I really like it here. There are flies, of course, and beggars, but it is green and has everything we need. The school has a large playing field and assembly field and a library. I can't wait to get started! As part of the faculty, the five of us volunteers will have a say in what we teach. I just can't wait to get going. We begin classes in about a week. I sure hope I can work in art.

Did I tell you how our teaching schedule works? We are given the national curriculum for whatever subjects we are assigned. I'll be teaching English, European history, African history, Ethiopian history, and geography. There is an outline and notes for each subject. The Peace Corps has given us the books for English, and we have a copy of each textbook for the other subjects. The kids don't have any textbooks. They have "blue books" in which they copy down every word the teacher says. Lynne teaches all English plus one class of 12th grade geography. I'm teaching 10th grade English and geography, plus 11th grade history and 12th grade history. It's a lot of work to get everything prepared, but it's interesting, so I like it.

Later—We've begun teaching. Our house is across the street from the school, just a short walk. Every morning walking down the dirt road that is our main street we are greeted with "Bambini, como stai?" from the little kids in the street. They are all probably around four years old, curly tuft on the top of their heads, long white shirts. They giggle and call to us as we walk toward school. During WW II there was an Italian fort on the hill above the town. The kids, obviously weren't here but grandparents apparently picked up some Italian.

Lynne will be home for lunch soon. We have two hours for lunch. In Ethiopia everything stops for two hours at noon. Also, when we don't have classes, we can come home. The schedule is much like that in college, so classes don't always meet every day. This really makes it nice. For example, this morning, I was done at 10:05 AM and don't have to back until 2:30. After the mail was delivered this morning, I had a chance to really sit down and read it.

Chapter 2

This afternoon, I have 12th grade history, which meets from 2:30 - 4:30 on Wednesday and Friday. It's good because you can accomplish a lot in two hours, but you really have to be prepared. Next year, Lynne and I want to teach the same classes, so we won't have quite so much prep work.

Our school is a secondary school. Most towns and villages have a primary school, grades 1 - 6. If they pass the national test at the end of third grade, they can go on to 4th grade. At the end of 6th grade, the students who pass can go to a secondary school (grades 7 - 12). However, secondary schools are only found in larger towns, so many students come from the surrounding villages and then need to find room and board. If they don't have relatives in the larger town, it makes it very difficult for them. Can you see why they are so serious about their studies?

At the end of every year in secondary school, they have to take a national test on each subject. Based on the results of the tests, they either continue in school or are assigned to another type of school, like vocational or health, and the rest either repeat the grade or drop out and return home. One of the things that keeps me busy is typing up what I need to teach, figuring out maps, taking notes from books, etc. By the end of two years, I should have a textbook down for each subject. So, best get at it.

Lynne and I are both well, although she has flea bites quite badly. Our single beds are topped with straw mattresses, which provide a home for various creatures but especially fleas. Our pajamas with the cuffs worked at keeping the fleas out for a while. Now, the bugs have figured out ways to get through, so I have large bites all over my feet, ankles, wrists, and hands, also some on my legs. Still, the pajamas do protect the rest of me.

We're really in the swing of teaching now. You know me—that's the greatest. I guess I just have to have something to do, even though I think of myself as lazy. My English, geography, and history classes have lots of preparation, but I like it. Not only do we have to cover certain periods of world history but also certain periods of African and Ethiopian history. This means I have to read like crazy to be able to understand what I'm teaching.

On the 3rd, 4th, and 5th of November, the faculty is going to take a mule trip to Wale Yesus, the church in the cave. I don't know too much about it but will let you know how it goes. I can't wait to see all of us on mules, especially our dignified director, Mr. Vyas.

I'd better close before I fall asleep on the table and start my hair on fire with the candle.

Love, Cindy

[*Please note: the spelling of* Woldia *fluctuates between this spelling and* Weldiya *and* Woldiya, *depending on the year, who made the map, and who was in control.*]

Looking back on this letter, I realize that it was written over time. We used Aerograms, writing on every bit of space on the paper. We bought them at the post office, and that is where Asmama or we took them to be mailed. They were prepaid mailers that folded up so that the recipient had to very careful to slice them open, not tear them open, or part of the letter would be lost. I continued writing over several days or weeks until the aerogram was full.

In these beginning weeks. I remember moments of disquiet and even homesickness. We were so busy trying to adapt to this new situation that we rarely gave in to those feelings. We were intent on keeping each other's spirits up and on doing a good job at school. Just having water to drink, food to eat, turning on a light, which meant lighting the Coleman Lantern, filled our days. We were responsible for our students, for Asmama's livelihood, and for teaching the national curriculum because the volunteers who came before us were excellent. Before this, both of us had only been responsible for ourselves, and we had had the support of family and friends, who, if nothing else, were full of advice. Now we had to figure out things with only each other as a guide.

October 10, 1967

Dear Barb,

Would you believe I'm learning to cook? Really, I am. We take turns making supper, or we do it together. Lynne is a really good cook. I've had beginner's luck so far. My crowning glory was a coffee cognac pie. We had the other volunteers over for supper, and it was a great success. Unbelievable for me!

Our small stove has three burners on top and a small oven. It is on the wall opposite our back door. The burners and oven have to be lit with a match. The metal box containing the safety matches hangs on the wall just to the right of the stove. A gas cylinder is connected to the stove. When it is nearing empty, it's time for a trip to Dessie. We keep an extra cylinder "just in case."

The kitchen also has a large metal container with a spigot for our water. Each time it gets low, we put a water purification tablet in the bottom section. After we boil the water, we pour it through the top filter. Once the water drips into the bottom and combines with the tablet, it's safe to drink.

As part of teaching, I also have a period of supervising the library. I'm doing that now. The kids in here today are a noisy bunch. So far, the students in my classes have all been very good. Many of the students are quite poor and have to ask the shopkeepers or teachers to help them. We have hired another student, Ayelu, to take care of the garden and run errands. We pay him $6.00 a month, which buys his food. We also have an 11th grade girl, Almaz, who stays with us, and we also pay for her food. In return, she does dishes at night and irons plus any other odd chores that might come up. So now we have three students. Jackie and Don have three, so that helps six. There are so many more who need extra help. We have to figure out how to help more.

I have to close the library now. I kept it open an extra half hour for the 11th graders. Now I have a faculty meeting, so I have to get over to that.

The next day—

I am once again cooking. This time it's a cake! What a cake. Lynne assured me the thing wouldn't rise. Guess what? It did, and now the insides are coming out all over the oven. It looks like a volcano. It's probably burned, too, because our oven doesn't heat evenly. I don't know how Ma ever baked a cake in a wood stove. We're going to eat it even if we have to scrape the burned part off. It is my practice for making a birthday cake for Andy and Jackie. We're having them over to celebrate their birthdays.

The ladies

Don & Jackie

Lynne

On Saturday, we were invited to the home of the Indian teachers. They share one large house. They had us for tea. The tea was quite sweet and very good. They also served a pastry that looked like potato puffs made from milk and sugar. Then they had a dish that looked and tasted like barbequed chow mein noodles. Finally, we had very crisp fried rolls, also sweet. Everything was good. It was really fun. The wives are so friendly. They told us to come over, anytime, just anytime.

The cake is out of the oven. It doesn't appear to be burned, but we'll see in an hour or so. I'm reading *The Blue Nile* by Alan Moorehead. It's a history of Ethiopia but written like a novel. I am enjoying it, though I usually don't read nonfiction.

I'm going to go frost the mess I call a cake. Andy and Lynne just got here to try a piece. It's nice to have two hours for lunch. Oh, and we're going to start Amharic lessons again. I'm off to school now. Write...

Xoxo, Cindy

As of December 2020, I am once again reading *The Blue Nile* by

Alan Moorehead. I don't remember reading it before, so it is like a brand-new read. It is a most readable book. Some author's styles and language do not hold up over time, but Moorehead is just as fascinating now as when I read it fifty years ago. I am enjoying it very much.

When I began to read these letters, I thought I would remember everything in them. That has not been the case. There are large parts of the letters that do not bring back any memories. I have had help in recalling some details from my RPCV's (Returned Peace Corps Volunteers) friends — Carl, Roger, and Susan.

I think Lynne and I were awesome for how we coped with all of the situations we encountered. What do you do with a living room full of baby chicks? I am also a bit chagrined with some of the decisions we made and how little we reflected.

We had the confidence of youth, the sense of immortality that seems to go with being young. I can only recall one time when I really thought we might be in danger, but it didn't stop me. We were in Uganda, and our encounter with death was brief, but you will need to read on to discover that incident. At that time, we were certain we had years and years — infinity ahead of us when we could make up for any wrongdoing. Now, I fully realize there are some things I can't make amends for and that my time is finite.

October 24, 1967

Dear Barb.

Here's the answer to a couple of your questions about our school. At Itegue Taitu Bitul Secondary School there are five Peace Corps teachers, four EUS (Ethiopian University Service) teachers, and two Indian teachers. The rest of the staff are Ethiopian. Our Director, Mr. Vyas, is also from India. In Ethiopia, before students graduate from the university, they are required to do a year of national service. This service could be in a community development project, or a health project, or the armed services, but many students choose to do a year as a teacher in a rural area.

Tadesse is one of the EUS teachers. He and Lynne have developed a close relationship, really more than that; she's in love. This has caused a bit of tension among our Peace Corps group.

Jackie often says that in Woldia, Peace Corps volunteers get one really good year. Their first year, the 1966-1967 school year, had been theirs. They were hoping to break the cycle and get two really good years, but apparently not with us. For the three volunteers who preceded us, their uncomfortable year was 1965-1966, and then voilà, 1966-1967 with the Schlenger's was wonderful. I think she is telling us to hang in there, next year will be better. I really don't understand this, but I haven't been around very many newly married couples before. I don't know if it would be easier to be married or more difficult. What is it like having to adjust to another person and at the same time to a new culture? What if one of you loves it, and one of you hates it? The married ones I know at home were my friends before they got married. It's too complicated for me. I just know it's uncomfortable and not easy for anyone.

Today is Andy's birthday, and tomorrow is Jackie's, so we're having them over for supper tonight. I made a chocolate cake during my lunch break (2 hours). I put the batter in two pans this time, so it didn't go all over the place. It looks pretty good. After my last period class, I'll frost it.

We have a puppy, and he's getting pretty big, so we're going to start house breaking him.

Later—

Lynne made beef stroganoff for dinner, which was delicious. Everyone was tired, so when Don and Jackie left, I thought Andy would go, too. He stayed for another hour and a half. I was ready to kill him! Both of us feel badly for him because he lives alone and doesn't seem to be friends with other volunteers who were sent here from Nigeria. He's starting to make a pest of himself. He's at our house every minute of the day, except to sleep. When we're ready to eat lunch and he's sitting here, what can you do but invite him? Cynthia, do shut up! It was better this week. He was only at our house for supper twice.

Andy seemed to love being in Nigeria. He constantly compares Ethiopia and Nigeria, and Nigeria is always better. Recently, we were walking down our main street with Andy and one of our students, Mulugeta. It was raining quite hard. We all had on our rain gear — hats, coats, boots. We used our umbrella to try to keep the rain off of bare-footed Mulugeta. Andy looked down at the boy and said, "Going barefoot in this weather sure makes it easy for you."

Mulugeta took a deep breath, looked up, and said, "Just because I don't have shoes, doesn't mean I don't feel the stones; it doesn't mean my feet never get cut, and it doesn't mean that I don't feel the cold."

Mulugeta has an eye disease that causes involuntary eye movements. One of the volunteers has a father who is an ophthalmologist (had to use the dictionary) and an eye surgeon. He's going to look at Mulugeta's medical records. We have to take him to Dessie for a couple of tests that the doctor wants him to have.

This Saturday, Lynne and I are going to Dessie. We've been invited to a Halloween party. It isn't because of our charm. There are only five single females within 400 miles: Lynne, myself, and three girls in Dessie. It should be fun even though it's a costume party. I've always hated those. I think we're just going to wear our rain gear. It's goofy enough with our high black rubber Czechoslovakian fireman's boots (a find in the mercado), big hats, and loud raincoats. Mine is transparent blue plastic with white polka dots and a white shiny vinyl hat. Lynne's hat is shiny black vinyl (looks like an LP), and her coat is clear, trimmed in more black vinyl.

We got our trunks last Saturday. Boy! That was a great day. It was so good to be able to change into something different. We've been wearing our dresses at least twice, sometimes three times, before they get washed. It's very dusty. You need clean clothes every day, or it's like wearing grease. It is really dusty and warm, not hot. I guess it seems worse than it is. Our house is down the side of the hill for the road coming in from Dessie. We don't have window panes, so with the shutters open, the dust blasts into the house whenever a bus pulls into town.

The two things I most like to do in the time I have alone are reading books and writing letters. You know, I've always loved reading. Remember the time I went by bus to visit Aunt Pat and Uncle Red? I must have been in about 7th grade. I took the bus to Minneapolis. There I had to change buses for Farmington. I found a place to sit and read for two hours. The loud speaker would announce the connecting bus, so I didn't worry. About an hour after the time for the bus to leave, I glanced up at the clock. I had been reading for three hours. I missed the bus, didn't hear the announcement. Yikes! Uncle Red wasn't too happy about having to drive into the city. I've been teased about that ever since. So, reading, I understand, but I never thought I'd want to write letters. Must be because it's so great to get them.

Neither Lynne nor I have to race to the shintabet to get out of dishes. We don't do them. Thank heaven! I hate doing dishes, and here it's a real operation. We put two large metal dish pans out on the back steps, fill them with water heated on the stove, one with soap, one without. Then, the person has to kneel down on the steps, and the dirty dishes get washed, rinsed, and dried, and put away. The water gets dumped by the side of the step. Almaz does them at night, and Asmama does them during the day. I do not miss doing dishes.

You wanted to know more about the students, so here goes. Yes, they are very different than the students in the USA. For one thing, it is a rare privilege to get an education. Many jobs require a certain number of years of school (not necessarily a diploma/degree) to get higher pay.

There is much more pressure on the students, and they work under conditions that are much worse than any faced by students at home. There is no electricity, so homework must be done by candle light or lantern. They can't afford the kind of lanterns that we use, our Coleman gives good light. They are very anxious to learn as much as possible as quickly as possible.

The biggest threat a student is faced with is being thrown out of class. This doesn't mean they are angels. They test a new teacher to see how far they can go. They want to find out how much you know and how well prepared you are to be teaching. On the whole, though, discipline issues just don't exist the way they did at home. There is no pressure to come to school; they're here because they want to be. This makes a big difference. Many of them have to make large sacrifices in order to stay in school for the entire year. Many go all day without eating, having a meal only at night in order to have enough money to stay in school for the entire year. As most of them come from the surrounding area, they have to find a place to stay as well as eat.

The food is very different than what we eat at home. The wat (stew) is very hot, and there are many different kinds. It is all eaten with injera (the sour dough pancake). You rip off a piece and pick up the wat with it. On Wednesdays and Fridays, they have only vegetable wat because these are fast days in the Coptic Church. One type of vegetable wat is spicy hot, similar to chile. The rest are just vegetables, which have been ground or mashed. They don't have the berbere (hot red pepper spice) in them. We eat this about once a week, sometimes more. The hotel serves it, so usually we go there on Friday nights.

Later, November 4, 1967

What a party. But let me start at the beginning. Besides the party, we needed to go to Dessie to cash our checks. There's no place in Woldia where you can cash a check, so you have to get enough money at the beginning of the month. Each month, someone has to go to Dessie to cash all of the checks.

On Saturday morning, we ran for the bus and started on our way. We almost missed it, so our things were misplaced, and we were rather disheveled too. The bus driver is our friend, so he found places for us to sit and got all of our junk put away. After a few miles, they started to feed us. First, we were stuffed with sugar cane. In order to eat it, you have to rip the outside off with your teeth, but it's really hard to do. The other passengers thought that was pretty funny. Then you suck on the sugar and spit out the fiber. At noon, the bus stopped for a short while. Here the driver insisted that we have a beer. Neither of us wanted a beer, but you can't refuse to drink it when it's right in front of you. I thought I was going to be sick. Then he gave us some roasted corn. They peel the husk off the corn and throw it in the fire, and when it looks like it's done, they take it out. Simple! It tasted pretty good. So, we waddled back onto the bus and took our seats. The next town we went through found us eating bananas. A boy was selling them, and the man sitting across from us bought them for us. He looked like a bandito, complete with a thinly curled moustache. Finally, we arrived in Dessie, stuffed to the roots of our hair.

In Dessie, we took a gari to Carol Sue's house. A gari is a small cart that can seat two people and the driver. It is pulled by a horse. You can take one anywhere in the city for fifteen cents. We stayed with the three female volunteers. There are also five guys stationed in Dessie.

We were soon at work making decorations for the party. We made beautiful ghosts, witches, cats, and spiders. We also made a donkey for Pin-the-tail-on-the-Donkey. Then we ate supper with the other volunteers. At nine o'clock, everyone started arriving. The five of us were outnumbered by about four to one. We were really covered with attention. For me, it seems a bit odd, as I am no femme fatale. We played games that I never thought I'd be caught dead playing, and I had fun doing it. We bobbed for apples in the bathtub. A couple of guys ended up taking a bath also. I won when we played Pin-the-tail-on-the-Donkey. We also played darts. Then Shane played his guitar and sang. He is from a town about 45 minutes away from Dessie. He has a very beautiful voice. He and Bill are having a party in three weeks and invited us down for that. Then we danced.

The National Service Teachers were there as well as the Peace Corps and a couple of contract teachers. Remember the National Service teachers are from the University and are required to teach for a year between their junior and senior years? They are really a lively bunch. They performed some Ethiopian songs and dances for us. They want to have us down for a party, too. That one better wait until December because I have four preparations, which usually have to be done on the weekends. We had a really good time.

We met volunteers from all over the area, and they weren't just American. There were a couple of volunteers from France, England, and Sweden. One of ours, yet another Carol (no 'e'), was so thin we almost didn't recognize her. She has amoebic dysentery and is going home next week. First, she'll be in Washington, DC in a hospital and then home. The party was very crowded, lots of beer, lots of folk music, lots of noise; there were prizes for the best and worst costumes, neither of which we won. Andy should have come. Later, everyone found a place on the floor to sleep. A few who wanted privacy went to the "motel." Morning was not pretty. We had a blast.

The bus ride home found us once again chewing on sugar cane. This time we convinced the driver that we would prefer Fanta (orange pop) to beer. The last leg of the trip was the worst. Probably because we had gotten so little sleep. The party lasted until three. It is so cold in Dessie I found it hard to sleep and woke up at least four times in the four hours that we had to sleep before getting on the bus.

Now we are back home, waiting for the noon bell to ring at school. I have a pile of paragraphs to correct for English. We both have monthly tests to prepare for this week.

The Ethiopian lady teacher, Weyizero Enkubaher, has invited us down to her house after supper, so we'll have to get as much done this afternoon as possible. Tuesday night, the Mission has invited us up for a Halloween party. The Indian teachers have invited us over for supper on Wednesday night for a religious feast that they are celebrating. This must be the fullest week that we've had so far.

Last night I made meatloaf, and this noon we had sandwiches. It really tasted good. We've gotten so that we make enough at night to have the next day for lunch. Tonight, Lynne is making stew. We got some vegetables in Dessie. It is very hard to get anything other than potatoes here. On Tuesday, Asmama goes to the market and buys potatoes, lemons, onions, garlic, eggs, and sometimes corn. Everyone comes to sell their products at the Tuesday market.

We can get coffee beans, tea, sugar, flour, cinnamon, cloves, flashlight batteries, and a few other small articles in the little shops here. When I say little, I mean tiny. Just inside the door is a counter which runs from one side of the store to the other. It is about four feet long. Behind the counter, sits the owner. Around and behind him, piled to the ceiling, is the merchandise. There is room for one customer, two if they're both quite small. It reminds me of Bush's in New Market, his amazing variety store, which though larger, holds the same kind of stuff, and it's just as dusty.

Time for a quick trip outside and then to bed—xoxo, Cindy

I don't remember how Tadesse and Lynne found time to be alone, but they did. I guess anything is possible when you're in love.

Tadesse was a more complicated human being than anyone I had known before. He could be arrogant and look down on other people. He made unkind and condescending comments to and about others. A couple of times, he didn't tell the truth about his responsibility in dealing with some of the students. That bothered me, though Lynne found reasons for his behavior.

His attitude and tendency not to own his behavior did not endear him to Jackie and Don, nor to the other EUS teachers. However, Tadesse's views did match those of the EUS teachers concerning the emperor, land reform, the role of the church, and foreigners. He was adamant about revolution and his intent to take part in it.

Thinking back on all of this, I know Jackie and Don really tried to build a community with us, but we weren't like the volunteers from the year before. From what we were told, those three stayed in Woldia and seldom went to Dessie. We did; we wanted the flirtations, the parties, and to see our friends and the bigger town.

Andy's contrast between Ethiopia and Nigeria taught me that when you're new to a place, and loved where you were before, don't compare them to your new acquaintances. I have carried this with me all of these years. When we moved to Bloomington twelve years ago, I often reminded myself of this — that my happiness is my responsibility.

Just a little memory about our trunks and clothes: for the most part, even with clean clothes, we only took a bath and shampooed our hair once a week in a big old mental tub in the spare room. We had an extra room because we both slept in one room and used the other bedroom for a changing room.

Now, I can't imagine starting the day without a shower. We must have had excellent deodorant. When we would get on the bus, the Ethiopian ladies around us would get up and move if they could. If they couldn't move, they would cover their noses with their shawls as our deodorant, lotion, shampoo, and soap were offensive to them. Lynne was an attraction with her light hair and blue eyes. Every once in a while, someone sitting behind us would reach over the seat to stroke her hair.

Finally, I can't believe that I loved writing letters, though, even today, I love to get an actual letter in the mail. I think that's why I subscribe to magazines. Perhaps that's why people like ordering online. Emails are fine, but a note, a letter, or a package is such an unexpected surprise; it just makes the day sweet.

We knew we would only be in Woldia for two years, so we didn't want to waste a minute. I later read a poem by an Israeli woman. I can only remember the gist of it, which was that she knew she would be going home, but those she was serving would be in that place all of their lives. I knew this, too. I wanted to make a positive difference. Now, I can only hope that I did. For me, life in Woldia meant accepting all the opportunities that came my way.

I had the attitude that wherever you are, you need to get to know the community. In college, I volunteered as a teacher in an institution for the intellectually disabled, some of whom were also physically disabled. In the small town of Loyal, where I taught in Wisconsin, I taught an eleventh-grade catechism class, an evening art class for adults, started an art club for the high school students, and organized a field trip to see the art museum and a gallery in Minneapolis for them. When the principal wanted to charge them additional money for the bus, I argued with him about the athletes who were transported to games out of town. They didn't have to pay another penny.

November 17, 1967

Dear Barb,

Last weekend, Lynne and I went to Dessie and bought some material there. We are having traditional dresses made. We are very excited and can't wait until they come. The material is very fine. It resembles cheesecloth, so the dress itself has a lining sewn into it. The hemline of the dress is embroidered with incredible designs and colors as is the edge of the shawl that you wear over the dress around your shoulders.

We also went to the Catholic Church there. We went to the Ge'ez service. Ge'ez is the language of the Coptic Church in Ethiopia, and they also offer a service in the Catholic Church. The church is run by two Franciscan priests, one Italian and one Ethiopian. There is also an order of teaching missionary nuns, but I don't know the exact order. The service was very long and exotic. The priests and the altar boys chanted back and forth with the men in the congregation for the entire service, except during the sermon, which we didn't understand.

This is the letter of churches. Our mule trip to the church of Yale Jesus was a success. The donkeys were patient and sure-footed, but six hours of sitting on a wooden saddle covered with a thin pillow has cured me of wishing for another trip very soon. We arrived at the pasture where we were to set up camp in the early afternoon. The animals camped here, too, as well as the goats and other livestock in the area. So, we were walking through, cooking in, and going to be sleeping with, guess what? Oh, yeah.

We rested for an hour and a half until the priests were ready to admit us to the cave. The cave was below us, around and down on the curve of the mountainside. A waterfall streamed down over the mouth of the cave in a narrow white band. The entrance was hidden by beautiful bright green ferns, broad leafed plants, and other shrubs. The sun shone down into the crevice in big yellow streaks. It is a wonderfully beautiful spot. The colors of yellow, green, blue, and violet were a stunning contrast to the red rock of the church. We removed our shoes, as is the custom, so that we could enter the church compound.

Once inside, we saw that the church is small, after all, it has to fit inside the cave. It was about thirty-feet square, slightly rectangular, the ends being a little less than thirty feet. At the front facing the cave entrance, there were two windows on each side of a double door. This was the longer side. On each end, there was also a door with a window on either side. The windows were formed of gray rock with very intricate Coptic designs similar to the crosses people so often wear around their necks. The walls of the church were formed from large blocks of red rock. The church is about eight-hundred years old. The priest was so dignified in his white turban, white robe, and fly whisk. A fly whisk is made of horse hair and bound into a handle, often covered with bead work. The fly whisk is usually a symbol of status and carried by priests or royalty.

We didn't enter the church, only the cave. Usually, only priests go into the church. The privilege of entering is reserved for those who are without sin. The priests began chanting at about 3 AM on Sunday morning. The congregation began arriving at about 5 AM, and the service was completed between 6 and 7 in the morning. Certainly gives you the whole rest of the day, but if this were my Sunday routine, I would no doubt spend it napping!

The Ethiopian Coptic Church is one of the oldest Christian sects in existence. The services have changed very little since its beginnings. Imagine, sleeping out in the pasture with our animals and our guides around, sounds of animals, tame and wild, the air clear and cold and the sky black. Looking up into the depths of that darkness, filled with pinpricks of the stars, I felt the curvature of the earth and the heavens. When the drums began at three in the darkness of morning, it was once again an ancient time. It was hard to relate this to the Christianity we know.

The trip back was miserable. We got up at five and began walking out at 6:00. The trail wasn't too bad, but the mules couldn't make it. After two hours, we were back in the saddle again, as it then began to be very rugged and steep. We met some wonderful people on the way. One elderly man helped all the women over a part of the trail which was very steep. Another man cut steps into the hillside for us. They were

On our way...

Wale Yesus

so wonderful. The day grew very hot, and the saddle became so much harder than the day before. I couldn't believe that a wooden saddle could actually feel as hard as a rock. I swore my behind was black and blue. This was not a trip for a tenderfoot (or a tender ass).

We will be celebrating Thanksgiving with lamb, but we will have mincemeat, pumpkin, and apple pies. Our area rep, Harry Bingham, and his family will be here. We are really looking forward to it. His wife is very nice, and his two little boys are so cute. We will also have several other people and are looking forward to cooking and having the house full of people.

In English class, we had a story about farms in America. The kids asked questions, and I told them as much as I could. I drew a picture of my stepfather, Buford's farm on the board. Then they told me about their farms. Some of the families go together to buy machinery, but most do not. One of the kids drew a picture for me. They store millet and have chickens and livestock (mostly cattle and goats). There are usually a few round buildings — a house with an outside shelf where the chickens sleep, a hut for storing the corn, and a pen for the animals. The millet is stored below the ground in a large hole, covered with boards, and then with dirt. When they need it to eat or to sell, they dig it up. I think it's a pretty good storage idea.

It started raining last night and has continued all day, so it is very cold. I have some history notes to go over, but then I want to get into bed as that is the warmest place in the house. The rain is very unusual for this time of year, and it has flattened the crops. Many people are worried that there will be another famine in the spring. I so hope not. Good night, my friend.

Xoxo, Cindy

PS: Next time you write tell me about this guy you met. Who? What does he do? Where did you meet him? All the details please.

November 27, 1967

Dear Barb,

We still have rain coming down in buckets. I have only two classes today, so when I finish typing this, I can continue using our trusty portable for typing the textbook notes. I have to use the textbooks and the National Curriculum to write the history notes. I think I told you before that the students don't have textbooks, so they take copious notes. I've finished the 11th grade European history text for this year and next year. I'm almost finished with the 12th grade text. I've just started on Ethiopian and African history. At last, the end is in sight.

Lynne brought a cassette player, tapes, and lots of batteries with her.

Our house is filled with the sounds of Joan Baez, Pete Seeger, Buffy St. Marie, and the Kingston Trio. I've never listened to so many folk singers. Lynne has a 12-string guitar with her but doesn't like to play in front of others. She is studying Spanish guitar. She asked me what I usually listen to, and I had to confess that at home we most often had Benny Goodman, Nat King Cole, Glenn Miller, Harry James, or the Ink Spots on the phonograph. She couldn't stop laughing.

I was very surprised to hear that Mom got her ears pierced. Lynne said she's way more swinging than I am.

I am amazed at how much I like it here, and I love my students. After teaching in Loyal last year, I knew that I would always be happy teaching, and even though I have little equipment, I love it! The students make up for any lack of chalk or books or other resources.

Please thank Mom's sewing club for sending the box of art supplies. I am really happy to be starting an art club. Each of the English teachers is getting the names of students who are interested. I'm hoping their results will be a bit less enthusiastic than my own. I have thirty students who signed up. We just don't have enough supplies. I was going to meet one night after school, but I decided we would meet on Saturday mornings instead. I can sleep late on Sunday.

I really appreciate being able to send the film to you for development. Did the photos of the celebration of Coronation Day turn out? Coronation Day is the national celebration of the crowning of Haile Selassie as Emperor of Ethiopia. This year, Jomo Kenyatta attended the celebration in Addis Ababa. The kids were so excited, first because there was no school and then because there were ceremonies and games. We met at the school where Mr. Vyas gave a Coronation Day speech about the emperor. Then we all walked to the square in the old part of Woldia and listened to Haile Selassie's radio speech blasted through loudspeakers. This year, he mentioned that at Haile Selassie I University there are now over 1500 students. He also stated that the number of secondary schools has increased. Finally, he talked about the National Literacy Campaign, which can be summed up as: Each one, Teach one.

Here's a photo of me that Lynne took and had developed here.

Coronation Day

After the speeches by the town tilick sews (important people), we went back to the school yard. The kids played soccer and had athletic contests. One of the contests looked like pole vaulting. The kids just flew over the top. There was also singing, which is very different from our style of song. The ululating is astonishing, very exciting.

So, I'm getting fat, huh? My clothes still fit, though snug, and you're right, I am putting on weight. I guess I thought the diarrhea was keeping me even but the dabo (hard rolls) and peanut butter every morning maybe isn't such a good idea. Other than that comment, how did you like the photos?

In answer to your vegetable question (is this connected to your fat observation?), in Woldia we can get potatoes, onions, small green peppers, and garlic all the time. We have Asmama buy our meat, eggs, and chicken in the weekly market. The chickens are alive and then Asmama kills them and cleans them for us, very fresh. We can get some meat at the butcher shop up the street, but it's better when Asmama shops because then we don't have to see it. In the butcher shop, the meat hangs in the open half door where flies visit, staying as long as they wish, snacking on the goodies and I'm sure gossiping about the weather and laying eggs. Great lunch if you're a fly. Sometimes the meat is so covered that it looks black and alive with quivering. Often, it is a mystery when it goes in the pressure cooker, but it usually comes out tender. When the meat hits the plate, the mystery is solved, and we find out if it's beef or goat.

When we go to Dessie, we stock up on carrots, beets, beans, lemons, and bananas. We can often get apples or oranges and sometimes, cabbage, cucumbers, squash, or unsalted peanuts. If you see recipes that call for mystery meat and a few veggies, send them along to me. We have a James Beard cookbook, which was part of our book locker, and it has wonderful recipes in it. Lynne is quite the cook, and she has this cookbook at home too. He has a great recipe for butterscotch pie. Hmm, that might explain a few pounds too.

On Thursday night, we've been invited to eat at the Lutheran missionary's house. The mission compound looks just like a little village in Minnesota with two story houses, running water, and electricity, but no snow. Should be interesting. I haven't figured out what I think about the mission; they have a hospital and a doctor, which is good for Woldia, but most people here have a religion. Most all of the Amhara are Coptic. There are also Muslims. In fact, most of the shopkeepers are Muslim. So why are there missionaries here? And what about us, why are we here?

Time to sit down and grade some papers, my dear aunt. Xoxo, Cindy

Since then, the only time I ever remember seeing a mass of insects covering anything like the flies covered the meat was in Mexico. Dennis and I were in Celaya visiting my daughter, Elana, at Christmas time, and we took a day trip to see the Mariposas (butterflies). As we climbed higher into the trees, Monarchs would flutter by. Finally, nearing the top of the mountainside, we found the pines quivering with what I first thought were pinecones, loading down the branches.

As we got closer, we could see these gorgeous golden butterflies with wings opening and closing covering the trees. Imagine so many butterflies that the branches were bent under their weight. Magnificent!

The question of missionaries Christian or Muslim was one that we discussed among ourselves. The need for Peace Corps Volunteers teaching in the schools was a question we attempted to answer at our completion of service conference. When the Ministry of Education was created and Haile Selassie tried to set up an educational system, decisions had to be made concerning language and printed materials. Ethiopia was receiving aid from the United States and Great Britain. Teachers from India were also hired.

He wanted to educate his people and unify the country, and he did that through language. Students came to school speaking whatever their home language was, and Amharic was introduced. In third grade, English was added to the curriculum. In grades 6-12, most classes (except Amharic and religion) were taught in English. The printed materials were in English because printing all curriculum materials in Amharic would have been exorbitantly expensive. Low-cost or free printed materials were available from Great Britain and the USA. Also, at this time, pilots and military personnel received training from both the UK and the USA. They had to be able to speak and understand English. It was thought this would prepare

Ethiopians to be able to deal with the outside world more effectively.

We didn't question this part of the equation. Our question concerned the quantity of those with degrees because we felt that if there were enough to replace us, that should occur. That was our understanding of what the Peace Corps should do. We should make ourselves unnecessary.

At this time (1967-1969), Ethiopia had enough university graduates to replace us. Most of these did not want to take jobs outside of the larger cities. The first cuts in Peace Corps Volunteers were in the areas of English and history. The country still needed math and science teachers. Finally, only those in community development were sent. After fifty years, I was heartbroken to see the deterioration of the school system in many places to overcrowded half-day sessions.

December 12, 1967

Dear Barb,

We will be teaching during our normal Christmas holidays as Christmas is celebrated in Ethiopia on January 7. I don't think I explained how the calendar works here. The Ethiopian calendar is based on the ancient Coptic calendar and is about seven years behind ours; this is because of a different calculation of the date of the annunciation of when the angel Gabriel announced to Mary that she would become the mother of Jesus. The first month of the year here is September, and there are thirteen months. Each month from September to August has thirty days. The thirteenth month, Pagumiene, has five days or six in a leap year. I get a bit confused, but it works out. Our Christmas break begins around the same time, and we will have sixteen days in Massawa and Asmara. But first, we will celebrate our Christmas and New Year here with friends and teach too.

Today, the Catholic Archbishop of Ethiopia, Asrate Mariam Yemmeru, came through Woldia. He stopped to bless us and give us holy medals. He is a very dignified and warm man. He doesn't speak any English, and our Amharic leaves something to be desired. He also tried French and Italian. Our Italian ("Bambini como stai?") and French ("la pomme de terre" and "oh-la-la") didn't seem as though they would help. Luckily for us, spoken language wasn't necessary.

On Sunday, the head of the Catholic Mission in Dessie, an Ethiopian Franciscan priest, is coming to Woldia to say mass for us. We won't have midnight mass, but we will have a Christmas mass.

I think I told you that the Baptist Missionary, Dennis Harring, has invited us for dinner on Thursday night. They live a short way from town and will come and pick us up in a REAL car. It will be the first time I've been in a car since we left New York, only Land Rovers or Jeeps. It's just as well that there are few cars because of the many fatal car accidents. Don't worry, we always take the bus (not that we have a choice). This seems to be turning out to be our week of religion. Dennis is a bit of a contrast from Archbishop Asrate Mariam Yemmeru, who was quite formal in a black hat and long black robe. Dennis is from Texas, very informal and friendly.

This weekend, we're getting a tree, making decorations, and baking cookies. The students are excited. We said they could help us with everything. Last weekend, Don was in Addis, so along with Jackie, we stayed at the guest house and with the nurses, Martha and Susan, at the mission. They have electricity and a fireplace in their home, and we were able to have a choice — a hot shower or a bath! I had a shower every day and washed my hair twice in four days. The nurses had us over for pizza. We also had a couple of bottles of Chianti, which was too much. I've never been too crazy about wine, but no one got sick, just happy. The new doctor came yesterday. He's from Wisconsin. His wife is short and cute. I haven't seen him yet. The house they built for them is really pretty. It's nicer than many homes in Shell Lake. They have everything but television.

I have to repeat the story that Martha, one of the nurses, told us. Before coming to Ethiopia, she worked in a hospital in New York. One day, a very well-dressed man came in and wanted a shot of penicillin as a precaution. He explained very quietly that he had spent the night with a prostitute. He also said that he wanted to pay right away. Thinking that he wouldn't give his real name or address, Martha gave him the shot and arranged payment for him. He left and she forgot about him.

That night, she had a date with an intern for dinner and the theater. Previous to that, they were going to stop by his parent's house to meet some other family friends for a drink. On the way, they talked about the day, and Martha told him about the man who came in for a shot. She mentioned the address he had given, which surprised her date because it was an address he knew. Hers was the biggest surprise, though, as she was soon introduced to the man she had treated in the morning. Whoa! How about that??

I'll write more after Christmas. Enjoy the holidays. Hugs to everyone.
Xoxo, Cindy

In the sixties, we thought little about language. We were living in another country and still had the arrogance to resent having to continue language classes. At that time, learning another language was not necessary to earn a college degree. Now, this seems to be changing in many states. We had such American attitudes toward language and culture, and we weren't even the worst of the foreigners. Oh-la-la, indeed!

I believe that Asrate Mariam Yemmeru was ordained in 1934. He served as Archbishop of Addis Ababa from 1961-1977. He was a priest for 56 years.

In 1985, I took a position as one of the first five ESL teachers in a district just west of Chicago. I was greeted with the attitude that I could "fix" the kids. After all, if they're in this country, shouldn't they speak English? Not be bilingual and bi-literate; just get rid of that home language and replace it with English. And the sooner, the better.

Often in traveling, I find the same attitude voiced by American expats or fellow tourists; if "these people" want to do business with Americans, they should learn to speak English. We are one of the few countries where citizens can be considered educated and only speak one language. I have also found that in many countries, Holland being one, a person with a high school diploma can speak at least three languages fluently.

In recent years, there have been many debates concerning the advantages of knowing more than one language. Both sides make claims about the methodology of studies, the number of participants, etc. To summarize an article from The Economist: slowing down the onset of dementia or getting an intellectual boost is not a reason to learn a language. The main reason for learning another language is that it allows you to talk to and know more people.

I have been a proponent of late-exit bilingual programs, or dual language programs, for many years. I don't believe we should take away a child's home language. In education, we want to provide equal opportunities for all children. Sometimes this isn't the best policy. We should be working toward equity. My favorite metaphor is this: if you have an African violet and a cactus in your home and you treat them exactly the same (equally), one will die. You must give the violet what it needs to thrive, and you must give the cactus what it needs. But when I was young and struggling to communicate in Amharic, I was relieved when I could use English.

CHAPTER 3

In the blackness of December among the darkening shadows, Camelot is morphing into Mordor.

December 28,1967

Dear Barb,

You are such a good friend. Thank you for the subscription to *Look* magazine. It came right on Christmas Day, so nice to get it. Day to day life here is just as it is all over the world, made up of routines.

Our Christmas was incredible, just so nice. The kids liked their presents very much. We gave one a zippered sweatshirt, one a pair of tennis shoes, one a blanket, and for Almaz, material for a dress. Of course, we added stocking stuffers — pens, pencils, candy, and gum. Kids at home would never be so excited over a pair of shoes.

Later the Schlengers, Andy, two volunteers from Wachale, Gary and Cliff, and us plus all the kids went "uptown" to eat doro wat (spicy chicken stew). It was a treat for the kids as they usually eat lentil wat. There was a dance troupe in town, so we also gave them money to go to that.

The Wachale volunteers had to leave in the afternoon so they could teach on Monday. That night, the five of us had dinner at Don and Jackie's complete with flaming plum pudding supplied by Andy. He also brought French cognac, which we drank as we opened our gifts. We've come to really like and appreciate Andy, and not just because of the cognac. It was a wonderful day. We now enjoy having him drop by and tell stories about his time in Nigeria. We've come to realize that he had no preparation for coming to Ethiopia. The orientation that these volunteers got was nothing like what we had in Utah. He puts in a lot of time preparing for his classes, which means a lot to me. Andy is also very welcoming. Whenever someone new comes to town, if they need a place to stay, he opens his little house to them.

The next day we taught. Lynne and I made dinner that night for Andy, Don, Jackie, and five US Army Mapping Mission guys. They were really appreciative. They seemed rather lost and didn't quite know what to do with themselves. After dinner, the faculty had been invited to a party at Andy's so all of us and the US Army went down there. It was a very pleasant Christmas, mostly because there were so many others to think about.

The Mapping Mission guys are coming back to spend New Year's Eve with us. We don't have to be at school on New Year's Day until 2:30. We're going to have dinner at Jackie and Don's and then a party. We're going to try to make potato chips and pizza for later. When Major Kingsbury (mapping mission) was here, he left us some blue cheese crackers and Planter's cocktail peanuts. We've got it made.

In the midst of Christmas, we also had the DDT workers come to our house to spray for malaria eradication. We told them we are too high to require this, but there is no point in arguing. They have a job to do, no exceptions. Everything had to come out of the house — all furnishings, dishes, clothes, everything! We didn't want to take the Christmas tree out, but they insisted. What was a dead tree doing inside a house anyway? So outside it went, and in they went to spray.

January 5, the new year of 1968

We had the party and now the Mapping Mission guys have come and gone. We'll probably see them again after vacation. We're getting ready to go to Asmara and Massawa. I'm sitting on our back steps trying to decide if I should write what's been going on. I think if I can just write this down, maybe I can figure out a way to straighten some of this out. I know you will understand and not share this with anyone else. It seems that Woldia is not, after all, a fallen piece of heaven.

Sunday, New Year's Eve, we had the party at Jackie and Don's, and on Monday we didn't have to be in school until 2:30. This party was a disaster. Lynne, Andy, and I were invited along with the Mapping Mission guys who were staying in town. Jackie and Don wanted Scotch to drink, but with so many people coming, we thought cognac and eggnog would be better as we could get more for our money. Some place along the line Scotch was purchased. The Army guys were to bring their own. This seemed rude to Lynne and I after we invited them. Andy had a friend, Ann, from Kenya turn up, and he brought her. No one told Jackie that she would be at the party. I had one drink of Scotch and then switched to beer as I didn't feel so well. Andy didn't drink any Scotch, and Lynne drank only one. Andy did it out of principle. Lynne was just having a lousy time.

Lynne left the party for an hour and a half to be with Tadesse. Lynne came back from her time with Tadesse and sat near the Christmas tree. The dog started chewing on an ornament. She picked it up and put it on the desk. Jackie asked what it was and when Lynne told her, she said, "I don't care, it's yours now."

All this stuff gets passed down from year to year. Lynne got up and went to the shintabet. In a few minutes, I went out to find her crying. We went back in, said our good nights, and left. From then until vacation, Don and Jackie weren't speaking to the three of us. Thank God for the US Army. They were great.

Finally, Jackie spoke to me. This is what bugged her.

No one drank the Scotch.

No one told Jackie that Ann, Andy's friend, was coming, and she didn't like her house being treated as a hotel. You know me, and this is something that drives me crazy about Mom. I feel this ain't the Ritz, but everyone's welcome, anytime.

And the last thing that bugged Jackie, Lynne left the party.

My dilemma is that I like all of these people. Don and Jackie have been really nice to us. How could this happen?

The only issue I've been able to think of is that this isn't 1966-1967, and we don't do everything as it was done then. We aren't the same as the three volunteers before us. Don and Jackie come from a small college that was very sorority-fraternity oriented, a bit like University of Wisconsin, Superior. You know how I feel about that. It's okay but... well. Last year one of the other PCV's, Stan, was just like that too. Every Wednesday was a sorority-fraternity social. It's not me. It's not Lynne, and it's certainly not Andy. Oh boy.

On a happy note, the Art Club is going well, and I want to get some more paint for it in Asmara. We have some wonderful paintings on our walls. The kids are so talented.

Xoxo, Cindy

The US Mapping Mission to Ethiopia was an operation of the US Army. The purpose was to create topographic maps of Ethiopia. They completed mapping the entire country by the end of the decade. The soldiers on the ground faced many dangers from the sweltering heat, disease, animals, and deadly snakes, as well as hostile and warring peoples. I tried to locate Major Kingsbury on the website http:\\ www.vetfriends.com/units2/660801/ethiopia -us-mapping-mission

I was not successful.

My first taste of Scotch was second-hand in Salt Lake in training, and it had awful memories. I was held down and kissed by an instructor who had been drinking Scotch. At this time in my life in

Woldia, I had never shared what happened in the dorm with anyone. I thought it was my fault. For years, the taste or smell of Scotch, especially on someone's breath, made me sick. Recently I've been to Edinburgh with Dennis and had a Scotch tasting. It was so much fun, but that was so much later.

At this time in my life, I would never just show up at someone's home with an extra guest. If I invited someone to the house and they had company, I would just want a tiny bit of advanced warning, but I would definitely want them to come. Absolutely. I rarely invited anyone home with me because I never knew how my mom would react to my friends. Now in our home, everyone is welcome, anytime. In fact, if I invite one person, what about this person? And then what about so and so? For me, the more, the merrier.

I joined a sorority when I was a freshman at Superior, but then I transferred colleges, and I just let it go. I just don't like excluding anyone. I find nothing wrong with the idea for others; it just wasn't me. Our oldest granddaughter, Alexa, joined a sorority at Indiana University. I think it was a very positive experience for her. She was far from her home in Florida, and I think this gave her a sense of belonging. We were thrilled that she was able to do that. My daughter once told me that my parties are crazy because I put all these people in a room who under any other circumstances would never come together, except maybe at a funeral. She asked me once if I understood that some of my friends can't stand each other.

January 22, 1968

Dear Barb,

We're back from the conference for first year volunteers and our vacation, back in the groove of teaching. It was a phenomenal vacation. I rode a camel, swam in the Red Sea, could never have imagined this.

Chapter 3

Our hotel in Massawa was built like a motel. One long row of rooms, all white with green slatted doors and shutters. The walls were about six feet high, and the ceiling was at least eight feet high above our heads, complete with a ceiling fan. There was a two-foot empty space between the walls and the ceiling. I felt like I was in a Hemingway novel. Haile Selassie's winter palace is here too. Beautiful. White-columned. Can't get too close, but it is splendid.

If the hotel was out of a novel, our vacation was right out of a movie. Before Asmara, we spent a couple of days in Massawa, a port city on the Red Sea. We were hardly there five minutes when we were invited to the Yacht Club. A YACHT Club. I've never been to a yacht club in my life. We sat there beside the pool under a canopy, having a few drinks with Abdulla Mohammed, a Muslim young man who, according to him, doesn't do much of anything but live off his wealthy parents. He was so entertaining. He also showed us a couple of really swanky yachts. One of them is just a little smaller than an aircraft carrier. It belongs to Roberto Barattolo. He is a wealthy cotton grower here. There's a picture of him on his boat in the National Geographic with the article on Ethiopia *(page 581, National Geographic, April, 1965)*. After we spent a couple of hours there, we went to another beach, took some pictures, and watched some fat Europeans waddle around in not much of anything.

That night as Lynne and I sat talking, all of a sudden, we heard, "Lynne? Cindy?" And who was in the next room but Bing from our training group and now a volunteer in Mekele. He had a student with him, and the four of us went to the Red Sea Hotel for a drink and dinner. It costs $35.00 a night to stay there. $35.00. What a place, very posh. I don't know what to compare it to at home since I've never been anywhere quite so plush. It's so beautiful, with a gorgeous pool. Patios, balconies, bars, everything.

After we ate, we were pretty well pooped out, so we decided to go to bed and get up early the next day. Our hotel was right on the sea and had a natural pool. It was right out of a Clark Gable movie (novels and movies, loved it). When I woke up, I looked at the clock, twelve-thirty. We'd slept half of the day away. I tore to the window to look out, yelling at Bing and Lynne to get up. Finally, they got through to me. I'd only been asleep for an hour and a half. The brightness was from the lights in the porch. Our door faced the long porch facing the sea. Relief. Since we were all awake, hot, and thirsty, we went to a poolside table and drank a couple of bottles of pop. After that we went back to bed and stayed asleep until morning.

The next day, we bought some fruit, cheese, crackers, and St. Georgis beer for a picnic. We hired a dhow. He rowed us out to Green Island and waited until we wanted to go back. We forgot our swimsuits, so we went into the water in our dresses. It was lovely—cool, clear, blue water. I taught Bing's student to swim. He could do a mean dog paddle by the end of the day. He was very quick to learn, and salt water makes it a little easier to stay afloat. When we got back from the island, I had a short jaunt on a camel. Can you believe it, Barb? Me on a camel? The Red Sea, the one Moses parted? WOW!

After Massawa we went to Asmara. It is a beautiful city of palm tree-lined streets, white houses, a red brick Catholic Church, lots of shops. We saw at least three movies, ate so much: pizza, chicken, salami, cheese, hamburgers, French fries. We had ice cream and milk. Delicious. And, of course, we went to some great parties. We also had American ice cream at Kagnew Station, which is a US Army Base. This is frowned on by the Peace Corps, so don't tell anyone. You wouldn't believe the base. It's really something out of what I imagine is suburbia USA.

That's the trouble, it's too much like home, and yet it isn't. I couldn't stand it here for two years if I lived like that. I can see why they get homesick and discouraged. The ones we talked too would rather be in Viet Nam. They feel like something is being accomplished there.

In Asmara, we also bought some beautiful olive wood pieces

decorated with porcupine quills that are native to this area. I also found an art store and got some paint for school. Finally, we attended the conference for first year volunteers. The first speaker (didn't write his name down) has worked for USAID in several developing countries. According to him, Ethiopia is the poorest country in the world. He believes short range goals will be achieved but that the achievement of long-term goals is impossible. He stated that even with maximum success, Ethiopia will only reach the level of present-day Malaysia by the year 2040. He was not hopeful. In addition, to that he felt the Ethiopian culture gives the country no preparation for development, but actually works against it. He stated that Europe had the Renaissance and hundreds of years of moving forward, standing still, and moving forward again before the Industrial Revolution. But Ethiopia has had nothing to prepare it for the 20th Century. He also said the only way to speed things up would be a completely totalitarian government, and that would carry a great price for the country. He believes that either way, the traditional culture will be lost. Only the showy things like dances, art, music would remain. It was depressing. I don't know what to think. There's not much we can do except go right on doing our jobs. I do love my job.

The final speaker was Ambassador William O. Hall. He came to Ethiopia in September, so we've actually been here longer than he has. His speech wasn't spectacular, but the Question and Answer session was really good. Hall was more hopeful than the USAID speaker. He led us to believe that the country is quite advanced, though still dependent on a single crop, coffee. He added that many other countries and some parts of the USA are too.

When we came back from our vacation and conference, it was a little better between the five of us. At least everyone was civil. Then came exams. They have a very complicated system here. It involves proctors, seating charts, hand checks, etc. Each exam is 2 ½ hours. None of us (the three new PCV's and national service teachers) understood what was going on except for the staff, who were here the year before.

Jackie explained what I was supposed to do. I was assigned to the library. I went there and followed the instructions I had been given.

Andy and Lynne didn't have to proctor the first morning. They, along with three of the four university students, were sitting on the school steps. Jackie came out to explain all of this to them. When Jackie is uncomfortable with something she has to tell you; she sounds a bit like a general giving marching orders. She just wants to get it over with. The first time she did it to me, I was offended. Since then, I've learned she's very organized, even a bit of a perfectionist, when she gets nervous. She's excitable. Lynne glanced up at her, got up, and left. Andy made a few of his inappropriate remarks. He can be obnoxious, but when he is, all you have to do is tell him to knock it off. Then he's fine. It seems none of us have learned to accept each other's shittier traits.

That night I got a note to go down to Jackie and Don's to see about second semester classes. After we talked about this, they wanted to talk about Tadesse. It seems he told a student that Lynne was his white mistress. The student asked Don what that meant. Also, one of the townspeople made a comment to the Schlengers about it. The image of the Peace Corps is very important to them. They wouldn't lie, so I'm sure this stuff has been said. If the gossip continues with the students, it could get very bad for Lynne in her classroom. This is one thing the Peace Corps warns about. Girls have been sent home for this if their relationships impact their assignment. Sometimes when she's around him, she acts a little giddy. I just don't know what to do about this. She already knows I'm not crazy about him because he's always putting people down and he's lied about a few things.

Exams end on Tuesday. On Wednesday I'm going to Asmara to meet Carole (the one from lunch in New York). She always has good ideas, so I'm hoping she can give me some pointers on how to handle this. On

Thursday, Lynne is going to Assab with Tadesse. I'm hoping that when I get back, everyone will be so busy with new classes, they won't be able to think of anything else.

So, Barbie, I'm back to lesson planning and organizing the Art Club.

Xoxox, Cindy

Haile Selassie's palace in Massawa was destroyed in 1990 in a direct hit during the Ethiopian-Eritrean War. I did a painting of the ruined palace in a class given by Colorado artist Joan Fullerton.

I am now one of those fat grannies on the beach. Oh, I was so judgmental. I've since realized that people should be who they are and enjoy themselves as much as possible — fat, varicose veins, scars, and all. I certainly wouldn't give up those days with my grandchildren.

I was not familiar with army bases and certainly not one in another country. I had never been to a city with suburbs. In 1970, I was living in Hoffman Estates, Illinois, a suburb of Chicago, and I kept asking, "Where's the downtown?" I couldn't get over a town without a main street or a main square; even the Post Office was in a strip mall.

I had no recollection of talking to anyone about Viet Nam. This part of the letter was astounding to me. It brought back memories, helped along with photos of Kagnew. At that time to the present, I have not been a supporter of the war. Unlike many Viet Nam veterans, Dennis (Very Significant Other) has memories of a beautiful countryside.

When we first visited Viet Nam in 2018, he was very concerned about what kind of a reception we would get. His fears quickly subsided. The people welcomed us. They explained that after thousands of years battling China and more than a hundred years of French colonial rule, the "American War" of 12 years was a blip, though, 1968 is removed in time from what happened in Hue in 1972. This reference reminds me of our 2018 visit.

As we toured the Imperial Palace in Hue, one of the Brits in the group asked our guide why it hadn't been restored. Hue is tropical, hot, humid, and damp, so everything needs paint. Puzzled, she said it has been extensively restored. Once we were back home, we watched Ken Burn's Viet Nam documentary series. I then realized exactly what she meant. The place had been almost totally destroyed, and due to the climate, it will always need paint. The country restored the buildings.

The conference in Asmara isn't even a blur. I have no memories of that conference. Therefore, I have no comment on them.

Finally, I understand the young woman, Jackie, much more now than I did then. Dennis has sometimes said to me, "You're not my boss." A friend of mine, who was also part of the ESL/bilingual staff in Illinois, once told me that I could be intimidating. I never imagined that anyone would find me harsh or bossy. I think it happens when I just want to cut to the chase, get it done, or it happens when I'm listening and don't say anything because I'm focused. It seems that puts the other person on the spot. Here was Jackie trying to get things done and giving directions to people she knew didn't want to hear from her.

February 20, 1968

Dear Barb,

Thanks for giving me some details about Bud, the guy you were seeing. I'm sorry it didn't work out, but I think graduate school is a much better idea. I really can't see you raising his six kids on a tree farm in the far north of Wisconsin. They would be so lucky to have you as their mom, but it sounds so isolated for you. All I can imagine is the winter. Brrr.

I finally talked to Lynne before she and Tadesse went to Assab. I told her about students asking about her and Tadesse and reminded her of some of the consequences. I did not mention what he had said about a mistress. At first, she was angry, but then calmed down so we could really talk. When she came back, she said she and Tadesse had talked. He explained to her that his family would never accept her and that he knew the coming year was going to be difficult. He has a strong commitment to the student union movement. She is determined to make the best of the time they have and will try to see him in Addis, but that it may not be possible. One of the demands of the students is to rid Ethiopia of foreign influence, so a Peace Corps girlfriend isn't an asset. I feel badly for her, but I am glad they were able to talk honestly.

Monday night, a couple of British volunteers are going to spend the night here. They are on their way to Lalibela on mules. It has been raining for the past two days, so with that and the wood saddles, I think the trip will be totally uncomfortable.

Tomorrow night we're having Andy and an Australian over for pizza. The Australian has infected flea bites, so we don't know how long he'll be here. He was here two weeks ago and stopped back so that he could see the doctor at the mission. Dr. Vesmek told him he needs to stay in one place until they are healed. He has a lot of swelling, and the doctor is concerned about possible disease if the swelling and redness doesn't go away.

We've started the fast for Lent now, so we can't buy meat. The fast is really hard on the kids. They can't eat until 3 PM. It's difficult for them to focus during the last two classes of the day. When they do eat, it is usually shiro wat, a kind of soup or stew of chickpeas, or it may be some kind of dish made from vegetables like lentils. They scoop it up with injera. Remember, the large sponge like pancake made from tef?

There's one restaurant that still serves meat. We're going to get an order of tibs (chunks of meat, peppers, and onion) to put on the pizza, along with cheese and sauce. Andy just came in with the beer. I wonder if I'll prefer warm beer when I get home. I kind of doubt it.

In two weeks, Andy and I are going to Dessie to cash our checks and buy groceries, especially fresh fruit and vegetables. It will give us a chance to visit with a few friends too.

In March, there's going to be a meeting of most of the volunteers between here and Addis. It will be in a small town near Dessie. Jackie and Don aren't going, but the three of us are. Four volunteers north of us are going to stay with us overnight on Friday. On Saturday, the Peace Corps has arranged for us all to go by Land Rover to the meeting. The Peace Corps is paying for our hotel on Saturday night, our meals, and furnishing our transportation there and back. We get to see our friends, and it will all be free. That's so great since we're saving for our Easter and summer vacations.

Summer projects are coming up. Lynne and I signed up to teach summer school in Addis Ababa either at the University or at one of the high schools. We can live with Carole, and the three of us will really have a good time. She lived next door to us in training. Remember the steak tartare? That's Carole. The three of us will travel together in summer too.

I love Woldia, but I would like a chance to be in another place for a bit. The first time I was in Addis, I hated it. Now, though, I'd like a chance to see another area. Transportation is much easier to find in the city.

One of the guys in our Utah group went home two weeks ago. He felt he wasn't needed here as much as he's needed at home. He wants to protest the war in Viet Nam. He's probably right, but the kids do make it worthwhile for me. I still feel I belong in a classroom. I love it; I love the determination and enthusiasm of the kids. When at home did you ever have a student worry that you were out sick and he might not get everything he needs by the end of the year? I had some kind of bug that caused vomiting and diarrhea for a few days. I went in on a couple of Saturdays, so I could cover what I missed with the classes.

We're out of Aerograms, that blue paper that forms a letter and folds up into an airmail envelope again, so that's why I have missed writing. The letters may be farther between until the post office gets more. It's just too expensive to use regular paper and envelopes.

Could you do me a favor and thank Craig, Ruby, Fred, and Viola for the cake and candy? It was delicious. We had it for lunch when the two nurses from the mission and Weyizero Enkubaher, a teacher at the school, were here. We made a casserole of cheese, tomato sauce, macaroni, and the sloppy joe mix you sent. It was so good. We also had creamed cabbage, garlic bread, and a salad of canned mixed vegetables and string beans, but again, so good. For dessert, we had Jell-O chocolate pudding that Lynne's grandmother, Babbi, sent, plus the cake, candy, coffee, and tea. We couldn't serve meat because of the fast. Very tasty.

Poinsettias grow all over the place here. As we hike through the countryside, all of a sudden there's a gorgeous splash of red. Such a welcome surprise.

Lynne's stepfather, Elmer, is coming to visit. He will probably get here in the early part of May. He's an officer in the Merchant Marines of the American President Lines, Ltd. He's been everywhere in the world. He shouldn't have any trouble being in Woldia.

We went to a funeral today (March 27). Ato Gorfu, who is an important man in town, was murdered. He was killed on Sunday and was buried on Monday. For about a week after the burial, people go to the house to mourn. The burial procession itself is rather unnerving. The priests beat drums very slowly and mournfully, and one priest blows a trumpet-like instrument. He usually only plays one note. The body is carried on a stretcher on the shoulders of four men to the burial place. The women follow behind, wailing. Many tear out their hair or shave their heads. Some even scratch their faces. When you go to pay your respects, you go into the house, sit down, and are given food and drink. The faculty all went together, for which I was glad. We took four cases of pop. We had been told to wear dark clothes, black if we had it. We sat there for about half an hour and then came back home. It was so sad. I hope we don't have to go to too many of those.

We now have two cats and two dogs. Our dogs, Duba and Juju, and our cat, Dingy, all get along. Our new cat is Maggie, even though he's a boy. He's named after Lynne's cat at home.

Our landlord's cat got sick and died, leaving behind five kittens, so we took one. Dingy's not too crazy about Maggie, but I'm sure they'll work it out.

We'll be starting Easter break on the 19th of April.

More later, xoxo, Cindy

I think when Tadesse and Lynne first started seeing each other, she hoped he might be "the one." We had seen more than one successful Ethiopian – American marriage in training and in Ethiopia. Tadesse, however, had no intention of marrying anyone at this point in his life. He was dedicated to the Ethiopian Student Movement. A white wife would be very far from his notion of ideal marital material.

I'm not sure either Lynne nor I understood this kind of dedication to a cause. Yes, we loved Joan Baez and Pete Seeger. Yes, we believed in the antiwar demonstrations, but we never thought that we would be killed for our beliefs. For Tadesse, that was a genuine possibility.

It was tough to avoid getting bitten by fleas. Snug cuffs on pajamas could only do so much. I had scars on my shins for years from flea bites.

Chapter 3

The murder of Ato Gorfu seems very far away. With the help of Berhane Mogese, I discovered that Ato Gorfu, who owned the gas station in town, was murdered by Ato Abate Hailu. Abate Hailu was living as a bandit in the countryside. He fled Woldia after allegedly being involved in the attempted Coup d'état in December 1960 against Haile Selassie. He used to come to town disguised. He killed Ato Gorfu because he suspected him of having an affair with his lover. Authorities arrested Abate Hailu and sentenced him to four years in prison. After he was released, he again went undercover to fight against Haile Selassie's regime. He was killed in action in 1973. Both men have relatives who still live in the area.

I don't remember that we were afraid after it happened. We were living in a compound in a house right behind our landlord's. We also had two dogs and though they were still puppies, they were very noisy. Our landlord, Ato Fantew, also had watchdogs. I think we were simply trusting in our belief that somehow no harm would come to us. Our protection seemed to be our youthful confidence and the watchful eye of Ato Fantew.

I cannot imagine what Weyizero Enkubaher thought of this food. It was so different from her typical fare. Anything with cream in it was made from powdered milk, so the creamed cabbage and pudding would have been less than delicious, I'm sure. By this time, we should have been used to cooking at a much higher altitude than what we were accustomed to, so perhaps the macaroni was at least edible. I cannot imagine serving this lunch to anyone I know. Poor James Beard, rolling over in his grave.

April 20, 1968

Dear Barb,

Sorry it's been so long between letters. The post office has been out of aerograms forever. Even if I had time, there's not much to write as I've been busy teaching and not much else. *Look* magazine has continued to arrive, and we all enjoy it. Once we finish, it goes into the library for the kids. Many thanks again.

I'm quite sure we'll be teaching in Addis this summer. School ends July 5th, and summer school begins on the 17th and ends on August 27th. Then we have a big break when we plan to go to Uganda, Tanzania, and Kenya. Carole will do at least part of that with us.

Our Peace Corps Rep, Harry Bingham, was here last night for supper. We kept insisting that next year we do not want a married couple, any combination of single people, but he can't make any promises. He went back this morning. He told us a little bit of news from Addis. The University students are rioting there. Everything is pretty quiet here. We have had conversations with the EUS teachers about the strikes. Lynne is quite worried about Tadesse as he has told her that he intends to take part in doing whatever he can to overthrow the monarchy. The EUS teachers seem determined to promote and support revolution. They expressed the view that anarchy would be better than the present system. Their major issues seem to be land reform and the power and wealth of the Coptic Church.

This morning, I need to correct the 12th grade exams. They take the leaving exam given by the Ministry of Education during Easter vacation. The students are free then until graduation. This week, the director told me I'll be teaching all English classes next year. We have materials for that, so it's a good assignment, though I am hoping he'll switch me to history and geography.

Later, April 27, 1968

I'm in Addis now on Easter vacation. I've seen two movies here, *The Sound of Music* and *Harper* with Paul Newman. He is so handsome.

The other night, I had dinner with Steffan and some of the other

Swedish volunteers. It was a riot, just so much fun. They have a beautiful house. They wanted to know where Dad got the middle name of Segried. According to them, it should have been Sefried for a boy. They thought maybe he was named after his mother. We listened to Swedish music, and then they decided to teach me to bowl. Bosse, Erik, Steffan, and I went bowling. How chaotic. I am not coordinated, though I did enjoy myself. After that, we went to an Ethiopian night club. Frankly, by then I was too tired to appreciate it.

On Saturday before we left for Addis, we went to the engagement party of Tesfaye, the industrial arts teacher. He is marrying a tenth-grade student. Before they marry, she will finish twelfth grade. Once they are engaged, they may choose not to marry for four or five years. They are both secure now that they are engaged. He may go to India to study for a few years next fall. The engagement means that neither can marry anyone else without being in danger of going to prison or having their families brought to court. The girls don't have too much choice in these arrangements, but the parents usually abide by their wishes. We enjoyed the party.

We were happy to be invited. So far, Tesfaye is one of our worst faux pas. We invited him to dinner one night. We don't know if it was him or us, but the date got mixed up. He showed up at our house for supper, and we weren't prepared. We were embarrassed, and we didn't want to embarrass him. We pretended it was the right night. Lynne threw something together with hamburger, rice, and celery. We have a grinder just like Ma had that fits on the edge of the counter. We push chunks of meat through it, turn the handle, and voilà, hamburger! It was as blah as it sounds. We served this to an Ethiopian man, who is used to lots of spices. After that flub, we were so happy to be invited to the engagement party.

Love, Cindy

This is what I was able to find from the time when the Ethiopian University Service teachers were challenging the government of Haile Selassie:

> "According to Swarthmore College's Peace and Conflict Studies various student unions within the University joined together to form one organization, the University Students Union of Addis Ababa (USUAA). The focus turned to overthrowing the government, not just asking for reforms. The Struggle, a politically charged student newspaper replaced a more conservative one. The movement was driven by anti-Western influences and the US military presence in Ethiopia. In March 1968 they protested against mini-skirts at a fashion show. The students saw the style as un-Ethiopian. In 1969 one of the student demands was the expulsion of the Peace Corps."

We often talked to the EUS teachers about their ideas concerning government. I was most concerned about a plan for what comes next, what they saw as an acceptable form of government. I was told repeatedly that anything would be better than what they had. I would then ask, "Anarchy?"

And they would reply, "Yes. Anything would be better."

Looking back, I would love to have a conversation with them again. Did it turn out the way you hoped? Was it worth the sacrifice? I would really want to know that all five of them made it through those terrifying events, but I am not hopeful. We understood the danger for these men in Ethiopia, but at that time, we did not realize that Viet Nam and the civil rights movement were causing college and university students in the states to boil over. We were very late in becoming aware of the deaths that were taking place among our leaders, both white and black, in African American organizations, and among student protestors.

May 10, 1968

Dear Barb,

Liberation Day was May 5th. It marks the ousting of the Italians from Ethiopia by the British. We wore our national dresses. We had to get help with the netela (shawl) from Ato Fantew's wife, Zenebech. They have to be folded and put on in a certain way.

On Saturday, May 4th, some of the students had a meeting behind the school. They decided to present a list of grievances to the director, Mr. Vyas. Most of the complaints were against two teachers, an Indian and an Ethiopian. The complaints were based on punishments given to the students. Punishment for tardiness, disrespect, etc., are often delivered at morning assembly in front of all students and staff. The student comes to the front of the assembly to Mr. Vyas. He delivers a hard smack across the palm of the student's hand with a thick paddle. A National Service teacher was also named for insulting many students.

It is against the law to hold a meeting without permission of the government. On Friday, an 8th grader who is about thirty years old got drunk. He was in jail for beating a prostitute. On Saturday, he was involved in the meeting. Again, he was drunk and arrested.

On Sunday, Liberation Day, the students and teachers paraded from the school to the Municipal Building. Before we arrived, everyone who was at the meeting was herded into police headquarters. We had been warned by the Peace Corps to be careful about what we say in class because there are CID (secret police/informers) among the students. This must be how the students were identified. There was a flourish of guns and shouting, and the students were reprimanded. When it was discovered that the meeting was not anti-government, everyone was allowed to leave and continue to Old Woldia. The thirty-year-old was again, released from jail.

On Monday morning, the students assembled as usual on the field in front of the school and then refused to go to class. Mr. Vyas told them they were being given a free education by the government, and they were only hurting themselves. They milled around, refusing to go into the classrooms. About a hundred policemen arrived, all armed. Several government officials and a judge came also. At the third period, the students returned at last.

At the break before 4th period, they again refused to return to classes. Some of the students did come back. They were taunted by the others. Many of those who came back were 7th graders and the girls. Later at the noon break, some of the students had rocks thrown at them. All of the striking students assured the five of us that the Peace Corps wasn't involved, and they didn't want us hurt.

In the afternoon, the police were again at the school. Most of the students went back to class. The ones who were considered by the police to be the major instigators were taken into the compound, beaten, and put on a truck. They sat there most of the afternoon surrounded by police.

We were told severe consequences for a strike can happen for many reasons. One reason given to us is that the educated are elite. Education is a privilege for the few. This causes resentment on the part of those without an education, like the police. In Ethiopia, exams are given at the end of 3rd, 6th, 8th, 10th, 11th, and 12th grades. Students move to the next grade only if the National Exam is passed. Most towns have a school through third grade, and many through 6th grade. Many towns do not have a school with grades seven through twelve. That means a student must have some means of support for room and board. A student must be determined, resourceful, and lucky to achieve an education. The students are given a double standard, respect and obedience to elders and superiority over those who are not educated.

Student strikes are not uncommon. The students believe they have a right to the best. If the teacher isn't giving it, he must either change or be replaced. I don't disagree. The students are also proud. Beatings and insults are degrading, especially in front of other students. Do you remember the 9th grade student I was upset about in Loyal? I was teaching American Government, and he never turned in homework. He had a wonderful sense of humor, and we had a good rapport, but I could not get him to turn in his work. Finally, I called his dad. His dad met him at the school bus with his belt and beat him with it all the way to the house. The kids on the bus saw it and told me. The boy would no longer even look at me. I apologized, but it did no good. I will never do that again. It was too much of a loss.

The police eventually left, taking the boys with them. The school compound was then filled with milling parents from the town, looking in the classroom windows trying to find their children to see if they'd stayed out of trouble.

It has been quite a chaotic few days. I hope all of the students still in police custody will be fine. We've just gotten a *Newsweek* magazine, so we've been reading about the student strikes all over the world. We also received a NY Times and saw the ad disapproving of US involvement in Viet Nam. It was signed by the student government presidents and student editors of about 500 colleges and universities. It included University of Wisconsin, Eau Claire. It was a surprise to read that.

Enough for now...xoxo, Cindy

Lynne was a graduate of San Francisco State and was familiar with protest demonstrations. I was not. I recall only one protest in 1966 among students at Eau Claire, which happened in the art department. The painting and printing sections of the art department were housed in an old Victorian-type building, formerly the home of a logging baron. It was white with columns, tall windows, wood floors, and a smell of turpentine and linseed oil throughout. The small rebellion concerned the senior show. Mr. Lee, the painting instructor, had submitted several paintings to be exhibited. Several of them were nudes, including three of mine.

Mr. Campbell, Art Department Head, was the jury for the show, and he did not want nudes on display because of possible criticism from the women's alumni group. The seniors involved were angry. Each artist was called in privately to his second-floor office. He sat behind a large dark desk in front of tall windows showing the huge old trees surrounding the house. He explained to each of us that the paintings were not suitable for a senior show because of the subject matter and because they were not well-crafted. In his opinion, there were only two which met the criteria for a senior exhibition. When he added the well-crafted comment, the anger died without another word being said. Still, I asked which were those paintings. I was secretly thrilled because they were both mine. I kept my face blank when I told him this. I don't remember if they were displayed or not. I believe they were. Other than that, all demonstrations took place further south in Madison.

This tiny show of independence did not prepare me for the commitment of these university students— their dedication to their cause or allegiance to their principles.

I found out later, through reading, conversations, and discussions with other RPCV that the challenge to Haile Selassie's government grew because of other African students coming to study in Ethiopia. These students were coming from countries that had rid themselves of colonial rule. Also, the EUS teachers were able to gain support from secondary students and even some elementary students because they were being sent into the provinces.

And then there was us — the US Peace Corps volunteers who mingled with students and faculty much more than Indian or Ethiopian faculty had done in the past. Think of our ideas about freedom of speech and the turmoil that was going on in our own country. We were protesting, marching, demonstrating, and killing each other and our leaders.

May 20, 1968

Dear Barb,

We've had a little excitement in the house. Four days ago, I heard scratching in the kitchen, but it wasn't Dingy or Maggie. In the morning I opened the drawer of our dresser to get my toothbrush. There was a long brown cord in the drawer. I reached in to find out what it was; it moved. I screamed bloody murder — a rat! Lynne never woke up (could be the gin she and Andy drank the night before). Then, I grabbed Dingy and shoved him in with the rat. He wanted nothing to do with it and tore off. Asmama came and chased it out.

That night, I woke up when I heard scratching under my bed. With a little help from me, Lynne woke up this time, but the rat scampered away. The next night, we set a trap but didn't catch anything. In the morning, the rat was hiding behind the wardrobe. Lynne decided we could kill it by slamming the wardrobe against the wall. So... we slammed! Boy, what a squeal! Lynne was slamming and screaming, "Die, you damned fool, die!" Asmama to the rescue again.

At last, a peaceful breakfast. But no, here came Dingy out of the bedroom with a rat dangling from his mouth. Since that morning, we've had little trouble with rats. Dingy's caught one almost every day either inside or outside the house. That cat is really earning his keep. He got his final rabies shot today, so he should be pretty safe too.

The Schlenger's and Andy are getting ready to leave for home. They've already sent their trunks to Addis. I think we're all ready for something new. Jackie said, "After you trip over the same people six times a day, seven days a week, for ten months, you're ready for new people and new places." Yep, true.

Jackie has been giving us food that they're not going to need. We're moving into their house after they leave. They had the nicer house, and once we have our classrooms all packed up, we will move down the road to the new house. Ato Fantew is still our landlord. The house is larger, and the dining room and living room are quite spacious. The shintabet is out back in a small wooded area, so we will still be using a can at night. The yard is bigger, too, and there's a banana tree in the front yard. A friend is going to stay in the house for a couple of weeks this summer. He's quite an artist and will paint something on one of the walls. He looks like Omar Shariff.

The dogs have gotten quite big, and they are covered with fleas. As a matter of fact, so am I. We've been spraying, but it doesn't seem to do much good. My feet are especially bad. They are covered with bites. We do have pills to stop the itching, or I would be crazy.

The chickens are doing well. They laid their first eggs today. Lynne was so excited she cackled. We're going to see if one will hatch. We're hoping to get more chicks.

Lynne and friends

Lynne's stepfather, Elmer, won't be here now until at least June. His ship is three weeks late for docking in San Francisco. She's going to write to see if he can wait until July 1st as we'll be in Addis by then.

I've been reading Hemingway lately. I read a book of his short stories plus *The Sun Also Rises*, *The Old Man and the Sea*, and *For Whom the Bell Tolls*. I wish I could get a copy of *A Farewell to Arms*, but so far, no luck. I can't believe I've never read him before. I think they're the best books I've ever read.

Lots of work with the end of school coming soon—-love, Cindy

As Jackie said, you begin to want a change when you see the same people day in and day out. Who knew that fifty years later, we'd be facing a similar situation with COVID-19, but I'd been in the Peace Corps, so wasn't I well-equipped to handle this?

Pretty much the same people day in and day out occurred when 2020 found us back home from Portugal on March 15th. We filled our last week in Porto with walking, wine, food, port, and one final tour to a sheep farm and artisanal creamery. On Wednesday, March 11th, President Trump made his famous speech banning entry into the USA after Friday, March 13th, which caused our children to fear the order would force us to stay in Portugal indefinitely. At about 1:30 AM, we got texts and phone calls from them asking us to change our flights. At 3:30 AM, I was able to get TAP (Air Portugal) on the phone. We could leave the next day for $7,200.00. This is where Dennis's cool head comes in. He said, "we need to wait." If I had a moment on my own, I would have probably booked it. In the meantime, the NY Times clarified his speech. The ban does not apply to US citizens. We did not reschedule the flights but went back to bed and called our travel agent the next morning. She advised us that our flight was confirmed, to enjoy our last couple of days in Portugal, and to wash our hands often.

That Saturday, the hotel stopped providing cleaning services, and the police closed the restaurants one by one. On Sunday morning, we flew to Lisbon and then on to Chicago. Entry into Chicago was effortless, the easiest we've ever remembered. We did not stop to see our kids or collect our cat. We picked up our car and drove to Bloomington with a short stop at the 24-hour Mejier Grocery store in Mooresville. We arrived home at about 1:30 AM, still speaking to each other.

Then, a fourteen-day quarantine began with little impact on either of us. Dennis went happily into his garden to enjoy the first yellow blooms of daffodils. I settled into the laundry and then ran across the story my friend Camille had given me in November. It was one I had written many years ago and had forgotten about. I started working on the illustrations for it and figuring out how to turn *Chocolate Sundays* into a picture book.

Chapter 3

We decided we needed a project we could do together. We had a thousand-piece puzzle purchased many years ago. We got it out, sorted the pieces, and began the process. It was spread over the dining room table. After six weeks, we gave up and gave it away. Instead, I helped Dennis plant sixteen pots of flowers and two raised beds of herbs and flowers on Mother's Day.

We have only left our street to pick up groceries or to keep doctor appointments. Our neighbors are delightful but getting less so with each passing month, proving once again that Jackie was right. Limiting contact with the wider-world gives way too much time for gossip.

My job took me to Spain frequently. My habit, when traveling, is to read books that take place wherever that might be, so I took Hemingway with me to Madrid. I just couldn't read him anymore; however, because of him, I was introduced to the writer Martha Gelhorn, whose *Travels with Myself and Another* I loved. I've since read that she refused to comment on her relationship with Hemingway. This book was about her travels with him; the part about China was remarkable.

Also, because of Hemingway, I read Beryl Markham's book, *West with the Night*. It was published because of his recommendation. I loved it too. I have since read *A Moveable Feast* and was reminded of why I liked him in the first place.

We live on a quiet street where Dennis finds contentment among his flowers. I write, read, and paint much as I have for most of my life. But on the other side of town, life may not be so easy. In the next state over, there may be suffering. Across the ocean, there may be starvation and even as we enjoy our quiet street we must respond.

June 25, 1968

Dear Barb,

It's the end of the school year. I've been proctoring exams. The tests are written by the Ministry of Education National Board. I have dysentery mixed up with a cold. I need to go to the shintabet, and my Kleenex is all used up. My nose is running down my face. I'm miserable. All my grades are finished. I stayed up last night to get them done. In the afternoon, Lynne and Jackie helped me as I've been sick most of the week.

Susan, the nurse at the mission, invited us up for supper tonight. She is extremely nice. Remember she went to Wale Yesus with us? She's going home in August. There are two nurses who have just arrived to take her place. Ruby is about fifty, and Carol Moke is around twenty-two. On Saturday, the Everson's (the minister) are having a tea for the leaving faculty at their house. I'm baking cookies to take, and Lynne is packing up our stuff to move to the new house. She hates baking cookies. Sunday is Parent's Day at school, so we'll be there most of the day. Also, the graduation ceremonies will be held then. I did the 12th grade certificates for Mr. Vyas.

I had to fail one student in English. He completely failed the final. I feel so badly. I hope he did okay in his other subjects. A couple of others failed too, but I expected that.

We're hoping to get Mulugeta into the School for the Blind in Addis Ababa. I've sent letters to the school, and it looks pretty good. Once the American doctor received his medical records, he said there wasn't any surgery that could correct his condition. It's degenerative and will only get worse. He has no sight in one eye, and the sight in the other is almost completely gone too.

Some of the students have already been notified about what they will be doing next year. Almaz has been assigned to a technical school where she will study community development and health work. After two years, she will be assigned to a job, probably somewhere in the countryside.

Itegue Taitu Bitul Faculty 1967-1968

Molla has been assigned to complete high school at the University Lab School in Addis Ababa. He has top grades and always receives high marks on his exams. The students are paid for 12th grade and college. He will automatically (unless he really messes up) be accepted to the University without having to take the leaving exam. Then he must teach for eight years after college graduation. Our 7th and 8th grade students (my favorites) are all planning to be back next year.

We have been given our assignments for the summer. We will both be teaching ESL at Haile Selassie University in the Department of Education. Our students are Ethiopian teachers who are working on four-year degrees. I'm apprehensive about this assignment as many of the teachers have more years of teaching experience than I do. I'm both excited about living in the capital and a bit scared. We will stay with Carole in the house she is living in. She is going to Israel in July to meet her parents.

Yesterday, Asmama came to see me even before he fed the chickens. He said Dinka, our water lady, had fallen by the river and broken her leg. I sent one of the students up to the mission to find Susan at the hospital. She sent down the jeep, which they use as an ambulance. Later, I went to see Susan to find out what had happened. It seems they found her lying by the river. Susan said the only thing they could find was high blood pressure, but they are also doing blood tests. She has been vomiting a few times too. She doesn't talk at all. Some of the locals told Susan she is possessed. She's in the hospital and will be given good care.

Jackie and Don leave first, and I'm sure they are glad to leave us behind. It has been a tough year for the five of us. I don't know why we didn't click. Everyone who meets them loves them. We have lots of friends, too, so I don't get it. I feel sad though. Next, we'll move our things down the road. The kids and Asmama will help us with the move. Once the kids go back to their villages, we'll catch the bus in the plaza to Dessie to stay overnight at the "motel." The next morning, we leave at dawn for Addis and arrive in the late afternoon.

I'll write more when we get settled in Addis.

Xoxo, Cindy

Once Jackie, Don, and Andy left, I never saw them again. I got a letter from Don asking about a box that I promised to mail home for them. I did send it, but I wasn't able to trace it. I hoped that eventually, it would turn up.

I had a similar situation when I left. I mailed several months' worth of film the same way I sent the package for Don, and it disappeared. It never showed up. For years, I would wake up in the middle of the night regretting that I didn't keep it with me. Lynne refused to let her film out of her sight and carried it home with her.

She made duplicates for me, but we didn't always do the same things. Then, one year, our home was flooded, and I lost all of the slides from my first year and a half as well as the duplicates. Once more, she made duplicates for me. Was this my Karma for not getting Don's box home safely?

Molla completed his university degree and taught history at a high school in Addis. He married and had two children. In the late summer of 1995, he was chosen to be part of a contingent to go to a two-week seminar at the University of Michigan, Ann Arbor. Once there, he decided not to get on the plane to return to Ethiopia.

One day, Lynne called from her home in Clayton, California to tell me to expect a call from Molla. He would likely show up in Chicago one day soon. She added that he was ecstatic to hear that I was single.

For the rest of that year (about six months), I did my best to try to help Molla, but he wasn't easy. He showed up at my door early one evening. He said hello, and then asked me to marry him. He promised he would be a good husband to me and a good father to my daughter and son. This romantic proposal took place in our living room with Elana and Nicholas looking on, mouths hanging open. I said I was in a committed relationship with Dennis, but that had little impact.

Barely taking a breath, he asked if I had any single friends. I replied that I was concerned about his wife and children in Addis. No reaction. Eventually, I asked why he didn't return to Ethiopia. He said he was a political refugee. He explained that he was persecuted and couldn't teach how the Amhara had united the country, Haile Selassie, or any of the things he had been teaching. He concluded by saying, "You cannot rewrite history, and that is what this government is doing."

I was able to put him in touch with the Ethiopian community in Chicago. He returned to my house to tell me that they would not help him. They were Eritrean. I wasn't sure how to respond.

After not getting on the plane to home, he had made his way from Michigan to Washington DC, where there is a large Ethiopian community. I saw him again when I had a Title VII meeting in Washington. We went out to dinner. At dinner, he chastised me for not meeting his mother. He said she lived in Woldia. I was dumbfounded because we had wanted to help students who had no family in the area. When I said I would have been happy to meet her, his reply was that it was my own fault. I could not respond.

I gave him the names and phone numbers of organizations that might be able to help. One of these was Catholic Charities. I called them for him, and I had frequent contact with them. Through them, he was able to get a lawyer. He didn't like the lawyer. She was a woman. He fired her. Catholic Charities called again. They found him another lawyer. I continued to be in touch with both the organization and Molla. He stopped calling. His number was "no longer in service." They stopped calling.

I have no ending to this story.

If you're interested in more photos from the year 1967-1968 in Woldia, and you have about 6 minutes, go to:

https://www.youtube.com/watch?v=q-0svrlMbW4

July 13, 1968
Addis Ababa

Dear Barb,

I had to pack a few books and the curriculum we've used to teach English. I wasn't sure what materials we'd have to teach with at Haile Selassie I University. We caught the bus in the plaza. Our plaza is a circular spot in the road with an AGIP gas station at the top of the dirt road that goes down past the school. This is our main street. Next to the gas station is our Friday night restaurant. We spent the night in Dessie. We left at dawn for Addis. Each time we board a bus, the driver vacates the seat directly behind him and puts us there. We arrived in the city late in the afternoon.

We're sharing a room at Carole's house. Her house is off a main road in a warren of small compounds among muddy alleys and streets. It's the rainy season, but we've got our rain gear and those trusty boots. The house is a vacation for us. It has a fireplace, hot and cold running water, a bathtub, a toilet, and a telephone, so many conveniences.

I usually walk to the university or, if the rain is really heavy, I take a taxi. The classroom where I teach is freezing. The students and I keep our coats on for the entire class. I believe the architect was from France. He was never in Ethiopia. He must have looked at a map and saw that Addis is close to the equator. He didn't seem to notice that it's 7,725 feet above sea level. The room has an entire wall of windows, all louvered so they can never be tightly closed. We are in the highlands, and summer is not only rainy, but cold. Addis is so high it's not necessary to spray for malaria.

The beginning of the courses is a blur. I was given my schedule and room and was expected to show up. It is very different than teaching in Woldia where there is so much preparation, which I must admit, I love. Here, all of the lesson plans are prepared, so all I do is present them and answer any questions the students may have. My first impression of the school and the education building, in particular, was that of a modern up to date university. Once inside, that began to change. The furnishings are bare bones: wood chairs with an attached desk arm, a blackboard, no chalk, a wood table at the front for the teacher, no chair. We only teach 12 hours a week. I'm afraid I'll be crazy without more to do.

The toilets in most of the women's restrooms have either a broken seat or it is missing. There are signs in the johns saying, "Do not stand on the toilets." I asked about this and was told that students from the countryside cannot relieve themselves by sitting. They squat on top of the seat and eventually the seat breaks.

On Saturday, we are administering an English test to all students. The results will allow us to regroup the students on the basis of proficiency and do a better job of meeting their needs. This is the first time I've taught a class with so many men. I hope it goes well.

Lynne got really sick late Sunday night. She scared me so much I called the Peace Corps doctor. He said to meet him on the main road so that I could guide him to the house. Carole was afraid to go with me, so I took the flashlight and went by myself. The road at night is pretty lively. The bunabets (coffee houses) are full, and there are many "ladies of the night" around. A crowd gathered when they saw me. With my fractured Amharic and their twisted English, we were able to communicate. They were lovely. To keep me safe, about ten of them stayed with me until the doctor drove up in his Land Rover.

He couldn't believe his reception. Back at the house, he examined Lynne, took a urine sample, and started her on an antibiotic. The next day, we found out she has a urinary tract infection. She's much better now and at the end of five days it should all be cleared up.

I spent the last two weeks in Woldia with stomach cramps and diarrhea. I finally went to the Peace Corps Medical Office here in Addis. They did some tests, including taking a stool specimen. In this, they found an amoeba. I'm on a twenty-day treatment for Amoebic Dysentery. I was perplexed by this because everyone I know who's had this has lost so much weight; they're skeletons. I asked the doctor if there could be a mistake because I've been gaining weight. He replied, "You're a good host. You eat enough for yourself and the amoeba." Great!

Xoxo, Cindy

The broken toilet seats were a mystery until I realized why they were broken. Not too long ago, I bought a friend a "Squatty Potty." She had complained of difficulty in pooping. It was a birthday gift, and we got a laugh out of it, but she swears by it. The "Squatty Potty" puts your body in a more natural position, much like that used by the women at the university. In a scientific study conducted by Ohio State University Wexner Medical Center and College of Medicine, 90% of the participants who used the "Squatty Potty" strained less, and 71% had faster bowel movements.

I think back on the night when I made my way through those meandering muddy streets and alleys and realize that I might not do that now. It would depend upon the neighborhood in Addis Ababa. The tourist area where we stayed when we were in Addis in 2019 would not be an area I would go out in by myself. The street people, not just those begging, were very aggressive.

The neighborhood where I did a workshop for Selamta parents in 2019 is an area where I would feel fine by myself. Selamta is an NGO that supports permanent homes for orphans and staffs each household with a "mother" and an "auntie". The interactive workshop explored and demonstrated how mothers and aunties could share a book with children even if they couldn't read it themselves.

When the Peace Corps doctor asked me to meet him, I didn't think twice about it. Carol did, and perhaps she was the wiser of us, but I enjoyed the company I found on the street. I enjoy those types of encounters wherever we happen to be a communication challenge between people of goodwill. It's such a wonderful moment when you both realize, we get it! We know what you're trying to say!

August 14, 1968

Dear Barb,

New plans for Lynne's stepdad, he's going to meet us in Nairobi.

I have a urinary tract infection along with amoebic dysentery. I'm on a sulfa drug treatment, and it's not serious. Most of us have something of the sort, including Lynne, but we're getting better.

On Sunday, we went to Debre Zeyit. It's about forty kilometers from Addis. The whole area is dotted with beautiful crater lakes. We sat on the shore and had a picnic. We had a wonderfully relaxing day.

Friday night, the new director of Peace Corps Ethiopia, Dr. Joe Murphy, gave a cocktail party at his house. He served kitfo, which is spicy meat, usually raw but this was cooked, and he had cold beer. He seems to be an exceptional person.

After the party, I went out to dinner with the Assistant Dean of the College of Business. I was impressed with the title. It was fun, and the food was good.

This weekend, I'm going to Sodere, which is another resort area south of Addis. They have a huge Olympic-size swimming pool heated by hot springs. If I have enough nerve, I'll squeeze into my swimming suit. Amoebic dysentery be damned. Where is it when you need it?

Do you remember my mentioning a guy named Rick? He was in training with us in Salt Lake City. In fact, he and Lynne were the first two people I met there. We met him for lunch last week. He said there was someone he wanted us to meet. Rick was sent to a small town in the south of Ethiopia, where he is the only volunteer. He is an excellent Amharic speaker. Really astounding. That's probably why he was sent to that town alone.

We have seen him a few times at our meetings/conferences. At our last meeting, he asked me if I would consider marrying him. He said it didn't matter if we were in love. We were friends, and we could have a good life. Marriage is not something I've ever considered seriously. I did think about it when I was scared right before going to Utah for training. At that time, Rodney told me I could always come back, that he would be there. Now, I think maybe someday, a long time from now, I might think about marriage. I told Rick that I think you do need to be friends to have a solid marriage, but I think you need love, too. He seemed to feel that would come. I think Lynne and I showed him attention that he didn't always get. He knew Lynne had other interests. He and I have always had an easy-going friendship. I can't imagine being the only volunteer in a town. It must have been very lonely. He seemed starved for conversation.

Lynne and I met him for lunch and met his fiancée. A big surprise. She is an eighth grader, sixteen years old, and one of Rick's students. She looked so young and absolutely frightened. This was the first time out of her town. Rick did get her father's permission to marry, but I couldn't believe his plans. He wants to get married before he leaves Ethiopia and take her with him to California. He wants Lynne and I to take her shopping for clothes. He also wants us to explain to her about menstruation and to buy supplies for that and show her how to use them.

Do you remember what Mom told me? When she saw the blood, she took me in the bathroom. I thought I scratched myself chasing after a ball. She gave me a white elastic belt with two padded hooks hanging from the front and back and a white cushiony thing that she got out of a blue box. She told me I would have to change the pad several times a day, every day, for several days every month, practically for the rest of my life. Then she left the bathroom, returning with a booklet for me to read, *Growing Up and Liking It*. You've got to be kidding me, and I thought wearing a bra was bad. I don't think we're going to be able to find that little booklet in Amharic.

This young girl's English was much like our Amharic. "Hello, my name is, how are you, fine." I don't understand how he got himself into this circumstance. I told Rick he has to go to the Peace Corps office and find out how to proceed. When it became clear to him that he really couldn't manage the situation, he did turn to the Peace Corps.

Lynne has also tried to see Tadesse but hasn't been able to make contact. He went to visit his family, and he can't take her to meet them. He also told her that he will be involved with the student organizations and won't have much time to see her. She is quite worried about him. We have also been to see Molla, who seems to be settling in well at the University Lab School in the summer program.

Getting ready for East Africa now. Can't wait.

Love, Cindy

Debre Zeyit is now called Bishoftu. Bishoftu is the original Oromo name. It has seven lakes and aspires to be a tourist attraction. With the Corona Virus present, I am sad for so many who could be working with tourists but cannot do so at this time.

I wish I had written more about Dr. Joe Murphy and why I felt he was exceptional. I have since tried to find additional information about him. He went on to be successful in many ways, including academia. He was director from 1968-1970 when he was ordered to leave the country because he characterized the Selassie regime as "a repressive dictatorship which cannot establish a social order with better answers to its problems than shooting and beating young people." He was back in Ethiopia to work on a project in 1998. He was killed in a car accident there on January 17th. He was sixty-four years old.

When Rick finally went to the Peace Corps, they did get involved, and the young girl was sent back to her family. Somehow, they smoothed it out. Today, it would be even more of a mess, but Rick was not a pedophile, just lonely, and in Ethiopia at that time, a girl could marry at that age. My own grandmother, Ma, was married at sixteen to my grandfather, who was ten years older. After the Peace Corps, Rick went back to California and took a job selling insurance. He was brilliant with languages. I have often wondered what happened to him, but I haven't been able to locate him anywhere.

Little did I know then that in two years, I would be walking up the aisle. I met my future husband in California, where Dominick was stationed on Treasure Island. Before we left San Francisco for Chicago, Rick got in touch and wanted to sell us insurance. He said he could put the military insurance into a policy with his company. My mother thought it was a good idea, but we didn't do it.

CHAPTER 4

A whiff of eucalyptus and we are returned to a wondrous empire.

~C. Mosca

September 11, 1968

Dear Barb,

What a trip this has been. I am pinching myself. We have seen gorgeous sunsets, exotic animals, and mostly wonderful people. We spent the first part of our trip at the beach in Malindi, Kenya, swimming and surfing in the Indian Ocean. The Indian Ocean! Our hotel had a pool in the shape of Africa! Each room is a tiny house. In the morning, one of the staff put a tea tray on a miniature table outside our door. I felt so spoiled.

We went snorkeling at the Malindi National Park in a coral reef. The boat's rocking and rolling in the waves made me seasick. Once we were anchored, we could get into the water, and I felt much better. When everyone else got back on the boat, I stayed in the water. I fed bread to the fish. Talk about beautiful! I was having so much fun as they nibbled at the bread. It tickled. I started to laugh, ducked my head, and swallowed half of the Indian Ocean.

One day, we rented a beach buggy (sort of a jeep with the top cut off) and drove about 16 kilometers to see the ruins at Gedi. Gedi was a Muslim city founded in the early 12th Century. It is located in the small Arabuko Sokoke National Park. It was the first real jungle that I've seen. I looked up into the canopy, and all I saw were tangled, dark green, almost black foliage, not a hint of sky. I guess, I mean it was everything I imagined a jungle to be, complete with Tarzan vines. I could see him swinging down through the trees, letting loose with that famous howl. I wanted to try it, but Lynne was afraid I'd break my neck. Anyway, she said it was too dark to get any decent pictures.

Before we left Malindi, we did some shopping. I sent two carved sculptures home, a few small carvings, and some colorful fabric. I love the bright colors of the fabric, such pure gold, green, turquoise, red, black and white in bold geometric designs. Just stunning. There is also a surprise for you in the package. Happy Birthday, Barbie. We went back to Nairobi and met Carole. Then we set off for Uganda.

We had talked to other volunteers and were going to try hitchhiking to Kampala. We got a ride from a white farmer out of Nairobi. He took us to a crossroads. He had to turn off the main road to get to his farm. The three of us were all alone on a road with little traffic, scuffing our toes in the dirt. Lynne was very unhappy. She kept explaining how hard it is to get a ride for three people. Finally, after several crowded cars went by, we got the point. We flagged down a bus that said Kampala on the front, got on, and continued to Kampala. On the bus, we met two British volunteers, Nick and Mike. They also wanted to go to Murchison Falls.

In Kampala, the five of us rented a car. On Sunday morning, we set off for the falls. We got to Paroa Safari Lodge at about five o'clock. The lodge is lovely, very much like a Holiday Inn, complete with showers in the rooms (not down the hall). It was the first shower I've had with any water pressure. It felt so good. Later, we sat on the patio and had tea while we watched the elephants move toward the river. Family clusters moved slowly among the bright green vegetation down to the water.

Afterward, we had dinner in the lodge. Carole had roast beef with all the trimmings. Lynne and I had Ugandan food, which was a cassava dish and something with peanuts. We swore it was delicious (filling

would have been more honest). We weren't going to let Carole gloat over her choice.

The next day, we had a boat tour up the Victoria Nile to the Falls. We must have seen about 1600 tons of hippos, and as for crocodiles, about 400 pairs of shoes and a few purses. We saw one on the bank that was a real granddaddy. We were so close there was no need for a telephoto lens. We looked straight down into those two rows of scary incisors.

Chapter 4

After lunch, a park ranger took us on a tour of the park. A gargantuan elephant crossed the road in front of us. The ranger was more than a bit agitated when we jumped out of the Land Rover to take a picture. We were driving through savannah grasslands and saw herds of hartebeests, Uganda Kob, waterbuck, and we saw a white rhino, which the ranger explained was rare to see.

After the ranger dropped us off at the lodge, we got into our car and drove to the top of the falls. How magnificent they were. I could have stayed there for hours, just sitting near the edge listening to the roar of the water. We watched the sunset over the falls — yellow, orange, pink, red, purple. Then we had to move on.

We had decided to drive from the park back to Kampala at night to save the one-night cost of a hotel. Mike likes to drive at night, so it seemed to be a great idea. From the falls, we went back to the main road out of the park. It was about 6:00 PM. This is the time when really cheap, crazy Peace Corps volunteers, Englishmen who've been out in the midday sun and wonderfully wild African animals should go home for the night. We barely got on our way to Masindi when our teens-weensy little car was surrounded by a herd of mammoth beasts crossing the road. Elephants definitely have the right of way. Nick, Lynne, and I were squished in the back seat of the dinky Volkswagen. The driver, Mike, was separated from Carole by the gear shift. The car shook as the herd wove around this unfamiliar yellow bug in the middle of the road. I fretted silently that a massive bull would decide to walk over us instead of around. We stayed absolutely quiet and hoped for the best. Were we deterred? Of course not. On we went to Masindi, arriving at about 8 PM. We stopped for supper and to rest a bit. It was almost midnight when we got started again. We were driving through very dense dark jungle, trees arching over the hard-packed dirt road. The only light came from our headlights.

About thirty miles out of Masindi, Mike stopped the car. We had been dozing, but suddenly we were all alert. Mike said, "There's a body in the road."

I told him we had to go back to see if we could help. He insisted that we could not. Small town girl insists that we must. Mike, without speaking, put the car in reverse, and slowly, using the side of the road, backed the car up, and then put it in drive. There in the headlights, in the middle of the sandy road, lay a dark body. The bottoms of his feet shone pale in the glare. I saw immediately why descriptions of violent death often include references to a rag doll. The man's limbs were in positions no living person could accomplish, joints twisted and bent backward. There was absolutely nothing we could do. The man's head was missing.

We drove on, planning to stop as soon as possible at a police station. Though the jungle surrounded us in all of its darkness, we were all bolt upright and wide awake. We came to the town of Kibangya and found a police station. We were so lucky that the police officer was kind and much wiser than we were. He tried to reassure us, telling us that an animal probably did this. Big mouth (that would be me) insisted that an animal wouldn't take the head. He patiently explained that it could have been a revenge killing. The head would be used in a ceremony. I insisted that he take our names and the name of our hotel in Kampala.

We arrived in Kampala, returned the car, said our good-byes to Mike and Nick, and went to the hotel for breakfast. The next day, we left for Nairobi. Once there, we met up with other Ethiopian volunteers and planned a short-day trip to Tanzania.

There were about six of us, including Alan Bridges from Berkley, California. We rented a van and drove to Tanzania. We visited Lake Manyara, looking up into the trees from the van's open overhead window. There above us were lions taking a snooze in the branches of the baobab trees. Luckily for us, it was an after-lunch nap. We stopped for dinner at Tarangire Lodge before heading back to Nairobi. On our way back, we watched the sky change colors behind Kilimanjaro.

Alan and I had the same reactions to Nairobi. We were the only two in our group that found Kenya sad. The restaurants were full of whites being waited on by Africans. Alan is Black and sees things from a different perspective than most of us. This was the first time we really talked. Both of us were uncomfortable in Kenya. We are looking forward to a return to Ethiopia.

On Friday, we will have been here for one year. How about that? More to come when I'm back in Addis.

Love, Cindy

Seeing the white rhino took on more significance as we looked back. In Africa, southern white rhinos now thrive in protected sanctuaries and are classified as near threatened. Northern white rhinos are now extinct in the wild (World Wildlife Fund 2020).

When we found the body in the jungle, my behavior was once again based on my small-town mentality. My advice: never, ever travel with a small-town schoolmarm. I don't know how I stayed out of trouble. I credit Ma (my deceased grandmother) for keeping an eye on me.

Looking back, I have sometimes thought that our innocence protected us: the innocence I projected in the back streets of Addis waiting for the doctor, the innocence and spirit of wanting to do the right thing with the Ugandan police officer. I remember that Lynne, Carole, and I were relieved and anxious to leave Uganda, but even there, although we experienced moments of danger, nothing came of it. It seems that for me, no matter what harrowing experiences I might have in Africa, it will always be precious. I will always see it with starry eyes, as full of life and possibility.

As I read these letters, memories of Lake Manyara and Tarangire

Lodge come flying back. In 1999, Dennis and I planned to go to Ethiopia and Tanzania, but there was a travel warning for Ethiopia. We went only to Tanzania. We landed in Arusha. I walked down the ramp and burst into tears. The smoke from the cook fires brought back overwhelming homesickness for Africa, for the years in Woldia and those I had lost and might never find again. John Hemingway explains, "If you go to Africa you may leave but softly, persistently Africa will call you back."

The next minute, I was in the customs line behind Dennis, who sailed through and was waiting for me just outside. The passport official scanned my passport and then took out my yellow immunization card. He looked up at me and pointed to a blank on the card, which Dr. Brull had failed to initial. I explained that she just went down the list initialing and had inadvertently skipped a line. A supervisor came over to check on the hold-up. He said very firmly, "This is a problem."

"What can I do?" I squeaked out.

"Well, what would happen if I came to your country?"

"Oh, if you came to my country, I would show you around. I would welcome you to my home and introduce you to my family," stammered the still small-town naïveté.

At that moment, Dennis appeared with a ten-dollar bill in his hand and said, "Will this help?"

And with that, we were in Tanzania!

On that same trip, Dennis and I attempted to climb Kilimanjaro, and it was quite the experience. Afterward, we stayed in the Tarangire Lodge, watching the elephants from the porch of our charming tent. They come down to the river to bathe and drink. It is an incredible sight.

We drove past Lake Manyara on our way to Ngorongoro Crater. In 1999, there were no longer lions sleeping in the trees. It was distressing to realize that I had experienced this, and our Tanzanian guides knew nothing about it. In 2019, when Sue left Dennis and me in Lalibela, she went on to Tanzania. She told us when we returned home that the lions are back in the trees. I was so happy to hear that.

September 30, 1968

Dear Barb,

Lynne's stepfather Elmer got here on September 23rd. He brought me a package from Mom. The clothes she sent are so sharp, and the nylons are really nice. Both Lynne and I can use them.

I had a really neat birthday. I got lots of cards from home, so I'll have to get busy and write. I haven't written much this summer to anyone. Lynne gave me an Ethiopian gold filigree cross on a gold link chain. It is just lovely. Both the cross and the chain are handmade. Another friend had been in Asmara. He gave me a cup and saucer that I had admired. Another guy friend gave me a book and a box of candy. What can I say? I had a really nice day.

Everything is a bit chaotic here right now. We are busy getting ready to go back to Woldia so we have lots of shopping to do for things like toilet paper, tampons, dried soups, and dried pretty much anything. Since I've been back from East Africa, I've been going out a lot with some really nice guys, but I'm ready for a rest in Woldia.

Yesterday, we met the married couple who will be in our town, Susan and Roger Whitaker. They seem nice, but it's a little too early to judge. Harry was a little nervous about telling us that the make-up of our group would be the same a married couple and a single guy. We didn't give him much grief, though, just said we'd try. We haven't met the guy yet, Carl Dean. So, here's to a new year.

We're flying up to Dessie on Friday, overnight there and then the bus to Woldia. Lynne's stepfather is coming with us. Elmer doesn't seem too shocked by some of the conditions he's seen in Addis Ababa. He says he's spent a lot of time in the Orient. So far, Ethiopia reminds him of Indonesia. I'm going to meet Elmer and Lynne for lunch today. Lynne keeps dragging me along. I would do the same with her if my family was here, but I'm sure Elmer wants to see her alone sometime. In Woldia, it will be almost impossible.

I was so happy to come back to Ethiopia. It was like coming home. I guess when I do come home, I'll be so excited, I'll probably burst.

We stayed in Addis for Meskel on Thursday, September 27th. Meskel is a religious festival that marks the finding of the cross on which Jesus was crucified. The national holiday is celebrated with an enormous parade of brightly robed priests, carrying all manner of gorgeous crosses, warriors on horseback with lion mane headdresses, and purple clad acolytes. A colossal bonfire, many stories high, is built in Meskel Square. Emperor Haile Selassie comes to the bonfire, which is then lit in commemoration of St. Helena's fire.

According to the Ethiopian Coptic Church, St. Helena in the 4th Century (mother of Emperor Constantine) found the cross in Jerusalem. She was told to light a fire, and the smoke would lead her to the cross. St. Helena then gave pieces of the cross to all churches across the known Christian world. Ethiopia claims to still have its piece. The ash left from the bonfire is used to mark a cross on the foreheads of believers (kind of like Ash Wednesday).

It was a remarkable event. I loved being there, and I think both Lynne and I got some good photographs. Jackie and Don did this last year and told us to stay for it. We asked Mr. Vyas for permission, and though I don't think he was happy, he let us stay. We'll be in Woldia on Saturday along with Elmer and the new volunteers.

— Xoxo, Cindy

Chapter 4

In February 2019, Dennis and I went to Ethiopia. Sue joined us there for ten days. Sue and I shared an office for a number of years. Over those years, our friendship has grown into an unexpected and cherished gift. She wanted to see where I had taught so many years ago. We got to Addis Ababa first, and then she flew in the following day. From there, the three of us flew to Barhir Dar to meet Cheru.

Cheru is a guide who owns his own business in Lalibela. Lynne and I missed visiting Lalibela when we were living in Woldia. Cheru is a friend of Rick and Elizabeth Stoner, who arranged our introduction to him. Rick is an RPCV (Returned Peace Corp Volunteer) and later was the Africa Area Director of Save the Children (2002-2008) based in Addis Ababa. He and Elizabeth have a home in Adwa, where they have built a Cultural Center on property that has been in her family for many years. They involve themselves in many projects that benefit Adwa, including a food drive during the COVID-19 crisis.

As part of our visit, I returned to Woldia and visited Itegue Taitu Bitul School. I received a warm welcome from the current staff and children. I saw my old classroom, which looks much the same as it did when I was there. It is now a pre-K through 6th-grade school. They are opening a new pre-K and wanted mattresses for naps. Off we went to the market to buy mattresses. We returned with them stacked on top of Cheru's Toyota truck. The science teacher, who is now in my classroom, knew Ato Fantew's family, so we dropped in on them for a wonderful visit.

My landlord, Ato Fantew, died due to complications from diabetes. Weyizero Zenebech, his wife, is still alive. We were taken to their home, which was where we lived our first year. The house where we lived our second year was taken from them during the Derg — the military junta that ruled Ethiopia from 1974–1987 after the overthrow of Haile Selassie. The Fentaw family hasn't been able to get it back. I was delighted to hear about their lives, and though they have had their share of sorrow, they have also had joy.

Ato Fantew and his wife educated their children and traveled to Europe. One of their daughters, Hannah, is married and lives in Germany. She was visiting when we dropped by the house. One of Ato Fantew's sons, Elias, was also there helping with his mother. Cheru put me in touch with another son, Mulugeta, a student of Roger, Susan, and Carl. I have been able to continue to hear from Mulugeta.

Mulugeta taught for about thirty years and then worked for the Ethiopian Human Rights Council in Dessie. During the worst time in Ethiopia, he was arrested and jailed. He eventually was freed but spent two years in Senegal and four years in Uganda in exile (US State Department Annual Report, 2009). I have also been in touch with his daughter, Meklit. She is a talented and accomplished 11th grader. She won a scholarship to Lebawi International Academy in Addis Ababa, where she is flourishing.

Weyizero Zenebech (Fantew) welcomed us and insisted that we have coffee, which in Ethiopia is much more than "put on the pot." The old house where they used to live is now a coffee house. So, one of the young granddaughters came up to perform the ceremony.

First, she prepared the table with a white cloth and the tray for the china cups. Traditionally, scented grasses are part of the ceremony, and she placed them on the tray rather than the floor. She washed and roasted the beans in front of us on a charcoal brazier. As they began to roast and turn color, the young lady picked up the metal pan on which they were roasting and walked around the room wafting the smoke so that each of us could enjoy the aroma.

While the beans were roasting, she placed a long, thin-necked, round-bottomed clay pot (jebena) over hot coals. After she roasted the beans to her satisfaction, she ground them in a thick bowl with a heavy tool. It looks similar to a mortar and pestle. Once the beans were ground, she poured the ground coffee into the jebena's thin neck and brought it to a boil. She removed it from the hot coals and filled the cups with coffee. She offered us sugar and served us roasted barley, popcorn, and bread.

It was incredibly traditional and lovely Ethiopian hospitality. I spent most of the day alternating between smiles and tears. I am completely overjoyed that, at 75, I was able to make this journey.

CHAPTER 5

"Don't let it be forgot, that once there was a spot, for one brief shining moment, that was known as Camelot.

~ Alan Jay Lerner

October 17, 1968

Dear Barb,

We are back in Woldia. Home at last. It seems we've been away much longer than three months. Our bedroom wall has a new painting from our summer guest. We now have an angel to watch over us. It's splendid. It reminds me of the many wide-eyed angels in the churches here, though the colors are pastel and more subdued.

I have classes all morning, every morning. I'm teaching all geography this year: 9th, 10th, and 11th grades. I am so relieved. I really didn't like teaching English. It was so regimented and grammar is not my strong suit. You must be able to tell that from these letters. Geography is a lot of work because none of it is the same. I taught 10th grade geography last year, but this year the National Curriculum has been changed. I love all of it and enjoy teaching it. So much fun. 11th grade is African geography, which I really like as I'm learning too.

Lynne and I are trying to figure out what we're doing next year and where it will be. She's thinking of some type of work with the Camp Fire Girls organization on the West Coast. She worked for them for several summers as a camp counselor. She really likes the organization. Of course, for me, I want to teach somewhere.

Chapter 5

I think Woldia was a bit difficult for Elmer. We each got him a bottle of Scotch when we went through the duty-free shop at the airport in Nairobi. When we got home from teaching on our first day of school, the first bottle was empty! Once the second one is gone, I'm not sure where we can get another. We need Andy.

In some ways, this year is much harder than last, and, in some ways, easier. The teaching, even with new subjects and new lesson plans, is much easier. I think I'm a better teacher than I was before. The kids, of course, are more familiar, and I feel more attached to them, but that was never a problem for me.

The harder part is thinking about the future, not just my own future, but that of America. The five of us have many discussions about this. Roger and Susan have been more involved and have more information than we have gotten here. I have become less tolerant of bigots and hypocrites. The election of either Nixon or Humphrey does not fill me with hope. The deaths of Robert Kennedy and Martin Luther King caused a horrific reaction here. I didn't write about this before. When I entered school the morning after we heard the news that King was shot, one of the teachers asked me, "What's wrong with America? You have so much. Why do they shoot people they don't agree with?" I didn't know how to respond.

After Robert Kennedy was shot, I was in the simple home of an old man up in the hills. He had a picture of John Kennedy on his wall. When Haile Selassie visited Kennedy in Washington in 1963, many photographs of Kennedy were available in Ethiopia. This man was so proud of his framed photo. I am disheartened by the violence we seem to accept.

Today has been totally depressing. The Lutheran missionary, Denny Everson, started a Scholarship Committee last spring, which I joined. Over the summer a chicka (mud and straw mixture) building was built to be used as a dormitory for students. The idea is to provide a place for students who are most in need to live and to get at least two meals a day. Seventy-one students applied. This afternoon we met to review the applications and interview students. Only twenty-four can be chosen. They have finally been picked, but it was a horrific process. I just hope we can get the money for the food. The town is supposed to help, but so far, the merchants have put off giving money until tomorrow and then tomorrow and maybe next week.

Our new married couple, Roger and Susan, and our new single guy, Carl, are doing fine. Roger and Susan are very politically aware and can be intense. At the same time, they are both outgoing and are able to see the funny side of things. Susan has a nickname, Smf. Before she was married, her name was Susan Mae Flocken. When they were kids, she and her sisters made up nicknames for themselves. Her initials were SMF, so she became Smf, which I think you pronounce Sm-uf. You can imagine, with my nasal voice, how it sounds coming from me. Roger and Smf are both slim, nice looking, and Susan is very attractive with a great smile. She had a few problems in the beginning. I remember being down and mixed up when we first got here too. Can you imagine getting married, going into Peace Corps training (even though it was the Virgin Islands), and then Woldia? They are really trying and seem to like it more each day. They were at our house for supper last night.

Carl was, too. He is very Mid-Western and went to Ripon College in Wisconsin. Carl seems to be pretty laid back, and he is always ready to laugh. I'm not sure, but I think Viet Nam may have had some influence in their decisions about joining the Peace Corps. Lynne and I both like them. This weekend, we're all going to Dessie to get gas cylinders for our stoves. Harry is gone, and we have a new area rep. He hasn't shown his face yet. We're hoping to see him too.

We're in Jackie and Don's house now. It's really nice. We have more room and a great garden. On a much lighter note, when Roger, Susan, and Carl first got here they needed a bit of help lighting their Coleman Lantern. We still have no electricity or running water. Hopefully by next spring, we will be getting some electricity. In the meantime, we have our trusty Coleman's. Once lit, they give really good light; and once you get the hang of lighting it, you can use the mantle more than once. Up the street I went, leaving Elmer and Lynne at our house. When I arrived at Smf (Susan's nickname) and Roger's house, Carl was there too. The lamp was sitting in the center of the round dining room table.

I took off the glass globe and put it on the table. Then I took off the remnants of the old mantle. Roger had filled the lamp, so that was done. I put on a new mantle showing them how to do it. Next, I lit the mantle, and once it was all burned and cooled, I lit a match again. I held the match to the bottom of the mantle. I bent over the burning mantle to be sure it was fine before I put the globe back on the lantern. All four of us were so intent on making sure the mantle was burning steadily we didn't notice the smoke streaming up from the middle of the group until I muttered, "What's that awful smell?"

We all looked up. Yikes, my hair was on fire! Oh boy, so much for the Coleman expert. I have a singed crew cut on the top of my head.

I wanted to type this afternoon (Saturday), but Director Vyas isn't going to the school. Monday is an Indian holiday, so the faculty have been invited to their house tomorrow. This is great because they always have so much food you don't need to eat before you go or after you come home.

Later—

Next weekend, we're going to climb one of the mountains in the back of Woldia. On the top are the remains of an Italian fort from WWII. There's not much left but the walls as the people from around here have dismantled it for use in their homes. It has a great view of the town and valley.

This morning (Sunday), we have to go clean the library. We want it open for students tomorrow. As soon as we get the library straightened up, we'll have to come back to get cleaned up to go to the Indians. Yum.

Love, Cindy

PS: Elmer is now on his way back to Addis Ababa and then on to San Francisco and his next trip out.

I was able to get in touch with Reverend Denny Everson and discovered that he went back to Woldia in about 2000. He visited the school and also went to the dormitory, which was still functioning. The town was providing food for the students. I wish I had thought about asking about that when we visited in 2019.

When we returned in 2019, the town had electricity, and many homes and businesses had running water, hot and cold. There were tuk-tuks all over the country and in Woldia too. We stayed at the Lal Hotel. The hotel has rooms in the main building and tiny guest houses. There are many gardens full of vegetables and gorgeous flowers, as well as paths lined with dazzling rose, pink, and white hibiscus.

After arrival at the hotel, we had lunch and then visited the school, bought the mattresses, and visited Ato Fantew's family. After a very full day, the three of us had supper at the hotel, accompanied by several beers. This was followed by a walk down the main street. Once we had gone down the road a ways, there were few lights. Sue and I, fortified by Walia Lager, displayed a bravado that sober Dennis didn't feel. Once we walked past the darkened school, he convinced us to turn back. As we walked back, I spotted our old bar-restaurant and hotel. It was right next door to the Lal. This was the place with the generator that Smf, Roger, Carl, Lynne, and I frequented on Friday nights. The bar looked well used. Though it was open, I didn't think it would be safe to even drink out of a bottle in that place, let alone a glass. The hotel in the back was sad and dilapidated, with its roof caved in— no service in a very long time.

That night, we fell asleep to the sounds of priestly chanting.

I regret that I didn't take the time to find the house where Lynne and I lived during our second year. Morning found us on our way to Lalibela.

October, 1968

Dear Barb,

A week ago on Tuesday, Lynne and Carl took a day off of school to go to the market. It is a sprawling and major market for this region. The products range from berbere (hot ground pepper), raw peppers, to vegetables, eggs, fruit, clothing, fabric, animals such as sheep, goats, chickens, cattle, mules, and horses. Asmama goes here every week to get our eggs, salt, sugar, and sometimes meat. The market takes place behind Old Woldia in a gigantic boulder-strewn field surrounded by a few trees. To get to the market, Carl and Lynne crossed a rickety suspended bridge crowded with townspeople. Those coming in from the countryside use the riverbed as a way to get to the field.

When Lynne was a kid, she had riding lessons and loved being on a horse. She persuaded us to buy horses so that we could ride further into the countryside. She promised lessons as none of us know how to saddle a horse, care for one, not to mention ride one. She's a fast talker. She and Carl were in charge of buying us some horses and saddles. Asmama went with them to translate and bargain. At the market, the merchants won't take Ethiopian birr (currency). They only accept Maria Therese thalers (dollars). These are actually large silver bullion coins. On the front is a side view of Empress Maria Therese of Austria,

Hungary, and Bohemia. Asmama helped us exchange our birr for these, though it wasn't easy.

They bought four horses for the five of us. Smf and Roger are sharing for now. Lynne's horse is white and cost $75.00 and mine is an Ethiopian version of a strawberry roan, says Lynne. He cost $70.00. His name is Strawberry and in Amharic, Dema. We go riding most nights after school. Lynne, Smf, and I need to wear our jeans under our skirts so that we don't offend anyone. We have had great times for the most part.

Tonight, we went riding and had a few spills. Carl's horse is named Dalish. We're not sure what it means. It could actually be something else as our Amharic isn't that great. We went for a ride in the dry river-bed. Smf and Roger were sharing their horse. Sometimes one of them walks and, often, they ride double. As we were riding along, something spooked my horse, and he took a sharp right turn up and over the bank with me clutching him around his neck with both hands. Then, Carl's Dalish spooked, throwing him off. Carl tore up his left arm near the elbow. Lynne was adamant that he get back on the horse.

Once back home we put the horses in the back yard and unsaddled them. Lynne rubbed down the horses and then patched up Carl. We swigged down a few beers while we rehashed what a good time we had. The five of us really do have such a good time whether it's talking about politics, school work, or what we'll get up to next. Asmama found us a boy who takes the horses out to graze each day for $4.00 (10 birr) a month. They stay in our backyard at night.

Tomorrow is Halloween. The Eversons are coming for supper. The Whitakers and Carl are coming for dessert. I just made a cake, which is in the oven now. I'm anxious for it to get done so that I can go to bed. We're going to ice it with orange frosting and make it into a pumpkin.

Sunday, we're going to the Police Chief's for dinner. He's new this year. We haven't figured out why we've been invited. He told Lynne that he likes Americans. Usually, you have to be important to be invited for a meal. The whole faculty would be invited to a feast, so we're not sure why just the two of us. I hope the injerra is good.

I'll let you know how it goes. This is it for now—xoxo, Cindy

PS: I'm reading *War and Peace* by Tolstoy. The cake is out. It looks fine. Hope so, off to bed. Happy Halloween!

The five of us out in the countryside: Lynne, me, Susan, Carl, Roger

Riding was a passion that remained with Lynne for her entire life. She passed the love of horses onto her daughter, Megan, who became a very accomplished horsewoman. She entered many horse shows and accumulated both trophies and ribbons for her performances.

After checking, I discovered that Dema actually means "bleed" in Amharic. If we wanted Strawberry as a name, we should have called him Enĵori.

At 75, Carl still has the scar from that fall.

November 12, 1968

Dear Barb,

We couldn't believe what the Police Chief served for dinner. We had soup, spaghetti, doro wat, vegetables, fruit, bread, injera, cokes, and beer. After dinner, he wouldn't allow us to leave until the Scotch was empty. I thought we would have to crawl home, dirt road, stones, and all.

Lynne and I decided to have a feast on Thanksgiving Day for the faculty. We have to teach that day, but we have enough time to get everything done. We're also going to invite the Police Chief and his wife. We're planning to serve two kinds of wat, injera, bread, and fruit as he did. During the meal, we'll also have tea, coffee, and pop. We're plotting to have Carl, Smf, and Roger over one night soon to talk them into helping us. I don't think we'll have to resort to any tough measures to do that. Ha, ha.

Last week, I was sick and missed school. The Peace Corps doctor sent up some medicine this week. It is guaranteed to knockout whatever is ailing me. If it doesn't, I'll have to go to Addis for tests.

Lynne is going into Addis in December to take the GRE (Graduate Record Exam). Thank goodness Eau Claire made us take that as part of our graduation requirement. I have no wish to do that again.

We're trying to save money this month for our trip home. Those horses eat like crazy, and they're so skinny. Lynne thinks they have worms. Saving money or not, when we went to Dessie, we bought new saddles for the horses.

We're really busy with the horses, lesson plans, reading, and writing letters. Don't say it; I know I don't write often enough. Mea culpa.

We're still trying to get Mulugeta into a school. He now has only partial use of one eye. There are only two government schools and one private school in Ethiopia. We got the run around in Addis, but they assured us that he could go to the school in Asmara. The director in Asmara called today. He said Mulugeta was too old. And he was poor, and the school costs $20.00 per month. Carl, Smf, and Roger said they would help us pay. We're going to call back tomorrow to see if they'll take him long enough to learn braille. He could then return to a regular secondary school. I am angry. Should we teach him to beg? He's such a smart boy. The school has facilities for 125 students and has only thirty. I really could scream. I'm so ticked off.

We are organizing a Girls Club. I am loving it. They are so enthusiastic. I hope we can get half of the things done that they want to do.

Later, November 25, 1968

Our faculty Thanksgiving was a success. We had such a good time. Everything was eaten, and people seemed to enjoy themselves. Later, when the five of us sat down for a cognac, Carl had some news for Lynne and I. It seems the good Chief of Police was hoping to have his way with one or both of us. Carl told him, sorry, but he took care of both of us. Good grief, I suppose the Chief heard that female PCV's are the whores of the state department. Good thinking and many thanks, Carl.

I'm in Addis Ababa. I flew in on Sunday from Dessie and will fly back tomorrow. I told you that I had a urinary tract infection this summer. The drugs I was given didn't clear it up, so they want to do a few more tests. Everything is fine now. It wasn't serious; it's just that the drugs weren't effective for me. Also, on Sunday, my legs began to ache and continued to do so all day Monday.

I asked the PC doctor about it. She sent me to a specialist at a hospital here. He said I need additional calcium and need to drink milk or take calcium tablets. I grew up in America's Dairyland. I can't possibly need more calcium. I drank milk three times a day until I was over twenty-one. He also said I would always have trouble because the problem is deep inside the muscle and nothing can be done until I'm older. I have a list of things I can and cannot do. I am not supposed to ride a horse, except occasionally, I am supposed to massage my legs every day, sit down as much as possible, and wear support hose. I hate support hose. I can't imagine teaching sitting down. I was shuttled between doctors all day.

When I went back to the PC doctor, she wanted to give me two pairs of her support hose. They are really nice. I can't take them. She needs them. She has an artificial leg. I told her I could get some. I'm sure you or Mom will send me a few pairs. Boy! I sure have written a lot about what is wrong with me, especially when nothing really is.

I'm going shopping in a few minutes. The stores are open until nine. Almost this whole day was spent in and out of doctors' offices. I want to buy some pumpkin pie filling and cranberry sauce to take back to Woldia for Thanksgiving. We're saving the nuts you sent for Christmas. We drank the chocolate liquor you sent, right away.

Much later, back in Woldia, November 28, 1968

I couldn't get the pumpkin pie filling. All the Americans had cleaned out the shelves. I did find some Ocean Spray cranberry relish, which is almost as good as sauce. I think we will save it for Carole Mendelson when she comes from Addis for a late Thanksgiving. I just finished washing my hair. I usually do it outside. After I heat the water on the stove, I go outside, mix in some cold water out in the yard, soap up, and then rinse the soap out over the grass. If I do it inside the house, I tend to make a mess on the tiles. I'm a little tired after the flight back. I always get sick on DC-3's, and this was no exception. After I baste the lamb, I'm going to close my eyes for a bit. Feeling sick could also be from the glass of powdered milk I just drank. Yuck. The doctor said she could give me calcium tablets. I'm going to write and ask for them. This is awful.

Tonight, after work, we're celebrating Thanksgiving with the lamb. The nurse from the mission, Carol, is coming down. Everyone else at the mission has gone to a conference, and she's alone. Of course, now that the lamb is in the oven, we've run out of gas and I have to change the cylinder.

Chapter 5

Woldia is so great this year. Lynne and I like the other three volunteers very much. Rog and Smf's parents sent a tape of Christmas music. We sat and listened to it, and Rog and I both got homesick. We had to tell dirty jokes to get out of the mood. We do dumb stuff like that. It really will be so hard to leave. I love this place and this country.

Carole is coming next weekend from Addis. We're going to have a second Thanksgiving or third if you count the faculty celebration. She's bringing a LIVE 14-pound turkey. It has to be live, no refrigeration. What a sight that will be. I can just see her on the DC-3 with a big white flapping turkey clutched in her hand.

I won't have any trouble not riding Dema after school. Actually, either Roger or Smf could ride him if they want.

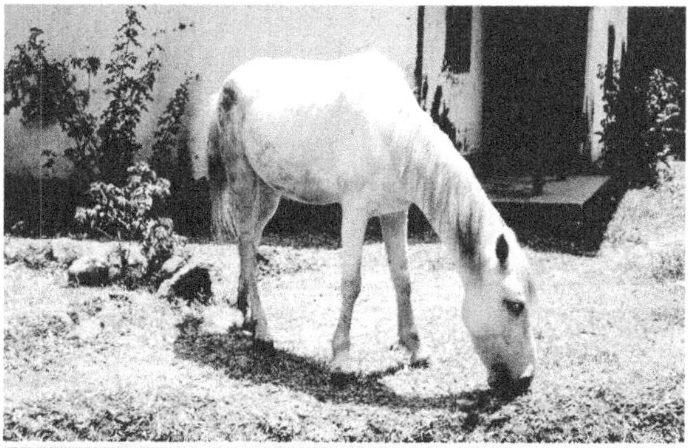

After school, I like to work on lesson plans. You should see the neat maps I've drawn. On Saturday, I love to ride, so I'm going to look at that as my riding occasionally. I love getting into the countryside. On one of my rides with Carl, we stumbled upon a little hamlet where a couple of families were living and farming. There was a stream nearby. A man was standing in the water clothed only in a white cloth. Standing there in the dark water, his black hair gleaming from butter, with the green hillside fields behind him, he was absolutely beautiful. Carl stopped to talk to one of the men, who told him the man had just gotten out of prison. That he was mad (as in crazy). Still, it was a stunning moment.

I have started teaching art to the 9th graders. I have each section for a study period once a week. I need to find a way to get paper. The Peace Corps won't furnish the paper, and the school can't. Right now, the kids who can get paper get the lesson and the rest study. I've gone through what I've bought and what Mom's sewing club donated.

More later alligator, xoxo, Cindy

When my mother saw the photos of our horses, before she could stop herself, she blurted out, "You didn't ride them, did you?" Her reaction was like ours to the Italian cookies, the first time we had them. We thought they were tasteless, but months later, they had become delicious. The horses looked acceptable to us. Now, looking at these photos, I can't believe I made that horse carry me. I should have carried him, poor thing.

I didn't know about mixed media or even much about collagé at the time, or in the art club, we could have made use of many more materials.

CHAPTER 6

"The winter is forbidden till December, and exits March the second on the dot. By order summer lingers through September in Camelot."

~ Alan Jay Lerner

December 12, 1968

Dear Barb.

Carl had Typhoid fever, so he is in Addis Ababa for tests to be sure he's completely fine. He was in Dessie in the hospital for a while. We were pretty worried. He was really out of it. Lynne is in Addis too, taking more tests for graduate school. Right now, Tazeze, Mulugeta, and Yohannes are sitting at the table with me doing cross-word puzzles, looking at magazines, and making Christmas cards, an idea they picked up from past volunteers. Since Lynne has been gone, I've been having the boys in for tea after school. They are really chatterboxes.

I've gotten lots of ideas for my classes, and it seems that my head is full of nothing else. Last night, I had dinner with Rog and Susan. That was fun. We listened to the Christmas music tape that their parents sent. Then we told stories about home like the time Dad got the idea to have a real Santa drop in for Christmas Eve.

Monday, the students are having a drama at school. That means no class in the afternoon. I don't always catch all of the Amharic but the kids just want us to watch them. They do put on quite a show.

Did I tell you that I saw Molla when I was in Addis in November to see the doctor? I had him called out of class. He was so surprised to see me. He almost dropped his book, pencils, and notebooks. He has a good sense of humor, really funny. Wish you could meet him.

December 20, 1968

Yesterday evening, Lynne and I sat at the dining room table correcting papers and writing lesson plans. The Coleman gave plenty of light for both of us to get our work done. We had finished dinner and were listening to a tape of Christmas music. Lynne was sitting with her back to the kitchen door. I was sitting to her left looking through the door to the living room. I was thinking that our tree looked really nice even without Christmas lights. We had the boys help us cut it down and bring it into the house. We put it up in the far corner of the living room. We had a couple of candles lit in there. Out of the corner of my eye, I saw something moving. It looked like a black line. I lit another candle. I walked into the living room to check on what I was seeing.

Holy cow! I screamed for Lynne and began cringing and stomping on the black line. It was an army of black insects marching diagonally from the tree, across the living room toward the dining room. Lynne jumped up and came in to see what I was yelling about. We stepped on as many critters as we could. We thought they were coming from the tree. Lynne grabbed the big flashlight and shone it on the tree. The tree was untouched. Over in the far corner, through a tiny crack between the door and the wall, came the bugs, hundreds of them.

We ran outside and around the corner of the house. The whole end of the house was black and swarming with bugs. Larvae were curled up on the back of each critter. We screamed for the boys to come out and help us.

Lynne and Tazezza ran back into the house to get matches and all of our magazines. When they returned, we tore out the pages and crammed some into the crack of the wall and the door leading into the house. The rest of the pages we piled along the shelf of the foundation.

We lit everything on fire. The bugs started popping. I was hysterical. I started laughing. All I could think of was the jingle for "Snap, crackle, pop, Rice Krispies." We watched the bugs ooze out of the wall and fall into the fire. Soon, there were fewer scattered insects emerging. After burning up all of our precious magazines, we went back into the house to stomp on any that were left in there.

The legs of our beds rest in large, clean, empty margarine cans, so we were pretty sure we were safe. Bedtime was nerve wracking. I kept imagining those critters with spawn crawling all over our house.

The next day, one of the boys went to get the Agriculture Agent for the town. He had trained in Lebanon as part of a USAID (US Agency for International Development) program. The man arrived at the house carrying what looked like a black stoppered wine bottle. He carried it very carefully. He took a length of ragged cloth from his pocket and tore it into several pieces. He laid them out along the foundation shelf. Just as carefully, he took the stopper out of the bottle. He cautiously tipped the bottle over each strip and applied a drop of black viscous fluid to each piece of cloth. Within minutes all remaining insects emerged from the wall of the house. Each one dropped down to the ground, writhed, and died. The end of the house was once again white. The man refused any compensation, put the stopper back in the bottle, and warned us not to touch any of the residue. He left with our abundant thanks.

So, Barb, that's our adventure for this month. I'm sure you're busy getting ready for the holidays. Give my best to all. Ho, ho, ho! Love, Cindy

December 22, 1968

Dear Barb,

Today is Sunday. We had the faculty over this afternoon for cookies, wine punch, and tea for our Indian families. I made the wine punch, which would have knocked most people over. Lynne said it would be a good marinade for meat and would surely tenderize it. One of the teachers visited several of the bunabets (little bars) in town before arriving at 3:00. He was so drunk, he needed support to come into the house. He sat down on the couch between one of the national service teachers (Mulugeta T., Mulugeta B., Stefano, and Tekele) and one of the Indian teachers. They tolerated him as long as they could. The Ethiopian teachers were embarrassed by him. Finally, in Amharic, they told him to leave. As Lynne walked him to the front door, he apologized profusely for being in such a state. We felt sorry for him. Actually, it was a shame he had to leave, as he was the only one to drink the wine punch.

Friday, the Eversons and Vesmeks (the doctor) from the mission came down. Another volunteer was here too, just traveling through. We had a small party with them.

Our tree looks so cheerful (without the bugs). Lynne made gingerbread men for it; the boys strung popcorn, hung candy, origami birds, which Lynne taught them, and with our inherited ornaments, it is festive. Our house now looks and smells like Christmas.

Monday night, Dr. Vesmek and his wife, Barb, invited all five of us to their house for dinner. Afterward, we're going to sing Christmas carols. Tuesday night, we're taking Mulugeta, Tazeze, and Ayelu uptown for doro wat (spicy chicken stew with a hardboiled egg for each person). The Whitakers, Carl, and their students are coming too. After dinner, we'll go to our own houses to give the boys their gifts. After this is done, everyone will come to our house for tea, cookies, and to listen to Christmas music.

I bought the boys presents when I was in Dessie last weekend. They have almost nothing, so I had a great time buying jeans, belts, shirts, shoes, towels, etc. We can't wait until they open their gifts.

Lynne was in Addis taking the Graduate Record Exam (GRE). She came back to Dessie on Sunday. I waited for her, and we both took the bus back on Monday morning. We both have first period free, so we got here in plenty of time. You know she is now part of my family, another sister.

While I was waiting for the bus to arrive from Addis, I bought a turkey for $20.00 to take back to Woldia for our Peace Corps dinner. Lynne said I paid too much for it as it was about the size of a hen. It was such a good turkey. It didn't make a mess or squawk or flop around at all on the bus. When we got off in Woldia, I carried the turkey and Lynne carried our packages. We got almost to the house. Then all of a sudden, SPLAT down the side of my trench coat. I think he knows what's coming. I really hate to have him killed on Wednesday. It's so much less traumatic to buy a turkey from the grocery store.

We've made gobs of cookies and goodies for Christmas - chocolate fudge with walnuts, the glass candy that Mom makes, pineapple cookies, melting moments, chocolate chip cookies, sugar cookies, gingerbread men, date bread, banana bread, and peanut brittle. When the missionaries were here, we had eggnog. We spiked it after they left.

Yesterday, we listened to a broadcast about the moon launch. It is incredible to realize that the Apollo 8 astronauts - Frank Borman, Jim Lovell, and Bill Anders are the first humans to orbit the moon, another world. It seems so scary to me. Sometimes, when I look up at the night sky, especially from here, I find the vastness so inconceivable. I feel like a tiny flea, absolutely insignificant. It took place at 4 PM here. The five of us toasted its success. We went on to toast quite a few other things. Then, we made pizza. This morning it looks like we launched a battleship in pizza sauce. The Apollo 8 broadcast sounded as though everything is fine. I hope it continues that way.

Have a wonderful Christmas. Enjoy the family and give them my best wishes.

Love, Cindy

Even at 75, reading this gives me the creeps all over again. I have no idea what the poison was that killed all the insects. We never had another bug problem. It could have been arsenic or DDT.

Even though I wrote home that we would sing carols, I can't imagine actually singing. I have the voice of a frog. In high school, I was in chorus, but I'm sure that was because I did all of Mr. Aderman's (our choral director) bulletin boards.

The astronauts would have the largest audience that ever listened to a human voice. The message they chose for Christmas Eve was the first ten verses of Genesis. They chose these verses because they are the foundation of many of the world's religions, not just Christianity. Lovell added, "There are more people in other religions than the Christian religion around the world. And so, this would be appropriate to that..." The mission took place as a response to President Kennedy's challenge to land on the moon by decade's end. It was such a turbulent and yet innocent time.

We cannot return.

We seem unable to shake off our cynicism and talk to each other kindly.

January 2, 1969

Dear Barb,

Thank you for the Christmas package. It was such a nice surprise for both of us. The nightgowns are too pretty for here. We have both of our beds in one room. We feel safer. Neither of us could possibly impress the other with a new nightie. It's also too cold for silk, so we're saving them for vacation.

Christmas was all I could have wished for, even though we taught that day. In our classes, we told stories, talked about Christmas traditions at home, and told about our favorite Christmases. I told the story of *The Littlest Angel*. I always get choked up, but the kids are getting used to my emotions.

Ethiopian music is based on a five-note scale called kignits. Earlier this fall, the kids asked about our music and wanted me to sing something. Not wanting to say no, I said okay. However, not wanting anyone to hear me, I took them out of the classroom, across the field, and behind the library. I sang the "Do, Re, Mi" song from *The Sound of Music* and to top it off, "Let's go Fly A Kite" from Merry Poppins. Sure enough, here came the tears. I love that song.

I also told the crazy Christmas story about the Crooked Mouth Family. Remember that one? We always have to give Mom a drink so that she'll sit down and tell us about the family: Mom, Dad, Brother, Sister, and the Little Sister, the only one who doesn't have a crooked mouth. They all try to blow out the candle so that they can go to bed and Santa can come. Finally, straight mouthed Little Sister comes to the rescue by blowing out the candle. I even brought a candle and matches to class so that I could demonstrate how Mom, Dad, Brother, Sister couldn't blow it out but then, Little Sister blows with her straight mouth and whoosh, it's out. The kids liked both stories, but the favorite was the Crooked Mouth one. I went into Carl and Lynne's classes and told the stories for them too. Lynne thought we were being cultural imperialists, but it was a fun day for the kids and for us.

Our kids opened their presents on Christmas Eve. They had a very full night with supper, gifts, tea, and cookies. I wish I could bring them home with me. Many of our students made cards for us. One of my ninth graders is the son of the governor. He brought us a huge bouquet of bright red poinsettias. They were gigantic and so beautiful. I've never seen any this large or stunning. They took my breath away. They were the centerpiece for our Christmas table.

All five of us ate Christmas dinner at our house. We had the poor bird

I lugged home from Dessie. Asmama had slaughtered it and plucked it for us in the morning. After dinner, we opened our gifts. We each got a bunch of silly ones that we had rigged up for each other. We also gave each other a serious gift. Lynne gave me a pair of fabulous handmade filigree gold earrings to go with my birthday cross. From Carl, I got a set of charcoal pastels. Susan and Roger gave me an exquisite piece of orange wool fabric covered with multicolored embroidery. The Muslim men wear it as a turban. Roger and Susan gave Carl a beautiful basket with a lid. When Carl opened it, there sat a hen. He's trying to raise chickens, so now he'll have two mother hens. We gave Rog and Susan an olive wood salad set with one large salad bowl and six small ones. The olive wood has veins of different colors running through it. It's so pretty. We listened to the tape of Christmas music that he sent. I can't imagine a better Christmas.

A day or so after Christmas, the EUS (Ethiopian University Service) teachers and the five of us hiked up a very steep mountain behind the school to attend the celebration for the feast of St. Gabriel. The priests and some of the faithful begin at midnight and continue into the following day. The churches are circular. When the service is about over, the priests come out, accompanied by the deacons and sub-deacons. In front of them are musicians who play sistrums and large drums. I've added a sketch. It is a bit rough but I think you will get the idea.

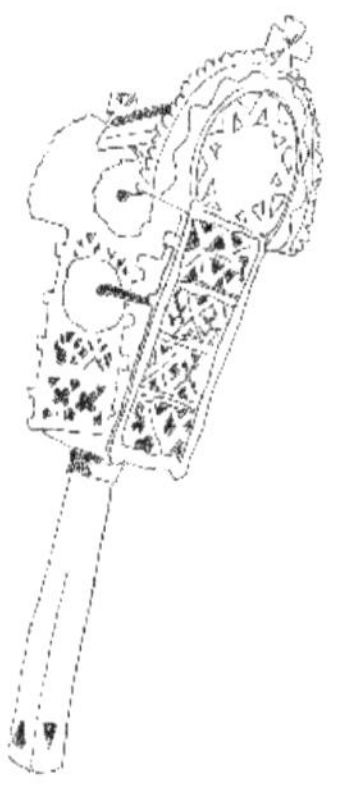

The disks shake back and forth making a pleasant metallic sound.

The priests carry large handmade silver or bronze crosses. The priests are shaded by velvet umbrellas of many colors — purple, rose, and greens accented with small glittering pieces of mirror. They all process around the church three times. It was quite a dramatic spectacle.

On New Year's Eve, we only celebrated a little bit. We taught that day and the next. We had an American lunch for supper. It started with Campbell's tomato soup, and then we had creamed dried beef on toast or as Mom used to call it with a giggle, "shit on a shingle." We also had potato chips that we had made, pretzels, olives, crackers, cheese, and gin. We struggled to stay up until midnight. It's rare that we stay up that late.

On New Year's Day night, we were at Carol's, the mission nurse. The missionaries from a town south of here were there, too, plus the Eversons and Vesmeks. We like all of the people at the mission. They have been very kind to us. This was an odd gathering as the missionaries from here didn't seem to like the missionaries from the other town. And it seemed to be true vice versa as well. As we joined in conversations with one group or another, they would share very ugly thoughts about each other. The "southern" missionaries were also very sarcastic about the Ethiopians they served. It was very uncomfortable. Not a great way to begin a new year.

The mission homes here are very much like what you might find at home. These homes are much nicer than the home I grew up in, except that they don't have television. We all left that party with a sense of relief. It was a beautiful night to walk home. When you look up at the night sky, you can imagine yourself back in the time of Christ. What's that sound beyond those trees? Are the camels you hear plodding along carrying the wise men? It's so dark and so clear and crisp. It makes for a phenomenal walk home.

1968 was the year I did not spend one day in the USA. 1969 will be the year I come home. 1967 was the year I left for Ethiopia. I was excited, nervous, and scared. Leaving here will be so sad. I love my students, this town, our house, our friends. I wish I could hold on to life as it is right at this moment.

January 29th is Lynne's birthday. I'm going to make her birthday cake. I found some birthday candles in Addis. We can't very well surprise her. We did think of one thing, though. She's been talking about ice cream. Tomorrow, I'm going to go up to the mission to ask if they'll make some ice cream for us. We'll have one of the students go get it while we eat dinner and then surprise her with ice cream and cake. We'll have chicken and potato salad as she likes it, rolls, and a vegetable. I bought her two LP's for her birthday—one on Ethiopian church music and one on southern tribal music both made by UNESCO. I also bought her a goofy gift. She hates to go out to the shintabet at night, so in an emergency, she uses an old margarine can. In Addis they have plastic chamber pots for little kids. I bought her a yellow one shaped like a duck. I can't wait until she opens that!

Happy 1969, may it be a wonderful one for you! XOXO, Cindy

I no longer have the charcoal pastels. I gave what was left of the set to a student when I left Ethiopia. I do still have the earrings, which I wear on special occasions, like my retirement. I also still have the beautiful piece of orange wool. I had it made into a long skirt, which I loved. Now it wouldn't fit on my arm, but I can't part with it.

February 17, 1969

Dear Barb,

Bad news, really bad news...we had to have one of our dogs shot, Juju. He got sick last week, foaming at the mouth. He refused to eat or drink. We called a vet in Addis Ababa. He asked us a few questions and told us he thought the dog definitely had rabies. He said he should be shot. Then we called the Peace Corps Medical Office. The doctor told us that whoever was exposed to the dog had to come in for rabies shots.

Chapter 6

The dog didn't bite any of us. Lynne, Carl, and I all tried to get him to drink water. He would lick our hands but wouldn't drink or eat. We all had small cuts on our hands from scratching bites, paper cuts, and who knows what. We all had to go to Addis.

Denny came down from the Mission and shot the dog. It was very hard for him to do and very hard for us. Asmama had to cut the dog's head off. The doctor at the Mission had to send it to a laboratory for tests. Then we all flew to Addis. From there, Lynne got sent to Asmara. She had a reaction to the vaccine in training. The shots had to start as soon as we got to Addis. The reason we got shots in training was so that if we should be exposed to rabies, we would have a week or so to get the rest of the shots. We got here on Friday, Valentine's Day. Carl and I had the first shots Saturday morning. There's very little chance that any one of the three of us have rabies. The Peace Corps just doesn't want to send anyone home foaming at the mouth. We had three shots during training, so we only need five more shots now. We'll fly back to Woldia on Friday. The shots aren't too bad. Carl and I are getting them in our arms, right one day, left the next. The bad part of all this is that we are missing a week of school, which impacts the kids. Before we got here, we had finished semester exams. We will need every week of the second semester. If I need too, I'll go into school on Saturdays to make up anything I might miss covering.

There isn't much for us to do here. We've only been here since Friday, but we've already seen four movies. Saturday night, we saw *Dr. No*. I didn't miss anything by not seeing it in the states. I would say, "No, no, don't go." On Sunday afternoons there are matinee shows that start at 12:30. They show three movies. We saw *Warlord, The Liquidator,* and *Hotel Paradiso*. The last one was the worst. I couldn't believe how awful it was.

Lynne flew from Addis Ababa to Asmara for her rabies shots. The Peace Corps doctor did not want to risk a reaction. She has to have her shots in the stomach. Carl and I went with her to the airport to see her off. We stayed around to watch the planes take off and land. Carole came out and met us for lunch. The restaurant at the airport is good with a great view of the runways. I tried brains, not sure whose brains, a calf, I think. It looked like a plate of cauliflower swimming in tomato sauce. It was served with a baked potato and a green salad. I liked it.

Tomorrow, after our shots, we have to go to the Ministry of Education. I want to meet with the head of the geography department. We have no books for 9th and 10th grades and very few maps. I just want to check to see if what I've been teaching is correct. Both of us have appointments to try to get materials for the school.

On Thursday night, we have been invited to dinner by a man from USAID and his wife. He knows a lot about the financial crisis that's looming. Some schools have already closed because either the students or the teachers are on strike. The teachers have not been paid recently. In some places, students have been taxed for attending school in order to pay the teachers. I don't know how any of this will affect us. It should be an interesting dinner. He was a PCV here with the 3rd or 4th group.

The Director of the Peace Corps, Joe Murphy, is going to send me some material from Libya for geography. I think he was a volunteer there. Carl and I met him when we went into the office.

Later, back in Woldia—February 25, 1969

We just found out that a troupe from Ethiopia will be dancing and playing Ethiopian music on the Ed Sullivan Show on March 2nd. Try to watch, okay?

We may be getting electricity before too long. I hope so as our Coleman is just about shot. I do get disgusted with it at times. Lynne's afraid of it. There's really nothing to it. Unless you get careless like I did this fall and set your hair on fire. Speaking of hair, mine is getting long and looks pretty awful. Susan and Lynne decided it would look good long. Neither of them will cut it. It's terrible.

Chapter 6

Lynne fell in love in Asmara. The guy who gave her the rabies shots, Jim, is her new boyfriend. She is really smitten and misses him. When she was in Asmara, she called and said she was getting bored there. I'm not sure why as Jim and four of his friends seemed to take pretty good care of her.

She said she bought out the town, so we've had a few surprises since she's been back. Do you remember that in one of my letters I mentioned how hungry I was for root beer? One of Lynne's surprises was real American Hire's Root Beer. It hailed the day she brought it out, so we even had ice. It was great. Yum.

Tonight, we're eating at Sue and Roger's. We made scalloped cabbage to take. We got the cabbage when we went through Dessie. We had coleslaw for lunch and tonight, scalloped cabbage.

Much later, March 3, 1969

We really may have electricity soon. Rog and Susan already have it in their house. We should have it next week. No more Coleman, yay. Tonight, we're eating at Carl's. He's making chicken. We've been eating lots of it lately as we can still get it during the fast.

On Saturday, we went to Woldia prison to buy vegetables from their garden. The prison is just outside Woldia in a little section called Adago. It was a shock to find the prisoners shackled at the ankles. At the same time, there seems to be some concept of therapy and work. Many of the prisoners were weaving cloth or embroidering or making baskets. They can sell whatever they make. The vegetables were beautiful. I bought beets, cauliflower, and cabbage. It doesn't bother me that I can't get meat. Finally, the end.

Take care, enjoy the spring. Xoxo, Cindy

When we had to have one of our dogs killed, I felt guilty that we had taken the dogs in the first place. I think we thought we were giving them a home and would be able to place them with the next volunteers. Once they were older, though, they spent most of the day tied up on the porch. We would take them with us when we went out at night but not often at other times.

I have never been confident of my skills in caring for a dog because they are so dependent and require so much. They also require discipline and consistency, which is not part of my skill set. Carl did tell us on the tape he sent home that Duba was doing well. If I recall correctly, he went to Ato Fantew, always the one who would rescue us. I don't really remember much about getting the shots except that we had a few days in Addis and then had to make sure we made up our time with the students. They did not demand this of us, but we felt it was our responsibility to do so.

Lynne fell in love with people and Ethiopia. I fell in love with Ethiopia and my students, but I never fell in love with a flesh and blood person while in the Peace Corps. I did have a crush on three volunteers, two from our group, Alan and Bob, and one who came from another training group, Roman. All three from California. But love? No. Many years later, I met Bob at a conference in Washington DC and spent an evening with him and his family. He had a wonderful wife and two beautiful little daughters. His wife told me their "love story." It was very comical because he was used to having women fall for him (as I knew). She didn't, and her straightforward manner won the day.

In Woldia, my experiences with the children and colleagues were fine, precious. Dating in the Peace Corps was fine, even fun, but getting into bed with anyone was grueling. I didn't know how to respond. I was rigid. Everything about a sexual situation was traumatic. This did not change for me until I was engaged to be married.

Chapter 6

March 21, 1969

Dear Barb,

I did my income taxes. I made $1,410.00. Uncle Sam owes me $15.00.

It's going to be really hard to leave here. It will be so hard to say good-bye to the students, especially those who've lived with us—Molla, Almaz, Mulugeta, Tazeze, and Ayala. I hope we've helped them more than we've harmed them.

The rain and cold have gone. It is once more beautiful weather here. On Saturday, March 8th Carol Moke (the nurse), Carl, Shifferau, and I climbed the mountain behind the main street in Woldia. As always, Carol and I wore dresses. We never go out in jeans; even riding, we wear them under our skirts. Women here do not wear pants, only skirts or dresses. Shifferau is a dresser (like an LPN) at the mission, and he is one of our students. He is in his late twenties, but he wants to receive his 12th grade diploma. Between his duties at the Mission and his studies, he is really busy, but he made time to take us.

It was quite a hike. Once at the top, we looked out over the tin roofs of the town and into the green and gold of the fields. The countryside is dotted with small groves of eucalyptus trees, a few cactus, scattered patches of wild flowers, including the bright peachy orange of the quince flower, and the tukuls (round thatched cone roofed houses) of the small farms. The view was stupendous. It was a shiny blue and golden day.

Yesterday, I spent the afternoon sitting down by the river. I spent most of the time talking to some little shepherd boys and some elementary students. Our garbled English and Amharic was a riot. Whenever one of us felt we had been understood, we all got the giggles. It was a fun way to spend a Sunday afternoon.

This past Friday, Denny took us in his Toyota on an excursion onto the edge of the Danakil Depression. We left at noon on Friday. We missed an afternoon of school but will make it up next Saturday. We weren't going too far into the Danakil, just on the edge of the desert, because we were coming back the next day, and we can't be driving after dark. We packed our canteens, some sandwiches, fruit, plus several extra jars of water into one of our duffel bags, and we were set to go to the hottest and most inhospitable place on earth.

There are no roads from Woldia into the desert, just trails and river beds. The Toyota is very sturdy and can go off the road. All the missionaries, Peace Corps area reps, and embassy staff seem to drive this or a Land Rover. We piled in. Roger, Susan, and I in the back, Carl, Lynne, and Denny in the front. Carl and Lynne agreed to trade with Roger and Susan on the way back. I would stay put unless I had to throw up.

We headed east, leaving Woldia behind. We soon found ourselves plunging down from the Ethiopian plateau. Descending from the edge of the Rift escarpment, we were jolted and bumped along. We clutched whatever we thought would keep us from being thrown around. We kept our mouths closed so that we didn't knock a tooth loose. When we reached the bottom, Denny made a sharp right onto a dry riverbed. This led us into ever more arid countryside. We traveled from Woldia at about 7,000 feet above sea level into the Danakil Depression at about 400 feet below sea level. What a ride.

Denny knew exactly where he was going. In a bit, we spotted a small boy watching over a herd of goats. Soon, we came to a tiny Afar village. The Afar are supposed to be among the most fierce in the world. The homes were domed structures with large pieces of cloth secured with ropes over the tops. Near some, there were small corrals of thorn bushes for goats and cattle near the houses. They seemed to know Denny. I think he brings them medical supplies. Gradually, people began to emerge from the dwellings.

The young women and a few of the men wore their hair braided and gleaming with butter. In the heat, cheeks and foreheads gleamed. Many of the women wore only a skirt tied at the waist. Susan was quite the attraction. She was wearing a baggy shirt. A small group gathered who wanted to touch her chest to see if she was a man or a woman. All three of us had on skirts but then here, both men and women had on skirts, but women were bare-chested.

One of the oldest women stared at Lynne, Susan, and I with our shirts. Her well-used breasts hung in flat triangles to her waist. She looked at us, the females, with contempt. I admired her pride, her confidence in herself, and her way of life. I am beginning to realize that the small town I grew up in might be viewed in the same way, as quaint and backward. I might wear a top, but I am just as naked underneath. It is sweltering there, and I was tempted to join the Afar women and take off some of my clothes.

A couple of the men had bandoliers around their waists. They brought out a folding chair for an elder. He sat down and put his rifle across his lap. We were to take a picture, which we were only too eager to do. Other young men had large curved knives sheathed at their waists. Roger snapped a photo of a gorgeous little girl. Her mother appeared to be at least one hundred.

After thanking the Afar villagers, we left. After driving for an hour or two, we were back in an area of vegetation. We found a place to camp beside a river, which made it cooler. That was a good thing because the tent was a bit crowded. We put up the tent on a small rise of the river bank. It was a big square canvas tent. Then we dumped the sleeping bags inside and explored the area. The riverbed was bordered by savannah vegetation — acacia and thorn-bush. Driving down into the Danakil and to our camp site, we saw lots of game. There were monkeys, baboons, huge turtles in the river, oryx, gazelle, jackal, and wart hog. During the night, we also heard many hyenas, but we didn't see any.

Saturday morning, Denny stated that this would be a good place to spot a warthog. We drove only a short way when he stopped and cautioned us to be quiet. He produced a rifle from the back of the Land Rover. It wasn't long before we heard grunting and snorting. Denny motioned for Roger to get out of the vehicle with him. He told Rog how to hold the rifle steady, concentrate, and aim. This was Roger's first experience with a gun. Rog pointed the gun at the warthog and shot. The gun leaped straight up into the air. The warthog gave him an "are you kidding look?" Denny took the rifle, aimed, shot, and we now had "pork" for a later dinner. The guys loaded it into the back, being careful not to cut themselves on the tusks. Cuts are not good, but cuts and who knows what germs can be horrific.

We also found an ostrich egg. Denny blew it out like it was a Russian Easter egg. That event was much less traumatic. By the time we got back to Woldia, it was almost dark. It gets dark here on the dot of six. Going up the escarpment in total blackness was even more terrifying than going down. We got home about 7:30, safe and sound with many a story to tell. I've never been so filthy in my life — ever. We went up to the Eversons for showers and dinner. Joey (Denny's wife) outdid herself. It was fantastic! Ham, sweet potatoes, rolls, everything.

Denny had the warthog butchered, and we even have pork chops. Dorothy and Peggy were here yesterday from Dessie. So, all seven of us had another big meal featuring pork chops. What a trip!

This Saturday we're going up to the Mission again for showers and a pork roast dinner. We're going to have Asmama boil the head and save the tusks. Lynne and I will keep the tusks from the warthog as a souvenir of this astounding trip.

Xoxo, Cindy

Peace Corps based our salaries on approximately what an Ethiopian teacher in a similar situation would make. I do believe that we made more than they did. In Wisconsin, the year before, my salary was $7,200.00. I didn't manage to save much more of that salary than I did of my Peace Corps salary.

Roger and Susan's recall and photos from the excursion shaped my memories from the Danakil experience. Carl swears we stayed overnight and that we also followed an Eland. The rest of us don't remember that, so Carl must write his own memoirs of Ethiopia. I recently found another letter which confirms Carl's memories of camping overnight in a tent. Also, according to Carl, Roger did wound the warthog. Denny said the bullets cost $2.00 each, so he did not want to use up another one. Instead, he ran over the animal with the truck.

I've been looking at some maps of the area, and I think we were probably camping in the area that is now the Mile Serdo Reserve. This is part of the Ethiopian National Park system. We were probably at about 500 feet above sea level. We were not in the salt flats or near volcanic activity.

In March, I was beginning to wonder about my purpose and if I was helping or hindering the growth of our students. I was certainly changing.

All that you touch,
You change.
All that you change,
Changes you.

~ Octavia E. Butler, Parable of the Sower:
O Magazine, September, 2020

In 2019 we were in Lalibela. Cheru took us to Asheten Mariam, a church at the top of a sheer faced cliff. My favorite tour guide, Gertaye, Dennis, and I climbed the near-vertical path that clung to the side of the cliff. Gertaye told me that I had heart as he and a lady guide took my hands, urging me and supporting me up the uneven and challenging stairs. I only imposed one restriction, "No photos from the back!" But Dennis never pays attention. At the top, we scrambled through the opening of the cliff wall. Once inside, Dennis and Gertaye took off their shoes and crossed the dark threshold into the church. I had decided to wait outside.

I sat down on a low rock shelf next to a blonde woman from Holland. I asked her about her travels. She said she and her husband had had the good fortune to travel to many lesser-known, more exotic places in the world. She added that she was beginning to wonder about the wisdom of their choices. She questioned the advisability of their travels, even though they had benign motives. She suspected that by going to these places, they were harming the people and the cultures they encountered.

March 26, 1969

Dear Barb,

We received a letter from Molla. We had tried to call him and talk to him, but it was not successful. He told us that he was disappointed because the telephone was not working. He said others had had the same trouble. He also told Lynne that he could not find out anything about Ato Tadesse. He said he tried to find him at Arat Kilo but could not.

He wrote:

I asked his friends about him, and they told me that they know nothing about him either (as I don't know about some of my friends). Two weeks ago, he was caught by the policemen and stayed at a place called Sundafa, about 40 kilometers away from Addis Abeba. I met him after he was released, but I know nothing about him now.

Since March 3rd students of both the high school and the university have boycotted classes...The student movement of this year is very serious and political. The government at the same time is very serious. It does not want to perform (give in) to the fifteen demands. Students also decided not to enter classes unless or until the government (negotiates) the fifteen demands. So, in my view, if both sides are serious, there will be no school this year. Some of the students left for their towns. Some of the students willingly handed over school property because they are very serious about these issues.

The policemen are also hunting for students now. Yesterday afternoon, they caught some. The issues are the improvement of taxation and the improvement of the educational system. Another issue concerns the boy who died in Debre Birhan. The hatred of the foreign capitalists by the students is another issue. We want them to leave Ethiopia. The need for another minister for the Ministry of Education is another issue. We want the government to decrease the number of foreign ambassadors and their staffs because we feel that it is not good for the development of Ethiopia. We also want the government not to spend a lot of money on unnecessary things. Students also want the government to send back the Peace Corps and Indian teachers to their homeland. (This is, of course, in my view a stupid issue because without them we are a herd of cattle in a pen). Another issue is the money which is paid for the ESLC (Ethiopian School Leaving Certificate) and so and so forth is illegal. The most important issue among the high school students is that the acceptance of the number of students who are allowed to enter Halie Selassie University is very few.

In my part I have some issues in which I am concerned about. For the sake of these issues, I don't care whatever trouble comes upon me (death, starvation, and so on and so forth). If the schools are going to be closed for the rest of the year, I would like to stay with you in Woldia.

Yours truly boy, Molla Tikuye

Lynne is worried but realizes that she cannot do anything about where Tadesse is or what he is doing. She is now making plans to be with Jim once they are both back in the USA. The situation in the country is becoming more tense but not here in Woldia. We are all fine and working.

Xoxo, Cindy

Molla had had several Indian and Peace Corps teachers who recognized his gifts. The Peace Corps teachers, especially, would have praised him and supported his studies in ways that Ethiopian teachers may not have done. They had also supported him with living arrangements, and he had been our language teacher. Molla, as a young man, was very bright and had a good sense of humor. I would like to reconcile that boy with the man who was willing to give up his wife and children.

Chapter 6

March 31, 1969

Dear Barb,

We have been enjoying some of the goodies Lynne brought home from Asmara. She surprised us by baking chocolate chip cookies after school one night. Then before we ate them, she gave us another surprise. There was a secret ingredient in them — hashish. The five of us sat in the living room nibbling on the cookies and giggling. Rog said the stems were going to be hard to digest. Susan curled up on the couch munching away and grinning. Later, when she got up to go home, her legs were covered with bites. Really looked bad.

I think I'll pass on that kind of a surprise from now on. I started out happy and ended up sullen. Lynne told me I owe everyone an apology because I got so down in the dumps. I get quiet and then morose thinking about leaving, and the hashish made it even worse.

Our Easter vacation starts on April 11th. We have a Termination Conference to attend. It will be in Dira Dawa. We'll be spending most of the time filling out forms, taking language tests, and seeing doctors and dentists. I want to get some more art supplies for the kids, too. Lynne wants to see Jim, so she will first go to Asmara.

Two Austrians went through last week. They are students at the University in Innsbruck. They left their addresses in case we got to Austria on our trip home. We had quite the party. Carol brought ice down from the Mission. We had the best drinks we've had in Woldia.

Short and sweet—love, me

After that evening, I passed on any kind of drugs and stuck to beer and wine. It was many years before marijuana and I came together again. According to the Red Hot Chili Peppers:

I got dosed by you and
Closer than most to you and
What am I supposed to do?
Take it away I never had it anyway
Take it away and everything will be okay.

I looked at what these lyrics are supposed to mean, and there are many guesses. For me, I think the last line says it all, take it away and everything will be okay! What a grump I was.

May 3, 1969

Dear Barb,

I just got back from our Easter vacation. I had to have a wisdom tooth pulled in Addis. I had to stay to have the stitches removed. All went well, and I'm back and ready to go. I'll need to go in for a Saturday or two to be sure the kids have all of the information they need.

The Ministry of Education has closed some of the schools in Addis Ababa because of the strikes. Some of our friends are leaving for home next week. I don't think I would like to do that. I need time to plan and get things in order. It would be too fast for me.

Our Termination Conference was fine. We got all of our paperwork completed. The dentist made my appointment for the tooth that had to come out. We got a chance to say goodbye to many friends. The hotel and the swimming pool were wonderful. We made the recommendation that we (generalists and English teachers) not be replaced. There are enough teachers in Ethiopia to do our jobs. Science and math are still needed. The director and administrative staff seemed to agree with this recommendation.

Before we went to the conference, Lynne went to Asmara. Carl, Rog, Sue, and I went to Sodere. We hitchhiked from Addis. We met some truly neat people there. We drank beer and swam all day. It was so fun. The ending of our two days was not. It ended with a tragedy.

A little girl drowned. Carl and the rest of us tried to get a doctor. Carl gave her mouth-to-mouth resuscitation. She had eaten injera, and it came up into his mouth, sour and soggy. It was horrible. Nothing helped. She had been at the bottom of the pool for about twenty minutes. I think this is an area where the Peace Corps or Red Cross could help. Most of the hotels for tourists have pools. The lifeguards can usually swim. They have not, however, had any lifeguard training. This pool didn't even have a long pole to pull people out of the water.

It was chaos. People were running everywhere, a woman trying to help, slipped and fell. It was so distressing, especially for the little girl's family. The mom started not just to cry, but to wail. She was inconsolable. We could offer little comfort to any of them.

Once we were back in Woldia, we had a three-day weekend from school. Carl, Rog, and Sue went to Dessie to meet some friends. Lynne and I stayed here. We went up to the Mission and had dinner with Carol. And we got showers.

Lynne wants to come home with me sometime. Do you think Mom and Buford (stepdad) might arrange to have a calf born at that time? Ha-ha.

Later, May 28, 1969

Sorry it's taken me so long to get back to this. We've been super busy with classes, and I have the kids working on a poster contest, and Lynne and I are trying to figure out where we're going on our trip home, and what we are going to do once we get home.

The weekend of May 16-18, Lynne flew to Asmara so that she could see Jim. He will be discharged from the army in early spring, 1970. Lynne is talking about getting married in April or May, 1970. Pretty serious. I find it hard to go there just for the weekend, it's just so tiring, but she was fine.

The weekend of May 23-25, Lynne and I took the bus to Mekele. Jim, his friend Gary, and Al came to meet us there. Al drove them in his jeep. The bus ride takes forever and is so dusty, uncomfortable, and loud. The driver plays Ethiopian music the whole way. At least on this bus ride we only had a few chickens riding with us and then not the whole way, only as far as Alamata. I wish I could read on the bus, but I would throw up after two pages. On Sunday, Al got the idea of driving us back to Woldia. We ate dinner and then drove back in the dark, almost the only vehicle on the road. We got to Woldia at about 3 O'clock in the morning. Lynne and Jim stayed in our house. They had lots to talk about. Gary, Al, and I went up to the Mission to get Carol out of bed. She is so good natured. I think she is the real reason Al so kindly offered to drive us back. After that bus ride, I certainly wasn't going to question his motive. They left the next morning at 6:30 AM without getting any sleep. Don't ask what we talked about all night; I nodded off. They were back in Asmara by 5 PM. It's a good thing, too, because they didn't have permission to come as far as Woldia. What is that — AWOL?

In art class, I have the kids working on an All-Africa Poster Contest. There are two categories: Kindness to People and Kindness to Animals. I will be busy working with each student individually for the next month. They are so talented. The school has to send the finished posters to Morocco for judging. I'm going to make some kind of certificate for each student who participated. I bought all the materials for the contest when I was in Addis. I swear I'll never save any money.

Off to bed, xoxo, Cindy

I remember little of the completion of service conference. We had to take a language test to see if our language had improved over the two years. The testers were generous with their scores, as I recall. We also underwent medical and dental exams.

The most relevant part of the meetings was when we were asked for recommendations concerning continued service in Ethiopia. This was when we were able to recommend that we, as generalists, not be replaced. As far as I can recall, this recommendation was accepted and was put in place.

Life experience before the Peace Corps shaped my encounters with death in Africa, and Ethiopia in particular. As I wrote earlier, I watched my grandmother die when I was five.

My father died from a heart attack when I was thirteen. My sisters and I stood on the back steps of the house saying good-bye as he, my mother, and Aunt Barb were about to leave for a wedding in Milwaukee. I refused to kiss him good-bye because I had to stay across the street with the Browns instead of being able to stay home while they were gone for the weekend. It was the last time I saw him alive.

Later, at my dad's viewing, my grandfather told me that children aren't supposed to die before their parents. That this wasn't right. This was the second son that he had lost. For years, I couldn't talk about this without crying. Can you imagine being so stubborn?

The death of Susan, the man in the jungle, the child at Dire Dawa, Ato Gorfu, our poor dog Juju, each of these deaths stunned me; all of them left a mark, but I think I came to Africa prepared for death.

I have told my children from the time they were little that no matter what happens, I will always love you. If you are angry with me and I die, don't worry, don't stress; I love you no matter what we may disagree about. Death is rarely a choice, but it is a reality, even for a naïve twenty-something girl.

June 4, 1969

Dear Barb,

It sounds like Lynne and Jim are planning to be married in May or June 1970 in California. Whatever job I have or wherever I am, I plan to be there. She asked me to be her Maid of Honor. I am thrilled, but she has to tell her friend, Mary Lou, at home that she will be a bridesmaid and not the M of H.

Denny, our missionary, bought a bunch of groceries from a USAID doctor who is leaving Ethiopia for a new assignment. He bought more than he needs and sold the rest to others at the Mission and to the five of us. Lynne and I didn't buy much, but we did buy a bottle of Kahlua for $2.20. It makes a tasty after dinner drink mixed with powdered milk. One way to get my calcium.

We've already pretty much packed our trunks. I'll pack my sari after we go to the Indian's party on June 8th.

We've had a few festivities already. Carl is just like our cousins Mikey, Lynn, and Steve, ready to get into trouble at the drop of a hat. The other night, Carl made a chocolate pudding cake. I said it was too heavy to eat, but it would make great ammunition. Wrong thing to say. Oh yeah, food fight — chocolate pudding cake and cold coffee all over the place. Carl couldn't stop laughing as he took aim and smacked one of us. Children, children. We did clean it up, though, no one else should have to do that.

I think exams will be over on June 26th. If we have them graded and everything turned in, we'll leave on the 28th. A new school has been built in Old Woldia, so Carl, Susan, and Rog will be teaching there next year. We'll take the bus to Dessie and then fly to Addis. I'm glad there will be some parties because I am so sad. Xoxo, Me

CHAPTER 7

"Ask a person if he's heard the story, and tell it strong and clear if he has not. That once there was a fleeting wisp of glory called Camelot."

~ Alan Jay Lerner

July 3, 1969
Addis Ababa

Dear Barb,

The round of end of year parties started on Sunday night, June 8th at the Indian's house. I wore my beautiful yellow sari that I bought in Nairobi. They all thought it was cool. I even got a smile from Mr. Vyas. His wife gave me some yellow bracelets to wear with it. She wants me to keep them. I had so much fun. Carl said I had my Colgate grin on all night. I'm not surprised. Wait till I tell you how we started the day...

Weyizero Enkubaher came over to the house on Sunday morning. She invited us to her house in the afternoon. We started the day's festivities drinking her homemade tella (Ethiopia beer made of fermented grains). It's not my favorite drink, but I am polite, so drink it, I did.

On Thursday, the 12th, we went to the National Service teachers' house for injera and wat. They are really nice guys, and it has been fantastic working with them. I think the system of a year of service is a great idea, one the USA could use.

Friday, we went up to Carol's at the Mission for lasagna. It was delicious, as always. We had showers before dinner. Yay.

Stefanos, second from the left in the light sport coat.

June 14th was Rog and Sue's first wedding anniversary. Yay, another celebration. What could we give someone for a paper anniversary? Of course, toilet paper! They had a good laugh at our thoughtfulness.

On Thursday night, the 19th, we gave a feast for the faculty, Ethiopian food and drink. It was at our house, but we'd arranged for all the cooking to be done elsewhere. We really didn't do much except have a great time. We wore our Ethiopian dresses and then packed them the next day. I can't imagine my life without all of these people in it.

The posters for the All-African Poster Contest were ready to be mailed by the end of June. They made the deadline. I can't imagine any of the students will get a prize but their work is gorgeous. The kids loved their certificates. The posters and exam preparation, giving, and grading kept me too busy to think about leaving. Usually, by bedtime, we were ready to sleep. On some nights, though, we laid there and talked or tossed and turned. I have been way up, laughing and happy, or way down and sullen. Lynne's been the same way. Luckily, so far, we've hit the same moods at the same time. When I'm in class, I'm always up. You can't help but be up in class because the kids are so great.

My Timex is just about going to make it home. It has to have a rest every once in a while. Then it works again. Lynne's watch is a total wreck. We'll take the travel alarm with us just to be sure we know we have something that works.

On June 29th, it was time to leave Camelot behind. Walking up the main street of Woldia to catch the bus to Dessie was so painful I can't write about it without starting to cry. We got on the bus, found seats, and looked down into those beautiful upturned faces we loved. I didn't cry. I sobbed.

So, Barbie, we are on our way to Europe, first stop Athens, Greece. Will send postcards or letters as we get to each place. We'll be using our Eurail passes and should be able to write from the trains.

Love, Cindy

Roger reminded me that one of the university students was Stefanos Seyoum (see the photo: second from left, in light sport coat). Stefanos ended up going to the University of Wisconsin, Madison for an advanced degree. I did some research, and with the help of Sarah Grimm at the University of Wisconsin, Madison Archives and Record Management was able to learn more about what happened to Stefanos. She sent me some valuable links that explained Stefano's life after leaving Madison with a Master's Degree in Finance and Economics.

He returned to Eritrea and joined the EPLF (Eritrean People's Liberation Front). In the struggle to win independence from Ethiopia, Stefanos became a brigadier general. After independence in 1993, Stefanos became Director General of Inland Revenue. In 1990, the Christian Science Monitor quoted Stefanos as saying, "After the war, the main responsibility of the ELPF will be to reconstruct the country and get the economy moving."

In 1993, Eritreans voted for independence in a United Nations monitored referendum. The government reorganized to include both EPLF and non-ELPF members. The assembly chose Isaias Afewerki as president. The ELPF became a political party. The state planned presidential elections for 1997, but they never took place. The constitution was also ratified in 1997 but never implemented (BBC news).

In his position with Internal Revenue, Stefanos began to question why Red Sea Trading Corporation was immune from paying taxes. Stefanos and ten others signed an open letter to Isaias Afwerki, calling for peaceful democratic reform and dialogue. In 2001, all who signed the letter and many journalists who published it were imprisoned in Eilla-Eiro Prison in the remote deserts of Eritrea. They were never charged or tried, never given access to their lawyers or to their families. According to Amnesty International, most of the cells were not cells at all, but metal storage containers of the type found on cargo ships. They would be inhumanly hot during the day and freezing at night. It is believed Stefanos died in prison in September 2007 as a result of infections related to chronic diabetes. By 2014, it was believed that all of the others had also died. (BBC)

Isaias Afwerki was described in 2009 by the US Ambassador in Eritrea as an "unhinged dictator." Some observers have called Eritrea the North Korea of Africa. Amnesty International has demanded reforms and the release of the political prisoners, which included the journalists. Many observers of Eritrea welcomed the peace agreement with Ethiopia but still remain skeptical that it will change anything for the Eritrean people. The reports from Amnesty International and the BBC are depressingly consistent in the descriptions of Afwerki from cruel, defiant, vindictive, merciless, to charismatic. According to Andebrhan Welde Giorgis, a former comrade and former Eritrean ambassador, Afwerki has a split personality, inspirational and brutal and dark.

I was hoping to find Stefanos alive and thriving. I imagined him, much as I had seen him last, a smile on his face. An honest man. His betrayal is so difficult to reconcile with my memories. I haven't been able to sleep. This wretched news is so distressing.

Leaving Woldia was so sad. It was much later in life that I learned that though it may be difficult to leave, it is much more painful to be left. When I copied this letter from the original that was sent to Barb, I cried again, missing that time and that place.

If you would like to see more photos from 1968 - 1969 there is a six minute video here:

https://www.youtube.com/watch?v=LNz7AjYjCW8

EPILOGUE

Dale Musolf did go on to travel. After serving in the Peace Corps in Nigeria, he became a helicopter pilot in Viet Nam. Dale certainly did not live his life in ticky-tacky little boxes. He was unique and lived his life taking chances and opportunities as they came along. He did not marry his high school sweetheart, but he did marry. The last time was to a beautiful woman from Panama. He worked there for Boeing, overseeing helicopter repairs until his death on May 3, 2017.

Lynne and I left for Europe with dreams of one day coming back to Ethiopia together. That never happened. Lynne did not marry Jim from Kagnew Station. In the fall of 1969, Lynne was working at the USO in the San Francisco International Airport. There she met and fell in love with Jim Fitzgibbon. They married in January 1970. I was Maid of Honor at their wedding.

After spending time at home in Wisconsin, I flew to San Francisco, where Lynne and I lived in Elmer's home. After an unsuccessful attempt at a return to nursing, Lynne went to work for the USO, and I went to work as a recruiter for VISTA (Volunteers In-Service to America) on college campuses in California and along the west coast. During this time, we wrote to and received letters from Ethiopia. It was difficult to send packages, but we could send money to Carol Moke at the Mission. She then purchased items for the students we had housed.

It was a difficult year for Carl and the Whitakers. The student strikes had spread, and finally, there was little to hold them in Woldia. I received the following letter from Roger and Susan:

Tuesday, February 17, 1970

Dear Cindy,

On Thursday at 9:15 AM, we leave for Cairo. Where does one begin to explain?

We have left Woldia, probably forever. We have left Mandefro, Asmama, Molla, Tazaze, Dingue, and all of what was a great life. On December 29, the president of the student union in Addis was shot dead. The following day 20 – 40 more university students were killed in a demonstration concerning the first death. Our EUS (Ethiopian University Students) quit and so did the kids. As of February 8, when we left, they were still out. Six weeks without a class, six weeks of sitting in an empty classroom, six weeks to magnify our frustrations, our disgust with ministry tactics, six weeks to envision a journey home. So, we left.

You can imagine what it was like: the appeals to stay; the tears that one is not ashamed to show; the sadness of it all.

We have now recovered enough to be excited about traveling at least somewhat. We've saved, afraid to leave a peaceful security, and yet excited about another turning point. The only way we can accept our decision to leave is to envision and anticipate a beginning and leave the thoughts of the ending for comparisons that are sure to surface later.

Carl will transfer; I don't know where. Ron is leaving the country. Things have indeed fallen apart. Woldia was Ethiopia to us, and at the suggestion of transferring, we of course reacted to the insensitivity of the suggestion. So many have left — ten this week — ten scheduled for next week. So, it has finally ended.

Cairo, Cyprus, Israel, Istanbul, Belgrade, Vienna, Prague, Copenhagen,

Amsterdam — till the end of March. Then to Sue's sister's in England for a few weeks. Then back onto the continent for Germany, Italy, Spain, and France. Then London, NYC. We should be home in June.

So, we're leaving — like a child bound for college. Afraid, uncertain, wondering. Yet, knowing it's for his and his parents' good — it had to be.

Love, Rog & Smf

Carl returned to Woldia alone to wrap things up before leaving for a meandering trip home. He made a cassette tape and sent it to Lynne and I. It was very heart breaking to listen too. It was so sad and brave as he cried his way through his last days in Woldia. And this letter came from Carl, written as he sat in an airport in India:

April 13, 1970

Cindy,

I'm in Calcutta waiting for my plane to Rangoon. I thought I'd write and give my impressions of India...it's a stinking, dirty, backward, hopeless country. It is especially hopeless. There are so many people here that they don't have a chance to develop. Ethiopia was a paradise compared to this. Statistic: India produces only enough food to feed 2/3 of her people on a subsistence level (UN report). Obviously, 1/3 of India's 550 million don't die every year. However, most everyone exists on a subsistence level. The people are lethargic, incapable of work. Money won't help this place. Only a vast reorganization of agricultural resources can help.

Well now, that's enough. Have you been getting my letters? Did you get my tape? Have you written? I'll expect a letter in Hong Kong — please. Tell me how life is and how disgusted you are. I've been getting more and more disgusted with "benign neglect," but since Carswell was rejected, the sun still shines. [The Senate rejected Nixon's appointee to the Supreme Court, G. Harrold Carswell, after reporters uncovered a speech in which he endorsed racial segregation as a legislative candidate in Georgia. Law experts also questioned his qualifications.] Really, Middle-America is revolting from the view abroad. How does it feel first hand? A job with the World Bank or USAID overseas is looking better and better.

Got a letter from David Sanders in Debra Berhan, and Woldia is still out. I still don't know yet whether I should have stayed or not. Please write and send me your summer address. If you're in Wisconsin, maybe we can see each other. And your telephone number. I'll call or write.

Love, Carl

PS: I'll write again after I get your letter in Hong Kong.

Seth was born to Lynne and Jim, followed by Megan. They brought absolute joy to both and, of course, the usual heartaches that come with children. She never got to see her grandchildren, though she was already worrying about them. She would have so loved being a grandmother. Lynne went on to become an amazing teacher, to inspire her students, and to especially love the most troubled of them.

I married Dominick in July 1970 after Lynne brought him home with her. He was a Marine who worked with Jim at the Armed Forces Police. We had a too-brief reunion with Carl, Susan, and Roger at my wedding in Wisconsin. Dominick and I had a daughter, Elana, and a son, Nicholas. We divorced in 1987. Lynne and I traveled back and forth from California to Illinois to see each other until my final trip to see her in 2001.

Eventually, the visits included Elana, Nick, and Dennis. All of them have been subjected to stories from Woldia. I have heard the Peace Corps criticized because many of the volunteers only did it as an adventure or a line on their resumes. There is something in the criticism, but the volunteers I knew were not motivated by either of those reasons. At the time, I didn't even know what belonged on a resume. Though, once I had to write one, I certainly included my time in Ethiopia. For me and many RPCV, life is an adventure; the people I meet are part of it, taking kids to the Art Institute in Chicago, a subway ride in New York. It is an adventure, and sometimes it is sad; all adventures do not have happy endings.

I loved teaching in the classroom, but I eventually moved from art back to ESL (English as a Second Language). I became the director of a large bilingual program in Cicero, Illinois, just outside of Chicago. It was because of that position that I met Dennis Schulz, who is my Very Significant Other. Elana, my daughter, and Nicholas, my son, have been the source of more laughter and more tears than I would care to remember.

Dennis has three daughters: Deanne, Kristin, and Kelly. And as is true for most of us, they are his delight, his pride and joy, and once in a while, his despair. Together, Dennis and I have eight grandchildren, and like all grandchildren, they are treasures.

Carl moved back to Indianapolis and went to work for Dean Brothers Pumps. He married Ann, and they had three beautiful daughters: Heather, Abby, and Laura. I hired Laura as a bilingual teacher. Those Peace Corps connections are pretty astounding. Carl and Ann have six delightful grandchildren. To use a Midwest expression, they are each the apple of their eyes.

Roger and Susan moved back to the East Coast. Both went on for graduate degrees. Susan became a speech therapist. Roger retired as professor emeritus from Georgetown University. Both Roger and Susan have gone back to Ethiopia. They traveled with Rick Stoner, Elizabeth, and Cheru. The birth of their daughter, Rachel, and son, Paul, further enriched their lives. They have three grandchildren and happily dote on each of them.

In 2019, Carl put me back in touch with Roger. Roger put me in touch with Rick Stoner and his wife, Elizabeth. Rick put me in touch with Cheru Abebe, who took Dennis and me on a fabulous month-long tour of Ethiopia.

For a five-minute video of the 2019 time in Woldia with Sue, Dennis and Cindy go to

https://www.youtube.com/watch?v=akY2eEvqwTA&t=1s

AFTERWORD

Today, my hope stems from the many young people I have enjoyed getting to know over the years and watching them grow. They are my hope for a new Camelot. One of my favorite lessons came from an ESL teacher who always started the year by drawing on her student's experiences.

To begin with, she would mark a world map with all of the places they came from. Then, she would give them an assignment. They were to research their own names and find out where their name came from and why they had that name. At the end of the unit, they would celebrate their diversity. One young man from China, however, wanted an American name. He pestered Anne every day to let him have an American name. After several days, she relented and said, "What would you like to be called?"

He replied, "Jose!"

Whenever I told this story at a conference, the audience would laugh in delight. One night, I told this story at my own dinner table to Elana, who was in college, and Nick, who was in high school. They didn't laugh. They were of the generation that was open and accepting. They didn't see their friends as being "diverse." Their response was, "What's the joke, Mom?"

Young people have taught me many lessons. Some of these teachers have been grandchildren: Alexa, who stands up for her beliefs and for others; Dan, who travels and finds beauty in Laos, a country he never imagined he would travel to; Jack, the kindest young man I know; Kylee and Ethan, both seeking and searching; Emilee, a brilliant young woman; Brooks, the happiest boy ever; Giana, our creative and imaginative little girl; and Meklit, the granddaughter of Ato Fantew.

I have gotten to know her because of our 2019 trip to Ethiopia. She is a talented and hardworking young woman who gets up every morning at 4 AM to be on time for school at Lebawi International Academy in Addis Ababa. She is an accomplished young woman and an inspiration to me. A letter from her follows.

A LETTER FROM MEKLIT

September 12, 2020

Hello Dear Madame Cindy,

My name is Meklit Mulugeta the daughter of Mulugeta Fantaw who once was your student. I hope you are doing fine. I'm very delighted to have reached you. It's such a small world, we are all so connected. The fact that you taught my dad even makes it an incredible coincidence. I am truly pleased. I am aware that my father told you a couple of things about me and my school. If you need clarification you can surely count on me.

My school is called Lebawi International Academy (http://lebawi.com/). I got a scholarship in 9th grade and right now I am an 11th grader. The process was quite challenging and still is. I have some issues with transportation because it's really far from my home. I find it hard waking early at 4 AM to prepare and leave at 5 AM. I get back home around 6 or 7 PM. However with God and my own efforts added it is all worth it.

Our school has radically changed me into the person I am and who I will hopefully become. Lebawi gives us the opportunity to use our maximum potential and believes in the hidden potential of human beings. It's motto and philosophy are really inspiring. We believe in the African ideology of "Ubuntu" —I am because you are. What's more I have been able to progress individually from the start of school.

I have been a member of the MUN club (Model United Nations) since

I started school here. So far, the school has held two conferences and in both I received the best delegate award. After realizing that I have an interest in global issues and international relations I wrote an essay this year for Human Rights Day. I wrote about Sustainable Development Goals (SDG's). Currently I am taking an online MUN class.

I also participate in the Lebawi Journal that students, faculty and others submit articles to. I am interested in being a journalist or a mass media communicator. I met the CEO of Twitter during the question and answer part of our Lebawi lecture series. I did take a picture of that fascinating moment. Our own President Sahle-Work Zewde came to visit our school. She is interested in improving the quality of education in Ethiopia. She was happy that a school like Lebawi exists. I take a lead in clubs like Obsidian Beats (music club) and Taekwondo. Both are part of our extracurricular activities. I am president of both. I have been awarded a certificate for participating in African Day. I composed a song and facilitated the presentation of it. I do have lots of things to tell you but I feel for now this introduction might be a little too much. I will love contact with you. And thank you so much.

Yours Truly,
Meklit

What started this, the date rape, has been forgiven but not forgotten. The hardest part of the whole experience was learning to forgive me, let go of the shame, accept that I wasn't at fault, accept that I didn't know what to do next, except to be quiet about it. Forgiving me was more complicated than forgiving him.

In writing this, I have had to look at myself and own up to how the rape affected my relationships after that. I was ashamed; how did I let this happen? I have had to learn that even if you invite someone into your house, you don't need to allow that person into your attic. It doesn't mean you're not a nice person if you have boundaries. I had artificial boundaries before, created by religion. I do not like to appear vulnerable. It is difficult for me to ask for help. It is difficult for me to abandon control. It took years for me to sort this out, and it took help from a therapist. Am I done? Never, I'm a work in progress.

Some of the stories in the letters do not have happy endings. Many times what happened next is not known. Reflection isn't a strength of mine, and telling the truth isn't either. It is easier to keep a secret. It is easier to appear strong and invincible. Reflection is a process, and apparently a very long process, but *The Girl at the Open Half-Door* just winked at me and said, "You are beginning to see the light."

LYNNE

In May of 2001, doctors diagnosed Lynne with Cancer. In October, I spent five days with her. She asked Jim if he would stay in the guest room so I could stay with her. I spent the first three days lying next to her in their darkened bedroom.

The first night, as I waited to fall asleep, I "saw" her angel take off his six-foot wings and place one under her and one over her. He took her in his arms, and she slept. I am not one for hyperbole; this is what I saw.

On Saturday, Lynne said, "Isn't it good just to lie around in bed all day?" I knew she would never get out of this mess. She was very tough, but I couldn't understand how anyone could believe that she was going to be okay. Perhaps I couldn't appreciate the chemotherapy. Perhaps everyone seems so defeated at the end of these horrendous treatments.

I would lie beside her and hold her hand. We would sleep and wake for trips to the bathroom or to the kitchen for water or tonic water. She would rally for a bit each day and then fall back asleep.

When I arrived at her home, she got out of bed to hug me and let me see how skinny she was, except for her stomach, which was filling up with cancer cells and fluid, though we didn't know it at the time. Even with the cancer eating away at her body, her wicked sense of humor would flash. She had a reddish wig that she wore if she had to go out. She said she'd always wanted to be a redhead, and this was her big chance. So, she twirled around to show off her figure, her hair swirling as she moved.

Seth came by on a Saturday to borrow lawn furniture for a party. She wouldn't let him take the two Adirondack chairs. They were for us. After he left, she wondered out loud if he would be okay. Did I think Dana could be a good mother to the yet unborn child? Who knows? Were we? Do our kids think we were good mothers? I would bet they could give us a whole list of how we failed. And who knows, regardless of their lists, the proof is in their lives, not ours.

Eventually, the pain became so agonizing that she needed to be in the hospital. Megan could see that, too, and convinced her mom to call the doctor. And with that, she was admitted.

We joked about a slumber party. I was relieved when we were there because there was always someone who knew what they were doing or could offer an option. She could get relief from the pain without explanations. She could be washed in relative comfort. It was easy to sleep there and to clean up. The staff was very accommodating with towels and blankets but mostly with making Lynne comfortable.

The hospital room was also brighter than her bedroom. We could let the light in. The room was sunshine white. Maybe the walls were painted a specific color, but my impression was one of sunshine. At her home, the low light came from a small lamp on the TV, but not here. I preferred the light for her and for me. Why is learning to let the light in so difficult?

Megan took me for coffee. Lynne insisted that I have a latte, though normally I would have had a black "coffee of the day." When we returned, she was so happy with it. "Isn't it good?"

"Yes," I agreed, "really good. Fancy place, this hospital of yours." Set in foothills of pine and starry nights and sunshine in the daytime, which you couldn't keep out even by closing the blinds. It was nice. A place to cut pain and let in the light. Comfort and light, a fancy place, with good nurses, too.

When it was time to leave the hospital, Lynne couldn't get out of bed. I hugged her where she was, and we both cried, afraid of what we knew. Eyes streaming, we made promises we'd never be able to keep.

In her embrace I felt our lives melding – the life we began so many years ago as young Peace Corps trainees, the over thirty years of friendship that followed, our life in Ethiopia living as people have since the dawn of time, under the night sky while unknown animals cry all around you, huddled by the light with the ones you love.

We parted that day for the last time.

Letters From A Wondrous Empire

ACKNOWLEDGMENTS

I OWE MANY THANKS TO MANY PEOPLE WHO HAVE ENCOURAGED ME, made suggestions, read, and helped edit this rambling epistle. The first encouragement came from the Unitarian Universalist Life Writing Group, who were the ones who first heard the introduction, years ago. If it were not for them, I would probably not have ever begun this project.

As I delved into the letters, I received support and renewal of memories from former Woldia Peace Corps volunteers Carl Dean, Roger, and Susan Whitaker. These conversations led to more research and reconnections to Ethiopia. We happily added Rick Stoner and his wife Elsa to our group. Ann Dean, and Dennis Schulz added to the discussions, and their patience is much appreciated. A heartfelt thank you for the memories and the wonderful Zoom conversations.

A big thank you to those who helped with the research, beginning with Sarah Grimm of the University of Wisconsin Archives and Records Management. She is a gem. She not only helped me locate Seyoum, but followed up with websites that allowed me to find out what happened to him. John Coyne, another RPCV and former Ethiopian Peace Corps staff member, put me in touch with Berhane Mogese, a lawyer in Addis Ababa, who graciously helped me locate the prison in Woldia and who has tried to find out more about Ato Gorfu.

A giant thanks to the first readers of the entire drafts for their patience and enthusiasm and suggestions: Pat Scholl, Sue Kosmoski, and Deanne Schulz. Without their encouragement, I would not have had the persistence to complete this project. Deanne had many amazing questions that helped me to focus on this long-ago experience.

And finally, a most heartfelt thank you to Ryan Archer, a most kind and encouraging editor who helped put some order into all of this. His searching questions helped bring back memories and emotions.

The mistakes are all mine either because of the perspective of youth or the faulty memory of old age.

REFERENCES

Butler, Octavia E. (2020, September). *Oprah Magazine.*

Connell, D. (1990, November 15). Eritrean rebels prepare for life after war - and AFTER MARXISM. Retrieved March 13, 2021, from https://www.csmonitor.com/1990/1115/oerit.html

Connell, D. (1997). *Against all odds: A chronicle of the Eritrean revolution.* Trenton, NJ: The Red Sea Press.

Connell, D. (2005). Conversations with Eritrean political prisoners. In *Conversations with Eritrean political prisoners* (p. 4). Lawrenceville, NJ: Red Sea.

Darby, K., & Lerner, A. J. (1967). Camelot the musical - camelot lyrics. Retrieved March 13, 2021, from http://www.themusicallyrics.com/c/203-camelot-musical-lyrics/1292-camelot-lyrics.html

Davis, B. (2006). Eye of the oracle quotes by Bryan Davis. Retrieved March 13, 2021, from https://www.goodreads.com/work/quotes/223913-eye-of-the-oracle

Eritrea must release prisoners of CONSCIENCE immediately and unconditionally. (2019, September 17). Retrieved

March 13, 2021, from https://www.amnesty.org/en/latest/news/2019/09/eritrea-28-prisoners-of-conscience-detained-18-years-ago-must-be-immediately-and-unconditionally-released/

Eritrea President Isaias Afwerki 'both charismatic And brutal'. (2018, July 13). Retrieved March 13, 2021, from https://www.bbc.com/news/world-africa-44824682

Estifanos Seyoum, eritrea. (2014, May 26). Retrieved March 13, 2021, from https://www.ipu.org/news/features/human-rights-cases/2014-05/estifanos-seyoum-eritrea

Ethiopia. (2010, March 11). Retrieved March 13, 2021, from https://2009-2017.state.gov/j/drl/rls/hrrpt/2009/af/135953.htm

Flea., Frusciante, J., Kiedis, A., & Smith, C. (2003). Dosed [Recorded by Red Hot Chili Peppers]. On *By The Way* [MP3 file]. Los Angeles, California: Warner Brothers.

Huijbregts, B. (2020). White Rhino. Retrieved March 13, 2021, from https://www.worldwildlife.org/species/white-rhino

Johnson. (2020, February 27). The advantages of speaking a second language. Retrieved March 13, 2021, from https://www.economist.com/books-and-arts/2020/02/29/the-advantages-of-speaking-a-second-language

Keane, F. (2018, July 09). Can Ethiopia's ABIY AHMED make peace with 'Africa's NORTH KOREA'? Retrieved March 13, 2021, from https://www.bbc.com/news/world-africa-44771292

Kenny, Nathaniel T. (1965, April). "Ethiopian Adventure." *National Geographic*, 548-82.

Lemma, L. (1979). THE ETHIOPIAN STUDENT MOVEMENT 1960-1974: A CHALLENGE TO THE MONARCHY AND IMPERIALISM IN ETHIOPIA. Northeast African Studies, 1(2), 31-46. Retrieved March 13, 2021, from http://www.jstor.org/stable/43660011

Peoplepill.com. (n.d.). About estifanos seyoum: ERITREAN politician (1947-): Biography, Facts, career, wiki, life. Retrieved March 13, 2021, from https://peoplepill.com/people/estifanos-seyoum/

Robbins, T. (1984). A quote From JITTERBUG PERFUME. Retrieved March 13, 2021, from https://www.goodreads.com/quotes/309821-like-the-arthurian-years-at-camelot-the-sixties-constituted-a

Shaw, A. (2019, January 9). Ohio state research finds Toilet STOOL may solve COMMON bowel issues. Retrieved March 13, 2021, from https://wexnermedical.osu.edu/mediaroom/pressreleaselisting/toilet-stool-mmr

Team, A. (2015, May 05). Eritrea 2015: Isaias Afwerki & his musical chair. Retrieved March 13, 2021, from http://awate.com/eritrea-2015-isaias-afwerki-his-musical-chair/

Theys, M. (2020, December 30). 64 famous Safari quotes that will inspire you to travel Africa. Retrieved March 13, 2021, from https://africafreak.com/safari-quotes

Made in the USA
Coppell, TX
09 September 2021

62073187R00111

MW00659253

PRAISE FOR

The Complete Guide to Teaching Dance

"*The Complete Guide to Teaching Dance* should be required reading for every aspiring as well as seasoned dance studio teacher/owner. Rhee stresses the most important thing about the dance business: that teachers are gifted individuals who pass on a legacy to their students, whether those students go into the dance profession or choose dance for its benefits of beauty, grace, and appreciation. This generous book of information is long overdue and Rhee should be lauded for his insight into a field of education that has so many facets."

—Charles (Chuck) Kelley,
master teacher, Broadway Dance Center, New York City;
administrator, Dance Educators of America training programs

"Rhee is a knowledgeable, experienced, generous teacher and a curious, energetic, fearless student of life. You will love this book of practical advice that is intended to help dance teachers achieve personal and professional success. . . . [I] intend to incorporate *The Complete Guide to Teaching Dance* into our pedagogy and arts management classes as assigned reading. . . . The book is pertinent and needed."

—Jo Rowan, Chairman of Dance, School of American Dance and Arts Management, Oklahoma City University

"My wife, Nancy, and I enjoyed watching Rhee Gold (and his brother Rennie) teach for us and then watched them grow into successful teachers and businessmen. After reading this book, I am more than impressed. I am absolutely amazed—amazed at how well written it is, at how easy it is to understand and enjoy. I am disappointed that a book like this did not exist when I opened my first school. This book should become the bible for all dance teachers and studio owners. It is fabulous!"

—Art Stone, Art Stone Enterprises, Smithtown, New York

"How I wish I had had the opportunity to read this book when I opened my studio in 1962, instead of learning by trial and error. Lucky young teachers!"

—Greta Leeming, Greta Leeming Studios, Ottawa, Canada

"Everything a studio owner needs to know is covered. Sometimes one gets stuck in a certain pattern of doing things even though times and needs change, and this book could certainly help a seasoned teacher remember why he or she started to teach in the first place. I believe this book should be in every dance educator's library."

—Marcia Aller, past president of Dance Masters of America and member of the Cecchetti Council of America

"*The Complete Guide to Teaching Dance* gives readers extraordinary insight into the fundamental processes necessary to succeed in the classroom as well as running, promoting, and improving a dance school. Mr. Gold uses his experiences in the world of dance to create real-life scenarios and provides ideas for level-headed resolutions to these situations. . . . This book takes you on a detailed journey through the intricacies of balancing art and business."

—Amber A. Perkins, director, Amber Perkins School of the Arts

"I thoroughly enjoyed every chapter of this book. After teaching for 28 years it was refreshing to read and remember why I decided on this venture so many years ago."

—Shelia Vaught, owner/director of Little Rock School of Dance and past president of the Southern Association of Dance Masters, Inc.

"As a school owner for 25 years, I have always wanted to sneak into someone else's studio and find out how they might be organizing their business. This is the guilt-free way to sit behind their office desk and rummage through their files! I found myself refreshed and full of new ideas that I'm sure will show not only in my studio's financial bottom line but on the lines that were forming between my eyebrows!"

—Diane Gudat, faculty member, Dance Masters of America and Dance Teachers Club of Boston teacher training schools

"I am always looking for new ideas and ways to improve the operation of my school, and this book enabled me to 'step out of the box' and look at some issues differently. I highly recommend *The Complete Guide to Teaching Dance* for teachers old and new."

—Nancy Chippendale, owner, Nancy Chippendale Dance Studios, North Andover, Massachusetts

"Rhee's book will not only remind you *why* you do it, it will inspire you to keep on doing it! I have taken new, refreshing ideas into my classes for younger students that have *automatically* improved and reinvigorated the kids and myself! *The Complete Guide*'s most important message is that teachers should value each other no matter what their background or experience is. It makes you think about the importance of a true spirit of community in dance."

—Melanie Sullivan-Coyle, artistic director, The Sullivan School of Dance, Queen City Jazz Company

"In addition to teaching students the love and art of dance, dance educators of today juggle many roles: choreographer, coach, surrogate parent, mediator, and entrepreneur. To handle all of these responsibilities, they need the support of many resources, such as that provided by Rhee Gold in his book, *The Complete Guide to Teaching Dance.* Material on dance is available from many sources, but information on running a successful business is much more limited. This book delivers from the horse's mouth!"

—Debbie Werbrouck, MDE, president, Chicago National Association of Dance Masters; owner, Debbie Werbrouck's School of Dance; artistic director, Patchwork Dance Company

"If ever a book should be considered required reading for dance educators, it's Rhee Gold's *Complete Guide to Teaching Dance.* Much of Rhee's writing could be considered a Credo for Compassionate Teaching: He emphasizes the positive influence a dance teacher can have as well as how harmful a less-than-caring philosophy can be to a child. Rhee shares a sense of insight that is integral to success as a dance educator.

"This is a handbook for the novice and a resource and restorative for the 'old pro.' All dance teachers should run to buy their own copy of this incredibly valuable publication!"

—Patti Goulding, national chairperson, National Dance Week

THE COMPLETE GUIDE TO

teaching dance

An Insider's Secrets to Personal Reward and Financial Success

RHEE GOLD

The Complete Guide to Teaching Dance
Rhee Gold

Published by Gold Standard Press
P.O. Box 2150, Norton, MA 02766
www.rheegold.com rhee@rheegold.com

All rights reserved. No part of this book may be reproduced or transmitted in any form or by any means, electronic or mechanical, including photocopying, recording or by any information storage and retrieval system without written permission from the author, except for the inclusion of brief quotations in a review.

Copyright © 2004 by Rhee Gold
ISBN 0-9749325-0-7

Edited by Cheryl Ossola
Jacket and book design by Mim Adkins

Dance illustration by Amy Scott
"On Reflection" articles reprinted by permission of *Dance Magazine,* 2004
Photo courtesy: Photodisc (front cover dustjacket); Eyewire (p. 1); Hoby Finn/Getty Images (p. 5); Cheryl Ossola (pp. 17, 47, 73, 83); Mark Anderson/Getty Images (p. 37); Corbis (p.53); Leanna Creel (p. 88); Rubberball (p.116, 129); Valeska Stupak (p. 147); and Stockbyte (p. 162); author photo (dustjacket) by Brad Fowler

Printed in Canada

Publisher's Cataloguing-in-Publication Data
Gold, Rhee
The complete guide to teaching dance: an insider's secrets to personal reward and financial success / Rhee Gold; foreword by Gus Giordano.
p. cm.
Includes index.
ISBN 0-9749325-0-7

1. Dance--study and teaching. 2. Dance school--Business management. 3. Teaching--Aids and devices.
I. Title.
GV1589.G65 2004 792.8'071
QB104-200133

Contents

PART II

SECRETS TO A SUCCESSFUL SCHOOL

Appendices

ABOUT THE AUTHOR

Rhee Gold is celebrating his 26th anniversary as a dance industry leader. He has been involved in dance since being introduced to it at his mother's school at age 3. He trained in ballet, tap, jazz, and modern with Sherry Gold, Gus Giordano, Lee Theodore, Frank Hatchett, Judy Bassing, David Howard, Sam Kurkjian, Beverly Fletcher, and many others.

At age 15 Mr. Gold became one of the industry's youngest master teachers, subsequently serving on the faculties of every major dance organization in the United States and Canada. He was a special guest for the Second International Congress of Dance in Rio de Janeiro, Brazil, and a guest speaker for conferences spanning the private sector, K–12, and higher education.

Mr. Gold has directed his own schools, including the Sherry Gold Dance Studios in Brockton, Massachusetts, and Dance Theatre of Boston. He has directed and produced the American Dance Awards, the North American Ballet Festival, and the North American Dance Championships.

He has served as president of Dance Masters of New England and as national president of Dance Masters of America. He is the dance industry's first public speaker, presenting lectures, keynote speeches, and seminars offering unique perspectives for school owners, educators, and dancers. As the founding chair of UNITY, Mr. Gold has worked closely with the leaders of most of America's dance-teacher organizations, helping to build relationships among all educators.

He has written articles on dance education for *Dance Magazine* and *Dancer,* and publishes the *Goldrush,* a newsletter for dance schools in the U.S. and Canada. His Project Motivate seminars for dance school owners, dance teachers, and students promote personal and professional excellence.

He founded the Rhee Gold Company in 2003 as a vehicle to expand ways in which he can offer his insights to teachers and dancers.

Rhee Gold, accompanied by his mother, Sherry, at his inauguration as vice president of Dance Masters of America, 1993.

ACKNOWLEDGEMENTS

This book, like the dance teaching profession, is a labor of love. But no amount of love alone could have yielded the final product—for that, I credit the wisdom, efforts, support, advice, and influence of others. My gratitude goes to all those who've shared in its creation, directly and indirectly, over a lifetime (sometimes when I didn't even know it):

The Higher Power who never fails to offer me the essential lessons of life and who always reveals exciting new roads to travel;

My parents, Sherry and Al Gold, and my family: Rennie, Tony, Kim, Tayla, and Jim;

All the Project Motivate attendees whose knowledge, inspiration, passion, and creativity influenced every page of this book;

My students, who taught me to accept responsibility for the impact a teacher has on their futures, both as people and as dancers;

My editor, Cheryl Ossola, who dedicated hours to this project and who never fails to help me sound good, and our proofreader, Amy Berk, who helped save us from the horror of typos;

KC Patrick, Barbara Kaplan, Bill Como, Richard Philp, and all my friends at *Dance Magazine*, past and present, who believed I could write before I knew it;

James and Ethlyn Bethel, Beverly Fletcher, Jeannie Castonguay, Mary Carmody, Sam and Etty Goodman, Nancy Sousa, Donald and Joanne Nelson, Helen Chopourian, Arthur and Nancy Stone, Patti Goulding, George Lon, Gloria Jean Cuming, Helen Levesque, and all my friends at DMA, UNITY, and UDMA.

My heartfelt thanks to you all.

FOREWORD

Sherry Gold was a disciple of the Gus Giordano jazz dance technique for many years. I hadn't yet met her family when one summer morning many years ago, I was on my way to teach class and it happened: Rhee and Rennie Gold, Sherry's twin 8-year-old boys, were hanging out the window on the third floor of my dance center, yelling, "Gus, Gus, Gus!" It was a glorious reception.

Through the years I've followed the careers of Rhee and Rennie (the "toy boys," as I refer to them affectionately). They've become well known and award winners as talented dancers, writers, choreographers, and teachers. Their contributions are part of why the dance world is where it is today.

And now, Rhee Gold has done it again. His book is filled with information essential to the dance teacher and dance studio owner of today. Throughout, he stresses the importance of knowing and following the basic fundamentals and principles of dance, of teaching dance, and most important, of living life. It's a message that has been close to my heart during the 50 years of running my own dance school and the 40 years of my dance company.

Rhee and some others in his generation provide a real structure for teaching and learning dance. Too often the young dance students of today simply mimic the movements they see in the various media without focusing on the foundation required for becoming good, and possibly professional, dancers.

Rhee's book entices people into knowing the fundamentals and lays out the basic dos and don'ts of teaching them. And it offers very good advice for running a dance studio effectively.

Gus Giordano, Evanston, Illinois

PREFACE

To understand why I wrote this book, you have to know my mother's story.

Flashback to 1964: My mom, Sherry Gold, was a professional dancer who married her theatrical agent and decided she wanted to be a housewife. After years on the road, beginning at age 12 when she traveled to Chicago to tap dance on the radio (yes, that's right—on the radio), my mother was looking forward to living a *Leave It to Beaver* existence. But there was this passion burning inside of her—you know the one—like dance is flowing through your blood and you just can't get it out of your system, no matter how hard you try.

The story goes that the neighbors asked my mom to teach their children to dance. But I believe the real reason my mother started a dance school was because she wanted my twin brother, Rennie, and me to grow up with dance flowing through our blood, too.

We had a very small home in one of those typical '60s neighborhoods, and my mom opened the school in our basement—with three poles, a tiled floor, and (maybe) six-and-a-half-foot ceilings. After enrolling more than 90 students in that tiny basement school in the first year, she decided her June Cleaver days were over!

As it turned out, she was a very good teacher. When I look back, I know the key to her success was her passion and drive. Her dancers wanted to be good because *she* wanted to be good! It was an atmosphere that she created within her school that still exists 40 years later.

My mom constantly searched for ways to expand her horizons as a dance teacher, taking master classes and workshops and networking within dance teacher organizations. I remember her traveling on weekends as an assistant for jazz dance legend Gus Giordano. Gus was one of her biggest mentors; before long, Sherry Gold was one of the country's most respected master teachers.

In the meantime, her basement school had grown to several hundred students, with cars coming and going all day, and the same neighbors who had encouraged my mom to teach their children now wanted her business shut down. My mother fought them for years. Once, a police officer armed with a cease-and-desist order marched down the stairs to find my mother on the floor with a "baby class." She said, "You're going to have to drag me out of here if you want me to stop teaching." Parents from the school, encouraged by my mother's rebellious attitude, marched on town hall with picket signs. The story of Sherry Gold's fight to keep her dance school became front-page news! Those years were lean in finances but rich in lessons; it was then that I learned to fight for what I believe in.

After three years of defying cease-and-desist orders, my mother moved her school. The years of turmoil were a blessing in disguise: Sherry Gold was famous in the area for her struggle to keep her dance school, and her business flourished.

By the early '90s, my mother had developed a national reputation as one of the finest dance educators in the country. Her students were moving on to professional careers and many had become respected teachers. Her hard work had paid off! But in late 1993 she was diagnosed with terminal cancer, and in 1994 she lost her final battle.

During her illness, this woman who used to work compulsively told me that if she lived, she wasn't going back to the school. She had burned herself out. She had discovered that there was a lot about life that she would like to experience—a life that had nothing to do with dance.

In my heart, I believe that conversation was my first inspiration for Project Motivate—and the seed of this book. I saw that many dance teachers were stressed or burned out. Jealousy is rampant in our industry; often these teachers had no one to talk to. Some of them regarded other teachers as the enemy. But I believe that dance teachers have too much in common to be enemies—how can we be, when we share such a love for what we do?

One summer weekend, I invited my former business partner, Gloria Jean Cuming, to join me on Cape Cod, and together we wrote down all the issues dance teachers have to deal with and the ways we could help make their lives less stressful. We filled a legal pad, and before long we launched the first business and motivational seminar for teachers and school owners, called Project Motivate.

Last year, I made the decision to devote more time to Project Motivate and to write this book. Teachers today need to realize, as my mother did, that success doesn't come from awards or accolades or the size of their school's enrollment. It comes from the knowledge that they have made a difference in the lives of the children they teach. And they need to learn, as my mother did too late in life, that their families and personal lives are just as important as owning or teaching at a successful school.

This book presents many of the topics covered over the years of Project Motivate, and it's my hope that it will function as a portable, ever-present source of inspiration, validation, and encouragement. It's my way of showing dance teachers how exciting and rewarding—personally and financially—our profession can be.

Enjoy!

PART ONE

Teaching From *the* Soul

"Education is not
the filling of a pail,
but the lighting of a fire."

William Butler Yeats

ONE

The Power of a Positive Attitude

'I like thinking big. If you're going to be thinking anything, you might as well think big.' —Donald Trump

The role of the dance educator has changed dramatically over the past couple of decades. Gone are the days of teaching children once a week and producing a dance recital at the end of the season. Today, dance training is an educational process that has a major influence on the young minds that dance through our schools for years to come.

There are more than 3 million children taking dance lessons each week in the United States. In many cases, students remain enrolled for up to 10 years; often they train several days a week. It is fair to say that some students are at the studio more than they are at home. Often, their dance teachers will spend more time with them than their own parents do. The dance educator's role is not only to teach the newest steps or the correct technique but to instill self-esteem, confidence, and life lessons that will influence the students to become the best they can be. You may have thought you were merely becoming a teacher, but instead you have become a mentor, surrogate parent, disciplinarian, part-time psychologist, and more.

Only a small percentage of students will move on to professional performing or teaching careers. Therefore, effective teachers understand that their influence and the lessons learned at the dance school are the tools dancers will utilize to help make them successful adults, whether or not they continue to dance.

Successful dance educators realize that teaching is as much about attitude as aptitude. Those with a positive attitude expect great things; they work hard and are likely to achieve their goals. It has been proven that positive-thinking people are happier, healthier, and more successful than those who carry a lot of negative baggage along on their life journeys.

Positive thinkers usually accomplish their goals—and enjoy the journey more. They are less likely to give up or lose control when the pressure is on. Their upbeat attitude makes a favorable impression on their students and parents, as well as other teachers, and they gain respect as good team leaders. Often positive thinkers find themselves surrounded by others who possess the same attitude—or perhaps they foster it in others—which makes for a great adventure through life!

Teaching is as much about attitude as aptitude.

Look for the best in everyone involved with your studio: your faculty or managers, students, and their parents. Find the things they do right, and comment on them; let them know how much you appreciate their participation. Come up with a positive way to express concerns, especially about sensitive issues. If you're angry, hold your thoughts until you are prepared to express your feelings without being negative. Don't underestimate your ability to handle problems, and try not to jump to conclusions. Often a little time gives us the perspective needed to make the right decision. Look at challenges as an educational process. Life is about learning from each and every situation; look hard enough and you will discover the reasons why everything happens the way it does.

A positive attitude does not appear on your mental doorstep by simply hoping for it. How you feel each day when you awaken is up to you. No situation or person can make you feel angry or hurt, unless you make the choice to react that way. Dwelling on the negative makes problems seem bigger, perhaps even overwhelming. Instead, go about your day expecting the best.

Very few things in this world are perfect, so try to recognize that falling short of perfection is not failure. There is no such thing as failure. There are only lessons to be learned. Focus on the future, aim high, and more than likely you will make it a reality. The choice is yours!

CULTIVATING CONFIDENCE

So you're working on developing that positive attitude, but you're finding a few stumbling blocks. You're not alone. Picture this:

Joanne is a successful dance school owner with more than 400 students. She's organized, passionate about teaching, and her educational philosophies are respected throughout the dance community. After a decade in business, her school has become one of the largest in the area. She's very confident about the policies and standards she's established. Or is she?

What happens when a parent questioning the class placement of a child approaches that school owner? Instead of responding with the confidence you might expect, she becomes inhibited, responding in a tense and argumentative manner. By the time the conversation is over, the parent is pulling her child from the school—not out of concern for the child's class placement, but because Joanne lambasted her for asking the question.

The recital can be another sensitive time. The performance is over; 20 parents praised the show. Then one parent approaches, complaining that her child was hidden in the back line. Despite those 20 positive comments, Joanne can't sleep that night—because of the *one* negative remark. This seemingly confident school owner allows one parent's criticism to be the only thing she remembers about her last production.

What's underlying this lack of confidence? Many dance educators have been through personal and professional challenges in an effort to pursue their passion for teaching. As a result, some are a bit sensitive to criticism—perhaps hypersensitive when it comes from a student's parent. This self-doubt may have started with childhood friends who didn't understand that a commitment to dance could be more important than going to the movies. Their peers seemed to think that dance was a silly or frivolous activity, not something you could dedicate your life to. It's during these periods that many dancers make the decision to quit training altogether.

Others, when they explained to their parents that they wanted to major in dance or open a school, were discouraged or ridiculed. Their parents thought dance was a nice hobby but not a suitable profession. Certainly, they would say, it's not something you could make a living at!

Those who have spent most of their lives trying to prove the validity of their choice of profession may be overly defensive. It's hard to feel confident when you feel that those you love question your judgment about a career choice, but only you know what's right for you. If you love what you're doing and believe you do it well, then act confident. Eventually, it won't be an act anymore.

Dance is a silly, frivolous activity, not something you could dedicate your life to—right? Wrong!

Then there are the spouses or partners who can't compete with their mate's dedication to dance. Confidence lacks in some teachers who've been divorced or seen several (sometimes more) long-term relationships come to an end. I've heard of many who have suffered verbal abuse over the amount of time and energy that goes into running a school. Not only do they find themselves alone, often they have the responsibility of raising children along with teaching or operating a school.

Some teachers doubt themselves because they don't have a degree in dance education, but they don't give themselves credit for the incredible amount they have learned through experience. Few, if any, colleges teach the skills needed to operate a studio or to instruct a 7-year-old in how to do a shuffle-ball-change. Those skills are acquired through years in the studio, or from mentors, or workshops, or even trial and error. Unfortunately, some dance educators with degrees do not look positively at private-sector teachers who don't have them. They don't acknowledge the many skills those teachers have—skills that are not being taught in colleges, universities, or conservatories in this country, and which are critical to the development of teaching excellence. Don't let the attitudes of organizations like these undermine your self-esteem.

The situations I've just described can shake the confidence of even the most positive-thinking person, at least at times. The key to maintaining a forward momentum is to focus on the fact that teachers have a significant impact on the lives of the children they teach. And the fact that they have pursued their dreams should be, in itself, a confidence-builder. But when those shaky moments occur—and they're bound to—think positively. They're only temporary.

ON REFLECTION

You Call That a *Real* Job?

All dancers and teachers have dealt with family or friends who think our dedication to the art of dance is a nice hobby. How many times have you been asked, "When are you going to get a 'real' job?" Although the question is a bit humorous, sometimes it's frustrating, especially if you're teaching forty hours a week or performing two shows a day, six days a week. How else could you define that kind of activity, other than as a real job? But then, by one way of thinking, it can't possibly be work if you enjoy doing it.

Mary is a successful studio owner who happens to be a single mom. For years, her financial responsibilities had been supporting her children and the dance school she had opened five years earlier. During the first four years of operating the school Mary lived every day under the stress of what she referred to as "financial fear."

She was constantly trying to figure out how she was going to pay the rent for the studio as well as her own home. Many times she had borrowed from her costume accounts or other appointed funds in order to make the rent. She once went to her parents for help, but they turned her down because they felt she should close the dance school and get a real job. But during those first four years, paying the rent wasn't the only issue Mary struggled with. Her children would ask why they couldn't have the same things or do the same activities as their friends. On top of the financial fear, Mary felt a great deal of guilt.

On the rare occasions when there was a small profit, the money went right back into the school. The studio required sound systems, special wood floors for the safety of her dancers, mirrors, and all the other essentials of a dance school. With much hard work and dedication she managed to build herself a state-of-the-art studio as well as a solid reputation for quality training.

In her fifth season, things started to change. Enrollment increased tremendously, with more than 200 students dancing through her school each week. Finally the financial fear she had lived with for four years was starting to dissipate. She added her name to the payroll for the first time. Her children were thrilled to be joining their friends at the movies and playing Little League baseball, and they even went on a family trip to Disney World.

That year, Mary found herself sitting at her parents' table for Christmas dinner. To her surprise, the same parents who wouldn't help her with the rent and told her to get a "real job" were now bragging that they always knew her dance school would be a success. The fact that she was making a living made her parents think teaching dance was a legitimate job. She wasn't upset with her parents' seemingly hypocritical comments; actually, she felt like they had become her biggest supporters. Through it all, her parents had helped raise her children and deep down she knew they loved her. Mary was pleased that she had achieved success with her business but also that she had gained the respect of her parents, which meant more to her than anything else.

All those years, Mary had been driving the car she had gotten as a teenager. With her success, she decided it was time to purchase a new car. Nothing too extravagant: a three-year-old minivan with 40,000 miles on it. She was so proud that she would no longer be embarrassed to invite anyone for a ride!

For the first time, Mary parked her car right in front of the school rather than hiding it in back of the building. Mary walked into the lobby and told a parent that she had just bought a car. The parent responded, "Wow, you must be making a lot of money at this little dancing school thing. Maybe you should start to give those of us who have been with you from the beginning a little discount." The comment came from one of the wealthiest moms in her school.

Mary didn't know how to react, but her professional instinct told her to smile and walk away without saying a thing. Meanwhile, her stomach was turning and her emotions had gone from extreme pride to total confusion. After all those years of hard work, she thought she deserved to make money. But apparently the parents at her school thought that teaching dance wasn't something you should profit from.

Mary was devastated and feeling guilty at a time when she

should have been patting herself on the back. After all, she had set a goal, stayed focused, and followed it all the way through. Didn't she and her children deserve the same opportunities as the families who attended her school?

After some time, Mary realized that no one had the ability to control her emotions. She had made the choice to feel guilty because of what that parent had said. She knew what she had been through to make her school a success. She knew that she and her children had gone without so she could give more to her students. She felt the aches and pains of all those hours of teaching every class in the school. Most important, Mary realized that the trip to Disney World was the best thing she ever did to create memories to last a lifetime for her and the kids. How could she feel guilty about that?

Today, Mary is a confident school owner with more than 500 students. She understands that she has a right to make money and is now sharing her wealth with a faculty of five and two office employees. She has Saturdays off and attended all of her son's baseball games as well as her daughter's two drama club productions this year. Now, when parents comment on her success, Mary's response is bold: "Yes, the school is having a successful season; it gives us the opportunity to offer more to our students. How are you doing financially?"

—Rhee Gold, March 2002
from *Dance Magazine*

"Whether you think that you can, or that you can't, you are usually right." —Henry Ford

TWO

A Clear Understanding

"Pleasure in the job puts perfection in the work." —Aristotle

The school must be an environment in which the art of dance is held in the highest regard, nurturing a passion for one of the oldest art forms in the world. As teachers, we must stay on top of the newest teaching methods, which are changing all the time, and we must understand our own limitations.

Today's successful dance educators have clarity of purpose, not only in their philosophical approach but in what they want to accomplish with each class. Such clarity requires thoughtfulness, self-knowledge, creativity, and an open mind.

A class should not be used to prepare for a performance; its purpose is the technical training of a young dancer.

AN OPEN MIND

First, make no judgments, of yourself or your dancers. Every dancer, regardless of aptitude, is worth our time and effort. We should get a thrill out of seeing young dancers accomplish a simple movement that they couldn't do when they walked into the studio. This thrill is what being a teacher is all about! If we work only with advanced dancers, we can lose sight of the reasons why we became dance educators in the first place.

Dance teachers who lack vitality sometimes suffer from low self-esteem. They become preoccupied with judging themselves, and it shows in their teaching. Walk into the classroom with confidence in who you are and what you do. The knowledge you've gained throughout your career makes you a success or you wouldn't be standing in the front of that classroom.

LIFELONG LEARNING

As dance teachers, sometimes we can get caught up in the business end of what we are doing. When that happens, it's easy to neglect our own educational process. An educator/artist must never cease to learn. Being part of an evolving art form means evolving with it. The dance teacher who opens a studio at age 20 and never again takes class or continuing education programs may be cheating her students; her nourishment is vital to her success and that of her dancers. Grab every opportunity to be the best educator possible.

The image you present in the classroom
should be a mix of self-assurance and vitality.

TEACHING FROM THE SOUL

Express your passion at all times. You are there to send out a loving and positive attitude. Remember that the reason you are working with these dancers is to encourage them to develop a love for dance. Some will be better technicians than others; however, they all can develop the passion to be the best they can be. Each of us knows that special feeling that takes over when we dance. It can happen onstage or in the classroom; you may not be able to describe it, especially to those who do not dance, but it's your obligation to pass that feeling on. Don't get caught producing a technically impressive dancing robot. A simple walk or arm movement can impact an audience as much as any jump, turn, or kick—if it is done with passion. Dance may be seen in the body, but it comes from the soul.

"The mediocre teacher tells. The good teacher explains. The superior teacher demonstrates. The great teacher inspires." —William Arthur Ward

Set the Right Example

If students are expected to respect the rules and policies of the school, then teachers must set the standard. It doesn't do much good to establish policies if you don't have the fortitude to enforce them.

First, dress like the professional you are. If you wear street clothes or non-dance attire, it detracts from the respect you hope to command and makes enforcing a dress code appear hypocritical.

Your behavior sets the model for the students. If you expect your students to arrive on time and be prepared for class, you must do the same. Teachers who are late or unprepared send the message that such behavior is acceptable. Once you make this mistake, it's hard to turn it around. Since a missed warm-up can lead to injury, encourage students to arrive early for class. For safety reasons, students arriving more than 10 minutes late (and thus missing the warm-up) should not be allowed to take class.

They should, however, be required to watch it.

A great way to encourage students to follow the school's policies is to offer positive feedback to those who do. For example, saying, "Thanks, Susie, for always being here early" is a simple yet effective way to encourage late students to arrive on time.

Discipline

Discipline and dance go together; students who understand discipline are usually the most successful dancers.

Teachers who are invested in the success of their students take responsibility for misbehavior in their classes. Discipline problems are often a reaction to boredom or a lack of interest in the material being taught. A class that is constantly moving and full of energy is less likely to encourage misbehavior. Don't give your students enough time to act up! You'll notice that it's when you move to the sound system to select your music or when your attention is pulled away from the class that most bad behavior occurs. Once a student has enough time to be distracted, it is hard to bring the focus back to the class.

Your voice is one way to keep interest high. A droning monotone can cause students to lose interest in the class. Use your voice, through words and tone, to communicate confidence, excitement, or compassion instead of fatigue or boredom.

Students will test the boundaries, and it is important to react immediately but calmly. Be consistent. If you react to certain behavior, such as a student hanging from the ballet barre, you must react to *every* student who hangs from the ballet barre. Sending mixed messages is more detrimental than not reacting at all. Never overreact; if you lose your composure, you're no longer in control. Sometimes you don't have to say a word—a simple look or a moment of eye contact can send the message that you disapprove of a student's behavior. This type of reaction avoids public ridicule, which can have a negative influence on the self-esteem of your students. Sometimes silence is the best form of discipline.

When you do speak up concerning misbehavior, be sure the students understand that it's the behavior you are upset about, not them. Avoid comments that make children feel like failures; when they understand that everyone makes mistakes, they are more likely to learn from the error rather than resent the criticisms. If you react to the situation in a respectful way, most students won't make the same mistake a second time.

Don't allow those who continually create problems to be in the back of the room or hide behind other students. Move them to the front of the room. They won't know it, but by doing so you're discouraging negative behavior and making them feel important at the same time. Try to keep those students with behavior problems separated from each other. When you bring them to the front of the room, place them on separate ends of the line. Be prepared to go overboard with compliments (and express criticisms with care), in an effort to establish trust.

The most important aspect of discipline is consistency; otherwise you send mixed messages about what's OK and what isn't. And be sure your students know it's misbehavior, not them, that's unacceptable.

Make sure well-behaved students are not punished for the actions of others. Although offering corrections in technique to the entire class can be useful in not making a student feel singled out, blaming the whole class for one student's misbehavior can have an opposite effect. The offending student may be ridiculed by classmates who feel they paid a price for something they didn't do.

Persistent misbehavior must be addressed. If students are continually disrupting the class, it may be time to ask them to sit out the class for a particular period of time. Never let them leave the room—they might consider that a reward for their misbehavior. If parents complain about their children sitting out for a portion of the class, explain that it is your policy to never allow one student to distract the class from the learning process.

TIPS | **Controlling Your Classroom**

- A constantly moving, high-energy class keeps misbehavior at bay.
- Use your voice to keep students on task.

- React to misbehavior consistently; sending mixed messages is detrimental.
- Sometimes silence is the best form of discipline.
- Comment on the behavior, not the person.
- Keep troublemakers in the front of the class, and separate them from each other.

Maintaining Enthusiasm

According to Barry Neil Kaufman, author of *Happiness Is a Choice* and many other books, there are "Three Es" for being a good teacher: Energy, Enthusiasm, and Excitement. Ask yourself, "Am I excited about this material?" If you're not, don't teach it. Students turn off to unenthusiastic teachers. It's not the content, it's the presentation.

Students take their cues from the teacher. If the teacher is excited and full of energy, then the students will be, too. Why settle for ambivalence and boredom? Bring a theatrical air to your class. Give the students more than they expected!

The best way to bring excitement to your classes is to be fully present in each moment. Leave behind your personal problems and visually attend to your dancers. Make eye contact with all of them many times during class.

Although classes always have a certain structure, usually consisting of a warm-up or barre, across-the-floor work, and combinations or variations, it's OK to be creative. Enhancing the class with change or the unexpected helps to avoid student boredom, while utilizing exactly the same movement, music, or format every week leads to a lack of enthusiasm in both teacher and students. The change can be as simple as starting a combination facing a different wall, holding class in a different studio, or using some unexpected music. Be aware that many children of the 21st century are accustomed to continual stimulation, so do what it takes to keep them focused and enthusiastic.

Students often lose interest during the first few minutes of class, so starting with something unique could make all the difference. For example, make taking attendance fun and educational by asking students to respond with the name of a dance step, like "shuffle" or "plié" rather than saying "here" or "present." Although this activity has nothing to do with learning a movement, it stimulates the mind with something unexpected. And know what you want to accomplish before you enter the classroom. Investing time in pre-planning eliminates the "dead time" it takes you to figure out what you want to do next, which is when you will lose students' attention. Habitually winging it instead of pre-planning eventually catches up with you because students can feel it. Planning includes organizing your music; teachers who spend too much time at the tape deck or CD player almost always lose their students' interest.

Engage your students' interest from the moment they step in the door and they're more likely to stay on task for the entire class.

Once class is under way, move around frequently so that the students have to pay attention to where you are. Students may lose focus if the teacher remains sitting in a chair or standing in the front of the room for the entire class. Offer a change of pace every 10 to 15 minutes. It can be as simple as changing direction—if you are facing the mirrors, instead ask the class to face the back wall for a few minutes. Or you could change a center floor exercise to become an across-the-floor movement.

Think about the level and abilities of your students; teach

movement that will be challenging but not discouraging. If the material is too difficult, students become frustrated, resulting in a lack of interest; even worse, they may feel that they aren't good enough.

Break the material down by starting with the basic movement. For example, if you're teaching a turn combination, instead of starting with the full turn, simply demonstrate what's happening with the feet, and then encourage them to try it with the turn. Often students will grasp movement more quickly if they see it broken down and demonstrated in the most basic terms rather than attempting it full-out right away. Try changing the material or the way you explain it. The element of surprise is a perfect way to maintain a student's focus.

It is important to realize that students' lack of interest might have nothing to do with the teacher or the material. They could be dealing with divorce, conflicts in the home, problems with friends, or abusive situations. Whatever the circumstance, dance can allow students to forget their personal problems for the period of time they are dancing. Self-expression through the art of dance and the release of tension through physical activity can help students cope with their problems and build self-esteem.

TIPS | **Define Your Teaching Style**

- Does your love and enthusiasm for what you do show?
- Is your voice animated and energized?
- Are you smiling and full of life?
- Does your body reflect the energy you want from the students? Are you or your assistant doing the movement full-out? (Your students will not know what "full-out" means if there is not a good example in the classroom.)

PLAN, PLAN, PLAN

Planning is an important part of thoughtful teaching. Before each class begins, know what you are going to teach, express, and accomplish. Pre-plan your class (even if it's in your mind), and organize your music. Consider setting a goal for each class, either for yourself or your students—or both. It could be to have the students accomplish certain movement or choreography, or it could be as simple as making sure you say every student's name at least once during the class.

TRAINING IS TOP PRIORITY

Good teachers are aware that they are dealing with precious bodies that need correct training in order to develop into healthy adults. Keep proper training, which requires an understanding of how young bodies grow and develop, at the top of your priority list. Create a comfortable environment. You are dealing with movement and young people in leotards and tights; inhibition could play a part in their attitudes. Do all that you can to make every dancer feel comfortable by being accepting of differing body types, personalities, and reasons for dancing.

Avoid moving your classes along too quickly, making sure you don't miss any steps in the process along the way. Don't be tempted to give your dancers what they are not ready for. Safety is your number-one concern, so be sure the material you teach is appropriate for the age level and technical skill of your dancers. A good class has a good structure: Start every class with a warm-up or barre, and end every class on a positive note.

If students show potential in areas that aren't our specialty, we must understand that it is our responsibility to guide them in the right direction, even if it means they move on to another school. Not an appealing thought? The alternative is to assemble a faculty who can take the dancers to their highest potential.

THOUGHTS ON GOOD TEACHING

Good teaching is far more than the sum of its parts, and there are probably as many styles as there are personalities. There's no reason to lobby for cookie-cutter teachers; individuality adds dimension to what otherwise might be considered protocol. Still, there are tried-and-true classroom behaviors that every teacher should be familiar with.

First, establish an environment where the students feel respected, nurtured, and safe.

- Be sure to say each child's name at least once in every class.
- The students in the back of the room may be there because they don't have confidence in themselves. By recognizing their needs and pointing out what they do well, you'll help them develop more confidence.
- Build class morale by finishing class on a positive note. "Excellent class today, dancers—thank you!" or "I really enjoyed teaching you today" are just a couple of ways to send the message that you appreciate their hard work.
- Teachers who create a competitive atmosphere within their classes are not doing justice to their students, so don't play favorites. Use different people to demonstrate or to start the across-the-floor work each week.

Offer constructive criticism in a positive way, without passing judgment. Egos are particularly fragile in the teenage years, so be sensitive to the ages and developmental stages of your students.

- Begin a criticism with a compliment: "Wow, Susie, that was much better! Now be sure to stretch your knees and it will be perfect."
- Tune in to a dancer's or class's tolerance level for criticism. Know when to stop.
- Offer as many compliments as criticisms. Recognition of achievement is vitally important, even when the student doesn't quite make the grade. Hearing positive feedback like "Good attempt!" or "Much better!" could make all the difference in your students' confidence levels.
- Sometimes it is better to make a general comment to the entire class than it is to single out a particular student.

Treat your students with the same respect you demand from them, and make your goals and expectations clear.

- What you say—and how you say it—does matter, so choose your words carefully. "Please be sure to stretch your feet" is so much better than "What the heck is wrong with your feet?" Generous praise never harmed a child.
- Humiliating a student in front of her classmates will harm not only the student but the entire class. Your students will now come to class in fear that they will be next.
- Better learning comes with building confidence in the student. The learning process stops for students who feel pressured, humiliated, or unconfident.
- Encourage emotion, expression, or passion during class if you expect to see it in performance. Students have to learn to emote just as they have to learn how to do a pirouette. Don't expect them to perform like they love

what they are doing if they are not encouraged to be expressive in the classroom.

TIPS | **Successful Dance Educators . . .**

- have a genuine love for children.
- bring out the best in their students by motivating and inspiring them.
- enter the classroom free of personal distraction, giving total focus to their students.
- sense and respond to the individual needs of each student.
- always have the welfare of the student in mind.
- know what is physically appropriate for their dancers.
- select age-appropriate music and choreography.
- understand that each student is an individual with something to offer.
- maintain control of their classes by disciplining, engaging, and directing their students.
- encourage students to learn from each other.
- build variety—in music, presentation, orientation, structure, even guest teachers—into their classes.
- continue their own education, in order to offer the best, most up-to-date technical training to their students.
- appreciate and respect their fellow dance educators.
- stand up for their beliefs or studio policies.
- believe that teaching dance is about passing on an art form.
- aspire to be the best educator they can be.
- understand that the value of dance is far greater than awards, trophies, or honors.
- want to be doing exactly what they're doing.

LEARNING THROUGH CHOREOGRAPHY

Think outside the box when searching for new teaching tools. Sometimes learning is most effective when students are given new opportunities rather than corrections or guidance. Give your dancers the chance to experiment with choreography and you may be in for a surprise. Consider offering a choreography showcase where your students have the opportunity to invent their own works of art. They could create pieces for themselves or for other dancers from your school. Maybe you and your faculty could do an oral adjudication of the young choreographers' work and choose one to be in the annual recital or to enter in a competition.

At times, we discover that our dancers have hidden talents other than the technical or performance qualities we so often look for. As educators, we must encourage our students to find what they do best, then nurture those qualities. Often teachers are surprised to discover that the dancer from the back row moves to the front of the class when given the opportunity to choreograph.

Choreographing is another opportunity to develop the minds of your students and round out their dance training. Serious dancers may find that being exposed to the choreographic process helps them succeed in the professional world, as dancers or teachers.

ON REFLECTION

Cutting Your Losses

How many students dropped out of your school last year? Do you know what it cost you? Dropouts were a hot topic of discussion at a recent Project Motivate seminar; I was surprised to find that some studios lost 30 or 40 students per year; others lost more. Since the average studio enrollment is about 200 to 300, those losses make a difference in the bottom line at the end of the season.

What kind of numbers are we talking about? For example, at a studio where each student brings in $600 per year in tuition and fees, losing 10 students per year costs $6,000. Over a 10-year period, that's $60,000. So based on that potential 10-year enrollment and a loss of 10 students each year, that compounds to $600,000 over 10 years, $1,200,000 over 20 years, and $1,800,000 over 30 years.

Studio owners should expect to lose students who don't want to dance. We've all dealt with the child who isn't happy in class but whose mommy wants her there anyway (often because mommy is the one who wants to dance). We might lose the student whose parents are financially strapped, making dance tuition less of a priority. Sometimes students stop dancing because they become more involved in school activities; some move on to drill team or cheerleading because their dance training has prepared them to excel in both. Whatever the reasons, dropouts are inevitable. However, a loss of 30 or 40 students every season just doesn't seem necessary.

Sometimes personality conflicts between a faculty member and a student are to blame. Some teachers may be relieved when that student finally does leave the school. But better communication between studio owners and their faculty can temper those conflicts and perhaps prevent dropouts.

Faculty meetings, especially through the first few months of the season, are a good way to brainstorm ways to resolve conflicts and engage students who seem disinterested. Moving a student to another teacher's class or asking him to help out in a lower-level class could keep a potential dropout enrolled for 10 years, simply because there was good communication within the school.

I have learned that 90 percent of studio owners compensate

their teachers by the hour, without regard to the number of students in their classes. But a class that starts with 20 students in September, then finishes the season with 12 students, has lost 40 percent of its revenue. That class may end up costing money to run by the end of the year.

Your faculty may need a financial incentive to retain students. One school offers faculty members five dollars for every student who remains enrolled in their classes for the full season. Your bonus could be different; what's important is to offer some sort of incentive. In most cases, nothing works better than cash! Your investment could pay off many times over throughout the life of the studio.

Business owners should never underestimate the power of personal contact with their clientele; it helps build loyalty, which contributes to the overall success of the business. For example, I have discovered that the dropout rate is much less in smaller schools where the owner does all or most of the teaching. If you are a studio owner who doesn't teach all the classes, be sure to get to know all your students and their parents. Make it a priority to spend time in the school waiting room and to visit the classes you don't teach.

Check your attendance records often. If a student has missed more than two or three classes in a row, consider making a phone call to find out why. Your call will offer students and their families the opportunity to express problems or concerns they may have with the school. You could find out that the student has simply lost interest in dance, or maybe you will discover a situation that needs your attention. Either way, the call won't hurt your business, and it could result in keeping $6,000 of income over a 10-year period. That's not a bad return on the investment of a free local phone call and a small amount of your time.

Adding to the dropout rate is an atmosphere in which some students don't feel they are good enough. This can happen when the school emphasizes competition or touts itself as the most professional school in town. Always remember, the average parent and child are looking for a once-a-week class with a year-end recital. The recreational student needs to know she is an appreciated member of the studio family. Developing a reputation that you train professional dancers is not always good for business. Producing good dancers is important, but having a neighborhood school where everyone can learn to dance—and enjoy it—is the way to go financially.

Studio owners who pay attention to their students' needs often direct the most successful schools. Positive word of mouth will benefit you for years to come. It's more valuable than a full-page ad any day!

—Rhee Gold, November 2002
from *Dance Magazine*

THREE

Image Is Everything

"The art of being yourself at your best is the art of unfolding your personality into the person you want to be. . . . Be gentle with yourself, learn to love yourself, to forgive yourself, for only as we have the right attitude toward ourselves can we have the right attitude toward others."

—Wilfred Peterson, *This Week*, 1961

How often do you observe similar personality traits from person to person? Human nature inclines us to operate like a filing cabinet; we categorize people in various ways, often by our interpretations of their personalities. Sure, we know better—but it's a way to simplify the world. When we look a little deeper, we find that each of us is more like a fingerprint; no two are exactly alike. Everyone is unique in character, disposition, and nature.

Like each of us, every dance school has a personality all its own. The energy, characteristics, and attitudes of those who direct, manage, and teach combine to create the personality of the school. And that feeling, that atmosphere, that intangible essence has a huge influence on the success of the business.

A TALE OF TWO TEACHERS

We see one personality type in the imaginary Betty Sue's Dance Studio; it's the best technical school in the city. It has produced many dancers who moved on to professional careers and it brings home high-score awards from every competition. Throughout the season, the school hosts guest and master teachers in order to expose its students to the best in the business. Yet Betty Sue's Dance Studio has only 100 students, while another studio (let's call it Mary Jane's), up the street, has 400. None of Mary Jane's students have ever moved on to a professional career, and she doesn't produce the caliber of dancers that Betty Sue's does. How could it be possible that Mary Jane's enrollment is four times that of Betty Sue's? Well, it could be that Betty Sue's Dance Studio is too professional for the average parents of an 8-year-old, whose sole goal is to have their child dance in order to learn grace and poise—and, of course, see the child in a tutu in the annual recital.

The reaction of those at Betty Sue's is to talk negatively about Mary Jane's. They also spend a *lot* of cash on the biggest newspaper ads, proclaiming their studio to be the "most professional in the city." Mary Jane is so busy attending to the needs of her 400 students that she doesn't even notice the ads in the paper. Nor does she care.

Betty Sue's marketing objectives seem to be about being better than the other studios. The problem with that approach is that it scares off many potential clients—and the studio owner doesn't realize it! Instead of spending time, energy, and money trying to clobber Mary Jane's, Betty Sue needs to regard the competition her school faces as a motivator and dig deep to analyze the reasons for the differences in enrollment.

Outstanding credentials and hundreds of trophies or big ads in the newspaper do not make a successful studio; it's the personality. Owners who appreciate and get to know their clientele build successful studios. They spend a good deal of time in the waiting room talking with the parents and building lasting loyalty. The teachers and staff are always upbeat and positive. Organization and quality service are at the top of the agenda. And every dancer feels as important as the next, no matter what their skill level. In other words, recreational dancers are valued as much as the stars of *The Nutcracker* or big trophy winners. These characteristics are what parents are looking for. The average parent knows nothing about the technical training; they only know that their child is happy—or not.

Personality, not outstanding credentials, hundreds of trophies, or big ads in the newspaper, makes a successful studio.

If you truly have the best studio in town, have enough confidence in yourself to resist reminding everyone. Instead, go after being a neighborhood type of school that offers all its students (not just the good ones) the opportunity to experience the wonderful world of dance. Once students have registered at your school, slowly introduce the dancers who show potential to the more professional programs. Parents will accept a gradual progression as they see their child's ability and interest develop; asking them to jump into an intensive program that they don't understand the need for, or that they may consider too expensive, can make them feel threatened. Not all dancers, even talented ones, aspire to a professional career. Always have a place for those who choose to be recreational dancers, and always make them feel just as important as your advanced kids.

THE PORTABLE PERSONALITY

As a dance-event promoter, I have encountered a wide variety of studio personalities, as represented by the schools' owners, especially through the dance competitions. I've met many dance educators who have it all together. Their success reflects their understanding that organization is key to a successful business; they are aware of it and they practice it. These teachers arrive at all events—recitals, community performances, competitions—early, with a friendly and relaxed attitude, as do their dancers. Confidence seems to be a natural characteristic for this group. You can see and feel their love for their profession and for the dancers they teach. It is simply who they are, and it comes across without much effort. When their dancers are onstage they project a genuine love for what they do—and more important, they radiate that same sense of confidence. Audiences (and judges, if it's a competition) feel it and respond to it, sometimes without even knowing why.

At the other extreme, I see many frazzled teachers and school owners at competitions. They are usually late and disorganized. Sometimes their students and parents panic because they have a performance in 15 minutes and there is no sign of the teacher. The teacher has the music and without it, there will be no performance because she never thought to send backup tapes. The parents are disappointed and outraged because they and their children acted responsibly: They arrived early, paid their participation fees, purchased their costumes—and here they are without music or teacher!

When the teacher does arrive, long after the scheduled performance, the kids are no longer excited. Instead, they are embarrassed and nervous. When they finally dance, they don't give the performance they might have because of all the stress they experienced while waiting for the teacher.

A teacher who acts irresponsibly risks a double-whammy of ramifications from her behavior. She has opened herself up to unfavorable comparisons if several schools from her hometown are participating and all perform on time, with the guidance of a teacher who's clearly in control. Her dancers and parents see that the students from the other studios are relaxed and ready to go without a problem. When September rolls around and it is time for registration, she will suffer and the other schools in town likely will benefit.

"We must become the change we want to see."

—Mahatma Gandhi

Even if the frazzled studio owner doesn't lose the students, she loses control. The example has been set, and the clientele follow suit: Dancers and parents start to arrive late for everything, sometimes without the proper shoes or a complete costume. The dancers have not been taught the responsibilities of a committed performer. Onstage, they seem uncomfortable and lacking in confidence. Because they are so influenced by their teachers, they emulate their attitude and consider irresponsible behavior acceptable, because they know no other way.

That frazzled personality affects every event the school is involved in. I have been to recitals, dress rehearsals, *Nutcracker* performances, and classes where it is obvious that the directors or the teachers don't have it together. Whether you've been in business for many years or just a few, your demeanor should reflect the fact that you are a professional.

Actions, priorities, and personality all have a definite influence on success. Make sure you are proud of what you represent and are open to change when it's needed.

DRESS CODE: MAKING A STATEMENT

A dress code lends a professional look to classes and sends the message to students and observers that the school's staff takes the training they provide seriously. A dress code creates an added sense of discipline in the classroom and equality among the students. The focus stays on taking a good class rather than comparing dance wardrobes. Plus, baggy sweatshirts or sweatpants make it difficult to observe the dancers' bodies well enough to offer the technical corrections needed to build strong dancers. Straight knees and proper body alignment are hard to see underneath layers of baggy clothing.

Another advantage to having a dress code is the additional profit for the school if it sells basics such as leotards and tights. If your school has one, say so in the brochure, on registration forms, and on the Web site. But whether or not the school has a dress code, proper shoes should be required for all classes.

If your school has never had a dress code but you are considering implementing one, the place to start might be with the ballet classes. Often I hear teachers complain that their students don't take ballet training seriously. If the teacher and students look like ballet dancers, they will probably take their classes more seriously.

There are legitimate reasons not to have a dress code. Teenage girls who are self-conscious about their bodies may feel inhibited in a leotard and tights; if they feel too uncomfortable, they may choose not to dance. And many boys struggle with our society's negative stereotyping about males wearing tights. It's OK to start the boys out in a pair of sweats and a solid-color T-shirt. However, once they move on to a more advanced level of training, they should be willing to wear a pair of black tights for ballet classes. Boys who take their dance training seriously need to understand the discipline of a dress code as well as its importance to their technical training. Those ages 10 and over should be encouraged to wear a dance belt.

Hip-hop and adult classes should be exempt from a dress code. Hip-hop dancers often come to the school expressing no interest in other dance forms, so a dress code might intimidate them. However, they frequently segue into other classes once they've been exposed to them, and they can be introduced to the idea of a dress code in those classes. Adults may feel the need to cover up more and variations in dress don't distract them, so permissiveness in attire is generally the rule.

FOUR

Preschool: A Different World

"There are two lasting bequests we can give our children. One is roots. The other is wings." —Hodding Carter Jr.

Teaching preschool dance classes is not about teaching technique or steps. Children ages 5 and under are on a journey. They're experiencing the wonders of the world every day. Everything is new, new, new! The dance school is one of those wonders—yet another place for young minds to explore. They'll touch your mirrors, lose focus, hang from the ballet barres, talk out of turn, and play with the sound system. This behavior shouldn't be interpreted as negative; it's a positive result of natural curiosity. These young beings are simply doing their jobs: gathering information about the world around them.

Preschool children are like clay; you're helping to mold their personalities, inspire creativity, develop a basic understanding of musicality, and so much more. You, and your words, actions, and ideas, are going to make quite an impression on those young minds.

The very young student will not become a proficient dancer or learn extensive choreography. The objective is to teach basic musicality and movement skills and to improve gross motor skills. Preschool movement is as simple as skipping, hopping, or clapping to a beat. You can enhance the children's imagination by utilizing imagery or "make believe." With imagery you can become clowns or fairies or—of course—a ballerina. Props are a great way to augment these classes. Use magic wands, beach balls, hula hoops, rhythm sticks, flowers—the list is endless. Just be sure your props are safe!

THE FINE ART OF DISCIPLINE

Discipline for this age level must be on the gentle side. Good communication with your students helps develop confidence, feelings of self-worth, and good relationships with others. Positive learning occurs when teachers set limits and encourage good behavior. Ask yourself, "Am I disciplining in a way that will encourage or discourage?"

Preschool dance: an opportunity to set the stage for a lifelong passion!

Tailor your limits to the age group in each class. You'll find a vast difference in the attention spans of a 2-year-old and a 5-year-old. Many children are in some kind of structured environment, whether day care or school, at very young ages, so they're already learning about rules, structure, and how they fit into a group. Dance class is no different; make sure you explain the rules simply and offer frequent reminders. Come to each class loaded with patience—especially for the remarkable frequency with which preschoolers seem to need to go to the bathroom, sometimes more than once during a class! Don't become flustered by the many interruptions you may face from these very busy, very curious youngsters.

You may be stunned by the noise level in a preschool class, but whatever you do, don't yell. Speaking in a quiet voice is more likely to gain their attention; try whispering and you'll see the entire class settle down.

If you have a problem retaining your students' attention during a class, it may not be their fault. It's up to the teacher to use creativity in finding ways to keep the children on task in the classroom.

COMMUNICATION

If you're towering over your students when you stand, bend or sit when you talk to them—become child size! Look the children in the eye when you speak, and help them learn to direct their focus. Teach them to listen by gently touching them to get their attention, or say a child's name before you direct a comment to him or her.

Praise builds confidence. Be sure you compliment every student during each class. Unkind words or loss of temper can frighten or alienate children; sometimes it makes them feel that they are not "good enough."

INCLUSIVENESS

Make no judgments; be sensitive to different cultures and parental beliefs and attitudes.

Welcome parents to be a part of their child's dance education. Consider inviting the parents into the classroom for the last few minutes of class. (Once a month is about right.) This allows the children the opportunity to include their parents in their love for dance, and including the parents often makes them more supportive. Who knows? They might even practice at home together!

The structure of the class must accommodate those who are more advanced in their development and coordination, as well as those who need additional help. Good dance educators understand that no two children will develop in the same way. This means some will move faster than others, especially at the preschool age. Consider staffing all preschool classes with an assistant teacher who can offer individual help to the students who lag behind, freeing the primary teacher to keep the class moving forward.

CASE STUDY

Preschool Success

An interview with Melissa Hoffman, owner/director of the Melissa Hoffman Dance Center in Londonderry, New Hampshire, for the past 14 years. She has served as president of Dance Masters of New England and is active throughout the dance community. She and her husband are the parents of four children. Melissa has effectively managed her personal and professional life by surrounding herself with an outstanding faculty and staff.

Why did you create a daytime preschool program?

Prior to opening my school, I investigated the demographics of the community; I discovered the average adult age was 35. We interpreted that statistic to indicate that the area would be conducive to preschool dance programs. The region has many wealthier stay-at-home moms. Another important factor was that there weren't a lot of preschool activities available within the community. Also, I believe preschool children are better behaved and possess a longer attention span before three in the afternoon.

How many preschool students take class each week?

We have about 200 students registered in our preschool program, which represents a bit more than 25 percent of our total enrollment.

What do you consider a safe class size?

We work on a 1 to 7 ratio in most of our preschool classes. The average size is 14 with one teacher and an assistant.

How many preschool classes do you offer?

The school is open for weekday preschool classes three days a week: Tuesday (four and a half hours), Wednesday (six hours), and Thursday (three hours). We also offer preschool classes on Saturday.

Please describe your classes and what you call them.

We offer Preschool I for the 3-year-old, consisting of an intro to ballet and a lot of creative movement. The class is 45 minutes.

Preschool II is for the 4-year-old. It includes an intro to ballet and adds an intro to tap. It's also 45 minutes.

Our class for 5-year-olds is Kinder-Movement. It's a full hour, consisting of half ballet and half tap.

A program similar to Kinder-Movement, called Dance Works, takes place after school; it's for 5- and 6-year-olds.

Do you offer classes for children younger than 3?

We have in the past, but it wasn't as successful for us. Age 3 on up works best for my school.

Do you offer a "Mommy and Me" class?

We did, but we eliminated it. The original concept was to teach half the season with moms in the classroom, then the second half with only the children. But there was a drop-off in interest for the second half of the year. Often the children don't want to leave their moms.

How much is the tuition for your preschool classes?

The 45-minute class is $40 per month and the one-hour class is $48 per month.

How do you deal with academic conflicts?

For children who attend academic preschool or kindergarten in the morning, we offer a 1:45 PM class, and for those who attend in the afternoon, we offer a 9:30 AM class. I never start a class earlier than 9:30; most of my families have other children and are preparing them to go to school earlier in the morning. So 9:30 seems to be the perfect time.

Are the preschool children included in the recital?

Yes, they are responsible for half of the recital ticket sales. Each class performs one dance, either ballet or tap, depending on their age and skill level. We almost always utilize props for preschool routines. Props tend to keep the classes in unison and children this age love them!

Do the preschool dancers usually remember their steps when they hit the stage?

Some do. But often we'll place teachers or assistants at the front of the stage to coach them, usually only with hand movements. I'm not in favor of coaching preschool dancers from the wings; it's a distraction for the children.

I've met many teachers who offer a separate preschool recital. What's your opinion on this?

We have considered it in the past. What stops us is the exposure the younger dancers and their parents have to our more advanced levels. I think it's important for child and parent to have the opportunity to witness what the future will hold when it comes to their dance education. Also, not including the preschool students in the regular recital would eliminate at least 50 percent of our ticket sales. I do try to have the preschool students dance in the first half of the show to reduce the fatigue factor. This helps the backstage moms, because their work is done by the end of the first act. Most of the preschoolers then stay for the entire show.

Do you offer classes for preschool students after the recital?
We resume preschool classes one week after the recital. Usually there are two four-week sessions. There are fewer classes and students enrolled, compared to the rest of the season. About 60 to 70 percent attend class during the season—nearly 20 to 30 percent are new students. It's a good way to generate a new student's enthusiasm before the fall registration.

Do you offer any other summer dance experiences for preschool dancers?
Yes, we offer two separate camps. The Preschool Camp, which meets three mornings a week for two hours, is for children ages 3 and 4. The curriculum includes dance, creative movement, arts and crafts, and basic gymnastics.

Our second program is Kinder-Camp, offered to 5- and 6-year-olds. It's similar to Preschool Camp; however, the students attend five days a week for two and a half hours.

Both programs are offered twice each summer and are always full. Tuition for the Preschool Camp is approximately $55 per session and Kinder-Camp is approximately $65.

In what way do you perceive your preschool programs to be beneficial to the success of your school?
Children who start to dance at the preschool age are often enrolled in our school until they graduate from high school. Ten of my first thirteen preschool students graduated this year!

Children ages 5 and under explore and discover every day.

Who teaches your preschool classes?
I have an excellent teacher who has great rapport with the children. She has a young daughter, which I believe enhances her understanding of working with young children.

What's your advice to teachers who have younger or teenage teachers working with the preschool level?
Although there are exceptions, I'm not sure if a teenager has the experience or patience it takes to work with preschool children. I consider it a specialized field as well as the future of my school. My advice is to invest in teachers who have a passion for working with preschool children.

Do you have assistant teachers in the classroom?
Yes, I like adult assistants in my preschool classes. Most are moms from within the school who have a basic dance background. I've instituted a "parent rotation"—a different mom assists with the class each week.

Do you compensate the preschool assistants?
Most of my assistant teachers have children in the school. Their compensation comes in trade for their child's training.

Are there many boys in your preschool programs?

Yes, at least 60 percent of our classes have at least one boy. When considering costumes, movement, and music for the recital, we make our boys look like boys!

Is it difficult to direct a school that operates all day rather than only during after-school hours?

I believe it is important to be "owner friendly" with our clientele, so I make it a point to be at the school during the day; however, I don't have to be there all the time. I have an excellent teacher and staff to keep the school running while I'm taking care of four young children of my own.

THE TRUTH ABOUT KINDERDANCE®

Many dance schools that offer programs for preschool- and kindergarten-age children call them Kinderdance—but watch out! Melbourne, Florida-based Kinderdance® is a developmental dance, gymnastics, and movement program for young children that incorporates academic readiness skills and focuses on building self-esteem. It's a nationwide, franchised program, so using this name without purchasing a franchise and using Kinderdance-trained teachers and curriculum is a copyright infringement. Get those creative juices flowing and come up with an original, unique name for your program.

Enhance a child's imagination with "make believe" activities, imagery, and props.

TIPS | **What's in a Name?**

Since you can't use the name "Kinderdance" unless you've bought a franchise, here are some ideas other schools have come up with. Start brainstorming!

- Kids in Motion
- Kids 'n' Motion
- Baby Ballerina Program
- Exploring Dance
- Kid Fit
- Kid Moves
- Dance-Toddler
- Toddler-Dance
- Boogie Babies
- Twirling Tots
- Creative Movement
- Pre-Ballet
- Preschool Dance
- I Can Dance!
- Creative Dance
- Tiny Dancers
- Tiny Tappers
- Baby Dance
- Let's Dance!
- Dance-a-Lot

ON REFLECTION

The Most Valuable Student

New studio owners have one thing in common: They're motivated. They'll teach just about anyone, simply to keep the school doors open. But some, as they become more successful, lose interest in teaching the recreational or novice dancers or the "babies" in favor of working with the advanced dancers. It's very gratifying to work with students who have developed strong basics, making it easier to teach and create choreography.

However, it's important not to lose sight of the value—to your students and your business—of offering your recreational and preschool dancers the best experience possible. It will make a definite difference in your school's bottom line. To me, teaching dance is about instilling passion, not simply about creating great technicians. The once-a-week teen jazz dancer with a size 12 foot can develop passion, and there are students who can execute eight pirouettes or a développé next to their ear who don't have it. Producing students who love what they're doing (and happy parents) leads to more dollars for your studio, through positive word of mouth (which I think is more valuable to a school's success than anything). And recommendations are more likely to come from the satisfied parents of recreational and preschool dancers than from the parents of advanced students. Some of those with children on a career track may become burned out financially or emotionally when dancing becomes a full-time commitment for both dancer and parents. They may not be the ones you can rely on for positive word of mouth.

Make sure your best teachers are educating the largest—and therefore most important—sector of your school. Those "babies" are your future, and the recreational dancers are your financial base, not only because there are more of them, but because they're not attending classes at a reduced rate, like the intensive dancers.

Some school owners turn to their advanced dancers to teach the preschool classes. I believe there are very few 16-year-olds who possess the experience needed to work with young children. It takes years to develop the skills and patience required simply to control a group of 3- to 4-year-olds, let alone grasp the concept of what's developmentally appropriate movement, music, or discipline. It's not about teaching technique, it's about teaching basic rhythm skills—how to skip or hop—or how to interact with other children. Sometimes simply helping a child develop an attention span that lasts the entire class is what it's all about. Preschool teachers should be specialists, with the younger teachers working as apprentices before taking on a class of their own.

I also don't endorse advanced students teaching the recreational dancers, especially the teen classes. Young teachers can have a tough time gaining the respect of their students and the students' parents. Teenage teachers may not understand the importance of a professional teacher-student relationship—that's knowledge gained through experience—choosing instead to become friends with their students. They have good intentions, but I believe the situation leads to a lack of respect from their students.

Recreational students are not striving to be professionals; they want to experience the joy of a physical activity and have fun. Preprofessional dancers may have trouble valuing that choice. A good teacher enthusiastically teaches every child, no matter what the skill level or ambition.

For performances, it's important that teachers guarantee their students look their best. Choreography for young or recreational dancers should be well thought out; it can be a challenge to make a group of beginners look good. The best teachers are innovative enough to create a year-end show where the audience doesn't see such a difference between advanced and recreational levels. Students and parents can sense which dancers you consider important. If recreational dancers think you're giving more to the advanced students, they won't last long in your school.

Don't let economy be the motivation for hiring a teenage teacher. The result could be a sad financial situation for the life of your school. Investing in those who teach the majority of your students is the smart way to go. Imagine the difference in your school's bottom line if you retained most of your preschool and recreational dancers each season. What's in it for you? Fewer marketing dollars spent, positive word of mouth, more growth, and the knowledge that you are offering the best dance education possible, to all your students.

—Rhee Gold, September 2003
from *Dance Magazine*

PART TWO

Secrets to a Successful School

"There is no point at which you can say, 'Well, I'm successful now. I might as well take a nap.' "

—*Carrie Fisher*

FIVE

Building a Strong Team

"The important thing to recognize is that it takes a team, and the team ought to get credit for the wins and the losses. Successes have many fathers; failures have none." —Philip Caldwell

All good leaders in all kinds of businesses know the value of a unified team that's focused on success. When it comes to the dance school, the team might include your office staff, faculty, and perhaps some volunteers. Ideally, each player wants what's best for the school and its students. No one does it alone; the bigger the business, the more good people it takes to keep it operating. As the team leader, you must be open to ideas, a few criticisms, and constant change. It isn't about you being the boss, it's about how you coach the team.

Strong teams have open lines of communication and work together to bring ideas to fruition. Having team members with varied perspectives enhances the decision-making process; different personalities and viewpoints can do nothing but help generate ideas. Another benefit of regarding your employees as a team is the sense of pride you instill in them when they know their input is appreciated.

Do all that you can to assemble a staff of caring people who have genuine love for the art of dance and the children. Make sure your office staff (particularly the receptionist and anyone else who might work at the front desk) bubbles over with personality and can't help but spread positive vibes at all times.

It's a well-known fact that a good team outperforms any individual.

Today's dance school owner faces challenges that were unknown a generation ago. The lines of communication between those in charge must be open at all times to deal with an entirely new set of circumstances. It could be dancers who bring emotional problems to class with them, or maybe it's a problem with a parent who is too involved. Whatever the situation, each team member must know how to handle it with style. Everyone on the staff should take the same position on any subject and understand how to explain studio policies and the reasons for them. For that reason, it's imperative to keep your team up-to-date with changes in policy, dates of events, and other important information. When the entire team is on the same foot, it creates an organized and unified image for your dancers and their parents.

HIRING HOW-TOS

Every school owner dreads spending the time and money to hire and train new faculty members only to have them be a disappointment. How do you know when you've found an excellent teacher who will work well with your team? Is attitude more important than experience? Is professional experience more important than a college degree? Hiring a high-powered staff is a complex task in which you must balance multiple considerations about each candidate with your studio's needs.

Former dancers who have worked professionally may seem like exciting prospects to an employer at first glance—but remember, a Broadway or company dancer may not have a concept of what it's like to teach a 7-year-old. Although many former dancers prove to be excellent in the classroom, professional performing experience does not *automatically* qualify someone to teach. Likewise, some impressive teachers have never had a performing career.

The single most important factor in hiring is to observe a prospective teacher in the classroom, preferably teaching several classes at various levels—beginning and recreational students as well as advanced dancers. A teacher who is excellent with the advanced level is not always good with the beginners and vice versa. No amount of interviewing or resume reading can substitute for seeing a teacher in action.

TIPS | **A Dynamite Teaching Demonstration—What to Look For**

- Does the prospective teacher arrive early?
- Does he welcome the students and introduce himself?
- Is he well prepared for the class?
- Is his appearance appropriate for the image of the studio?
- Does he have good control of the classroom and the dancers?
- Does he show respect for the students, making corrections politely and tactfully?
- Does he make an effort to remember the students' names?

(It's OK if he's not successful; the point is that he is aware of its importance.)

- Does he pay attention to all the students rather than focusing on the most talented ones?
- Are his exercises and combinations suited to the age and skill levels of the students?
- Does he show a sound understanding of technique and possess an ability to communicate that to the students?
- Does he demonstrate musicality and look for it in the students?
- Does he move among the students and demonstrate movements rather than planting himself at the front of the classroom?
- Is he energetic and enthusiastic?
- Do the dancers respond positively?

Create a job description, put it in writing, and then discuss it with each candidate. Be specific about what you expect from them above and beyond the class schedule. Do you require them to travel to performances or competitions? Are they available for the dress rehearsal and the recital? Are they available for your summer program? Knowing exactly what the job entails allows those candidates who aren't able to meet your needs to remove themselves from the running before the process goes too far.

Most schools require their staff to choreograph for recitals, competitions, and other performances. Good teachers are not always good choreographers, so request a video of the candidates' own choreography. Make sure they have worked with younger dancers, and look for versatility, age-appropriate movement and music, and effective use of space as well as solid technique.

It can be difficult, but try to determine whether you think the prospective employee will be a good team player. Does he have experience working with other teachers or schools? Does he seem outgoing and anxious to work with others? Do you think his personality will fit in well with those of your current faculty and staff? Always call previous employers to find out why the applicant was terminated or left the previous job. They can also provide valuable information on the candidate's work ethic and ability to be a part of a team.

The interview will give you a clear sense of a prospective teacher's personality and ability to interact. Taking into account the normal nervousness that accompanies any job interview, you can still expect a confidant person to make eye contact and present herself with ease. (See appendix 1 for a sample faculty contract.)

TIPS | **Interviewing Essentials**

Always request a resume, but be sure to discuss these topics in detail.

- Availability—full-time, part-time, weekends, etc. Do they have any other employment commitments they intend to keep?
- Previous teaching experience, including which levels
- What inspired them to become a teacher?
- A description of their training—what kind, where, with whom, when?
- Other training or experience, such as acrobatics/gymnastics, social dancing, or administrative skills
- Have they had any performing experience?
- Option of a trial period of employment
- References or recommendations

- Name of last employer
- Reason for leaving previous employer
- Reason for wanting to work at your school
- Where do they see themselves 5 or 10 years from now?

Wrong Choices Aren't Forever

A teacher who's not a good match for your school can have a dramatic effect on enrollment, so observe your faculty as often as possible. Don't be afraid to express your opinion; if you want something done differently, say so with confidence. Those who are invested in being a part of the school will appreciate your input.

If you do have a faculty member whom you (or your dancers) are not happy with, don't wait until the end of the season to do something about it. Replace the teacher as soon as possible; otherwise, the students may end the season on a sour note and decide not to return in the fall.

YOU'VE GOT 'EM—NOW KEEP 'EM!

Once you've put the time and effort into hiring terrific teachers, you'll want to keep them. Showing your appreciation for a job well done encourages loyalty and promotes lasting relationships with your employees. Give your teachers plenty of reasons to want to keep working for you.

Faculty Incentives

When determining which incentives work best for you, look for opportunities that will inspire your faculty to become better educators. The following ideas are just some of the many ways you can reward and develop your staff.

Educational Opportunities

Continuing education programs can give you an excellent return on your investment in a good teacher. The faculty member gains valuable knowledge, your students benefit, and ultimately the school is more successful. These opportunities include conferences, workshops, choreography seminars, dance conventions, summer programs, teacher training schools, or even a trip to New York! If you have financial constraints, consider offering to pay only part of the cost. Perhaps you can cover the cost of the seminar, but the faculty member pays for the accommodations. Or consider covering 50 percent of the total expenses.

Pay Their Dues

A great way to assure that your faculty continues their education is to pay their membership dues in a dance teachers' organization. As their sponsor, you are justified to require that they attend a certain percentage of the workshops or seminars offered by the organization.

Subscriptions

You can keep your faculty up-to-date about educational issues, news, and trends by providing subscriptions to dance-related magazines. This is an inexpensive, monthly reminder of what a great studio your employees work at!

Bonuses

Many studio owners pay their faculty an hourly wage without regard to the number of students they retain through a season. A good way to encourage teachers to present a welcoming, fun, and dynamic class is an end-of-year bonus based on the number of students retained. Whatever the amount—$5 per dancer, perhaps, or as low as $1—it will create a greater awareness of dropouts among the faculty.

The holidays are the perfect time to offer your staff a pat on the back. A bonus is greatly appreciated at this time of year (and halfway through the season is a great time to say thank you). Base the amount of the bonus on seniority and/or the number of hours taught.

The close of the season is the time to make a good final impression. The faculty has been through months of rehearsals, dress rehearsals, fixing costumes, lining up kids, and doing everything possible to create a good image for you and the studio. If you rely on their talents for your success, invest in appreciating them! Again, the amount is up to you, but a bonus equal to one week's pay is a good idea. If you can't afford that, give less; the point is to show appreciation.

Benefits

Health insurance is probably the most expensive incentive you can offer, but it is the one thing that usually keeps an employee for years. More than likely your employees will think twice before leaving a job that offers them health benefits, especially if they have children. If you can't afford to pay for full benefits, you may choose to offer to cover a portion of the premium, with the employee paying the balance.

Say "Thank You"

The best incentive you can offer—your appreciation—comes from your heart and not your checkbook! Taking the time to drop a note of thanks is an excellent way to show your appreciation, whether it's to a member of the faculty, an office worker, parent, or dancer. Those who look up to and respect you will love the fact that you took the time to write to them. At Project Motivate seminars, I often hear teachers say they simply want to know that their employers notice their efforts. Everyone needs to know they are appreciated. If any employee, parent, or student is deserving of praise, make sure they get it. It's even better to offer the praise publicly.

Positive Feedback

Observing classes is another way to let faculty members know you care. If you are happy with the way they handle their classroom or a particular situation, be sure to mention it. Go so far as to give them a couple of reasons why you are happy with their performance. They will then know you have put thought into your compliment and that you mean it!

Give Credit Where It's Due

If your school participates in competitions or other performances where a teacher is recognized for his choreography, make sure he receives the recognition he deserves. Some studio owners take the credit for their staff's choreography, which only causes resentment.

Acknowledge the Extras

For dance teachers, working in a 21st-century school means more than merely teaching classes and attending the annual recital. Many teachers today are expected to attend performances, competitions, extra rehearsals, studio meetings, and more. If participating in these activities requires employees to spend their own money or their free time accomplishing the task, you may need to start thinking about some sort of compensation. It could be an hourly wage, but it does not have to be equal to their hourly teaching wage.

Although teachers' attendance at the dress rehearsal and recital is expected at most schools, it wouldn't hurt to offer an incentive to help them enjoy the experience a little more. Also, consider offering the faculty and other workers lunch.

Having teachers or choreographers attend competitions or performances can be a big morale booster for the students; however, some commitments can take up an entire weekend. Asking an employee to come and "hang out" without offering some sort of compensation or incentive may build resentment. Consider offering a per diem for food and transportation expenses. You could add a surcharge to the dancers' entry fees to cover the cost of the faculty per diem expenses. For out-of-town events, you may want to consider covering the cost of a hotel room. It could be one room for up to four employees; the imposed togetherness can even help build morale!

The best incentive you can offer comes from your heart, not your checkbook!

ON REFLECTION

Handle With Care

School owners can make many investments to achieve success; however, the key one is in the classroom. Passionate teachers who care about their students, who hold dance in high regard and work as team players, make a successful school and should be handled with care.

Four years ago, Pauline (not her real name) joined the faculty of a community dance school. The business was in its second year and very small. Initially, she taught three hours per week at a rate of $15 per hour. Since two classes had only five students and another had fewer than ten, she felt her hourly wage was appropriate.

Pauline was motivated, so she donated her time to create choreography for performances to promote the school and attended teacher-training programs to improve her skills. By the end of the season, her classes had doubled. New clients were calling the school specifically requesting to study with her.

The following year, the school took off. Pauline taught more than 10 hours a week and continued to choreograph, much of which she wasn't compensated for. Pauline felt uncomfortable bringing up the subject of a raise, and the school owner never did. She kept telling herself that she was satisfied with the increase in her class hours, though she wondered whether she was being taken advantage of.

In her third year, Pauline was the school's main teacher and choreographer. She had gained a title—administrative assistant—still, there was no raise. She was teaching 20 hours a week, creating most of the choreography, and taking on part of the administration. Yet she was paid only for the hours she was teaching. Pauline felt resentful that her willingness to take on responsibility wasn't appreciated.

When the school entered a dance competition, the dancers did very well. A special choreography award was announced for one of Pauline's pieces, but before she could get out of her seat, her boss was onstage taking credit for the choreography.

Pauline ran out of patience. She accepted part of the responsibility for the problems; she thought she should have spoken up sooner. She talked to her boss, but the raise in pay was nixed right away; it wasn't in the budget. As for the choreography, her boss responded that Pauline was paid for her teaching and that included the choreography and the credit for it.

Pauline realized that she and her employer perceived the situation differently and that she had allowed it to escalate because she had lacked the confidence to speak up for herself. So she decided not to return the following year.

Without Pauline, the school's enrollment drastically decreased. The school's owner had misjudged Pauline's value. An increase in her wage and an acknowledgement of her contributions would have been a small price to pay to keep her enrollment.

Many school owners do appreciate their faculty but have financial constraints that don't allow them to offer higher wages. There are other ways to show appreciation . . . those incentives that come from the heart, not the checkbook: Recognize effort with praise; go a step further and offer the praise publicly. Give program credit and provide positive feedback. And don't underestimate the power of a simple "Thank you."

—Rhee Gold, May 2003
from *Dance Magazine*

THE ASSISTANT TEACHER ADVANTAGE

Assistant or apprentice teachers can be very helpful to your faculty, and using them provides a great opportunity to develop teaching skills in your students. You may train a student teacher who ends up becoming a future employee of your school! An in-studio teacher-training program is a great way to expand the learning opportunities available to your students. Those who work as assistant or apprentice teachers may find their interest in dance recharged, and they may feel even more connected to the school.

However, a qualified and experienced teacher must be in control of all classes at your school; at no time should an apprentice or assistant teacher be left to teach class on their own. It is acceptable to allow an assistant teacher to teach a particular part of class or present a combination as part of their teacher training; however, the primary teacher should be present and ready to evaluate and make suggestions to the assistant.

Teacher-training programs are best offered to students ages 14 and over. Advertise your program in the school brochure and other literature, and encourage dancers who show an interest in learning teaching skills to participate. Make sure the students understand that they don't have to be intensive dancers to participate; often, the recreational students make the best assistants. Plan to have monthly meetings where faculty can evaluate and make suggestions to the apprentices and discuss issues or problems within the classroom, plans for the recital, and any other teacher-related concerns. Try to schedule all apprentice teachers to work with the same classes during the entire season.

TIPS | **Recommended Rules for Apprentice Teachers**

Apprentice teachers

- must have the permission of their parents to participate.
- must make a commitment for the entire season.
- must attend monthly apprentice teachers meetings from September to June.
- will comply with the studio dress code at all times.

- will arrive at least 10 minutes before the start of their first class of the day.
- will dance full-out during all classes.
- may be assigned to tutor students in need of extra help.
- will set the right example for younger students at all times.
- are required to learn the choreography performed by their classes.
- will assist with their classes at all rehearsals and performances.
- may be assigned to teach a class on their own to be evaluated by the faculty (older or more advanced student teachers).
- will abide by all studio policies and act appropriately and professionally both inside and out of the studio.

THE SCHOOL MANAGER

If a school is flourishing and operating at capacity, the owner/director may not be able to handle both the artistic and business ends without being overwhelmed. At that point, investing in a good studio manager is imperative. Other than the owner/director, it is the most important position in the studio. A manager must be loyal, well informed, and love what she does. It's not a position that can be filled by just anybody if the school is to be a success. The manager is in essence the "voice of the school"; most inquiries will be directed to her, and she will be the person whom most of your clientele know best.

As the studio owner/director, you will be in constant contact with your studio manager. You will need a reliable person, dedicated to offering you and your clientele quality service. Once you've found the right person, do all that you can to hang on to her. Never consider this an area where you can cut corners or try to save money. The manager's salary could be one of your biggest operational expenses, but if you have the right person it will be well worth it. Pay her what she deserves and you will get what you need—guaranteed! And be prepared to provide her with a private place to handle financial matters. Money should not be processed in front of anyone.

The Ultimate Studio Manager Job Description

The ideal studio manager is highly organized, diplomatic, and a born problem solver. The job requires a people-savvy mentality and excellent communication skills as well as practicality and bookkeeping skills. Besides being a visible, positive presence in your school, what else might this all-important person do?

- Answer all incoming phone calls
- Recover telephone messages, return calls, and send out brochure requests
- Update mailing lists
- Retrieve mail from the post office
- Pay bills (once they are approved by the owner)
- Balance monthly bank statements
- Respond to email
- Keep track of late accounts; bill for tuition and other balances due
- Create the school's newsletter
- Distribute or mail newsletters and other information
- Update and maintain the waiting room bulletin board
- Prepare notices to be sent home with students
- Fill out costume orders

- Maintain inventory for dancewear sales
- Supervise the cleaning of the studio and offices
- Attend faculty and staff meetings
- Secure rental of auditoriums for school performances
- Track and manage registration or entry forms for activities outside the school
- Collect entry fees
- Attend all school functions, including (but not limited to) the dress rehearsal, recital, local performances, and competitions
- Keep track of employee hours and payroll distribution
- Notify students and employees of class cancellations due to inclement weather
- Maintain rehearsal schedules

Qualities to look for in a studio manager

You'll have specific needs to consider (it's important that you choose someone who complements your strengths and personal style), but most studios need a manager who

- enjoys working with children,
- has a good personality (a genuine smile makes a big difference),
- has good communication skills with potential and current clientele,
- has a professional (but not intimidating) demeanor,
- demonstrates knowledge of or has a background in dance or the performing arts,
- is informed about the school's programs, philosophies, schedules, policies, and practices,
- has good organizational skills,

- demonstrates competency in computer skills (and is willing to learn),
- has good business writing skills,
- is an astute observer who can keep you abreast on the pulse of the waiting room,
- will not tolerate gossip,
- is discreet and will keep your personal business or decisions private,
- is assertive enough to stand by your policies and decisions,
- enjoys being a part of the extra events, including recitals, competitions, and community performances,
- has basic accounting skills, especially if they will be working on taxes, bank statements, deposits, and so on.

Once you've hired a studio manager, communicate your objectives and lay out all your expectations both orally and in writing. Add responsibilities gradually as you identify strengths. Be patient and try to look for the positive.

Hiring a parent who has a child in the school can work well, but not always. Be aware that he or she might be too biased toward their own child to be able to do the job effectively. These employees may be more likely to get involved in studio gossip, and their friends with children in the school may try to take advantage of their relationship. On the positive side, loyal parents who know your philosophies and history can be your best advertisement.

If you hire one of your own family members, make sure he or she will respect your authority. If they have a difficult time dealing with that, it can make working together difficult. However, the right family member is usually a person you can trust to look out for your best interests.

No matter whom you choose, make sure you invest in this person. Pay them what they are worth, praise them when they do a good job, and choose your words carefully when you express disappointment.

Successful Faculty and Staff Meetings

Always approach meetings well organized and with an agenda. By putting aside time before each meeting to focus on what you want to accomplish, you'll be sure not to waste anyone's valuable time. Your professionalism when directing meetings will influence how your employees respect you as a leader. Since your goal is to come up with a consensus on the particular issues at hand, that means you need to pay close attention to what your staff has to say—and they need to have a clear picture of your objectives. If possible, give them the agenda a few days before the meeting so that they have time to gather their thoughts. That way, they'll come prepared to offer useful feedback and suggestions.

- ***Listen to your staff.***

Ask for the reasons behind the statements, and don't make assumptions. Be open to others' reactions to your ideas and carefully consider what they have to say.

- ***Encourage all members to participate.***

Don't assume silence means understanding or agreement. Every once in a while, poll the group and have each member state their own view.

- ***Differences in opinion are OK!***

Alternative viewpoints are a good thing. Disagreements are natural and helpful because they help increase the amount of information that will eventually allow you to come up with the most informed decision.

- ***Search for alternatives that meet the goals of all members.***

Don't assume someone must win and someone must lose. When there's a stalemate, look for the next most acceptable compromise for all members.

- ***Avoid changing your mind only to avoid conflict, and don't just argue your point of view.***

Come up with ways to combine your ideas with others' points of view. Listen to the criticism of your ideas—those comments may lead you to a new perspective.

- ***Balance power.***

If one or two group members have more power or authority than the others, ask them to state their opinion only after the other people have been heard.

- ***Make sure there is a clear understanding of decisions.***

Check to see that all team members understand the decision and can explain it to your customers.

- ***You're in control.***

Be sure staff members don't carry on their own conversations during the meeting. Position yourself in a place of authority (head of the table) so that you can control and view the entire meeting. Always thank the staff for attending and express how much you appreciate their input. If possible, let them know where and when the next meeting will take place and give them an idea of what the agenda might be.

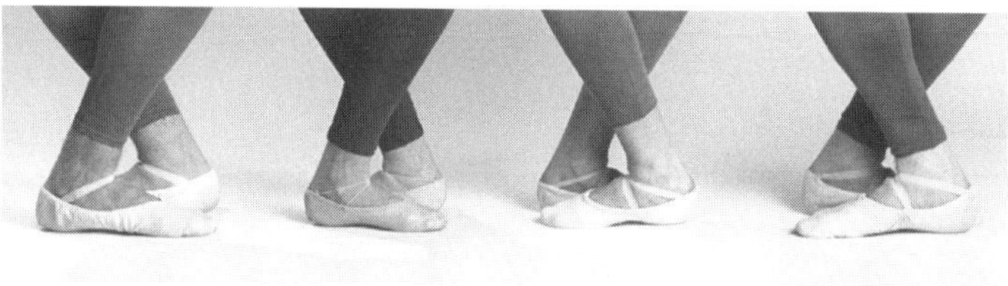

SIX

Get Ahead With Goal Setting

"Obstacles are those frightful things you see when you take your eyes off your goal." —Henry Ford

By defining what you want to achieve, you take greater control of your career and life, which is what most of us seek. If you want to make your life more fulfilling or your business more successful—or if you just want to experience more of those "memorable moments"—then goal setting is for you.

Worthwhile or positive goals are not a reaction to jealousy or competitiveness; they do not hurt or diminish the rights of others. Instead, they arise from an honest and critical look at what you want your future to be. Setting and achieving those goals will have a positive effect on you, as well as those who benefit from your accomplishments. Perhaps you want to enlarge the studio or hire a great ballet teacher. When it happens, you will benefit each of your students and your faculty; it becomes a win-win situation.

Once you set your goals and start to achieve, they become the motivation for new ones. The doors fly open to numerous possibilities and you develop a level of enthusiasm that can do nothing but make your business and personal life better. Watch your confidence soar as you develop that feeling of success!

Operating a successful dance school usually takes a cohesive team of dedicated personnel. You might even regard students and parents as part of your team, since without them you wouldn't have a studio! They, as well as your staff, benefit from the success of your business. Going public with your goals can act as reinforcement and motivation for you and helps clarify the roles your team members must play to help you accomplish your goals. What better place to outline your short- and long-term plans for the future than at your meetings with those who can help you reach them: your staff.

Worthwhile goals arise from an honest and critical look at what you want your future to be.

GOING FOR THE BIG STUFF

The second-floor space with two brand-new studios, beautiful hardwood floors, and new sound systems does not happen overnight. That's a long-term goal you write on a huge piece of paper and tape to the refrigerator. You look at it every day to be sure you're on the right track.

The short-term goal is to maximize the space you already have. By offering the best-quality dance education and service possible, you can increase your enrollment, which can then generate more income to pay a bigger mortgage or rent. Assemble a team of employees and faculty who have the same vision you do, then expand your programs until you're busting out of the walls of your current space. You will have no choice but to spend that extra income on that long-desired second floor.

One of the best benefits when you do open your expanded studio is the opportunity to enjoy it without worrying about how you're going to pay for it. By analyzing where you want to go and setting smaller, incremental goals you end up achieving your big goal in a controlled, manageable way. Then it's time to post *another* big goal on the refrigerator.

So You Want to Hire a New Ballet Teacher

At $9 a head, you will need fewer than three students per ballet class to hire the new ballet teacher at $25 per hour. How do you accomplish that goal? Go through your card file to look for students who could benefit from a ballet class—or an extra one. Make a phone call to the parent to explain what this class will offer their child and let them know what a great ballet teacher you've hired. More than likely, the fact that you took the time to make the phone call will be enough to sell the extra class to the parent. Do this a few more times and you will have accomplished your goal by taking some very small steps. Another excellent teacher and more class options mean that your school is now offering students a stronger education and will probably attract more students, which will generate more income. There's that win-win situation!

Be Ready to Swerve a Little

Sometimes we set goals only to find ourselves learning something new, which takes us to an unexpected place. It's not a bad place, but it's not what we had in mind at the start of the journey. Part of successful goal setting is learning—and sometimes, redefining our goals—along the way. We gain new knowledge that sometimes makes the original goal less enticing, but as a result, a brand-new goal emerges. Don't let a swerve or two disappoint you; it's a good thing.

Here's an example: You opened a dance school with the goal of teaching children. But then you started an adult program to make extra money. As it turns out, you like teaching the adults; it's exciting and rewarding for you. It seems like people are coming out of the woodwork to take the classes. What started as a once-a-week class has turned into five days a week, and now the program is at capacity.

All of sudden you find yourself revising your original goals. The children's program stays, but now your goal is to focus on the booming adult program that, as it happens, you love to teach. Our circumstances and environment are always changing, so expect your goals to change as well.

You may think you know exactly what your goals are—but be prepared to change them as your business develops and grows.

Finding Balance

As admirable as it is to have clearly stated goals, it's important not to let them turn into obsessions. A positive family and personal life have to be part of the equation. Knowing when to pursue your goals and knowing when to forget about them for a while is an important balance that must reached. Otherwise, you may reach your goals but be too emotionally drained to enjoy them—or worse, have no one to share your success with. So plan on scheduling personal time into your day, every day.

INCREMENTAL STEPS TO SUCCESS

You've defined your goals, shared them with your staff, and are ready to get started. Easier said than done, right? Keep reading to see some examples of specific goals and the steps you can take to make them a reality.

Goal: Become a Better Educator

To develop my teaching skills, I will

- go to New York or Los Angeles (or any nearby major city) and take a class that will challenge me;
- gather books, videos, and other resources that inspire me to be the best educator I can be;
- open myself up to new styles and techniques, even if they are not my specialties;
- communicate, network, and share ideas with others in my profession;
- join a dance teacher organization and benefit from the classes or seminars they offer;
- attend a teacher-training school;
- attend a convention and take as many classes as possible while I'm there;
- keep myself in good physical shape so that I can continue to teach and demonstrate the proper technique;
- pre-plan each class and do it with the attitude that I am going to give my all to my dancers;
- give myself time off to rejuvenate the spirit that makes me love what I do.

Goal: Jump-Start the Educational Process

To provide the best possible education and learning environment for my students, I will

- hire the best ballet teachers I can, because I realize that ballet is the foundation of a strong dancer;

- take my dancers to master classes or bring master teachers to my studio;
- take my dancers to see Broadway shows or company concerts that will inspire them;
- treat my students equally and fairly (each one deserves the best that I can give);
- spend as much time as I can on my less-advanced dancers, resisting the temptation to focus all my energy on the advanced dancers;
- hire the best faculty and staff I can;
- give 100 percent of my energy to every class I teach.

Goal: Rejuvenate My Choreography

To create choreography that I will be proud of and that will meet the needs of my students, I will

- use steps that are age appropriate and do all that I can to educate my dancers at the same time;
- spend an entire day listening to music of all kinds;
- choreograph something totally different from what I have created in the past;
- attend 10 dance performances in the next 6 months;
- take a chance and choreograph that number I have been thinking about for 10 years. (I won't base my success on how others see it, but on how I feel about it.)

Goal: Upgrade the Studio

To make my facility and business the best it can be, I will

- increase my enrollment by 10 percent this year;
- create a welcoming and friendly atmosphere;
- upgrade my sound systems or flooring;

- move to a larger facility;
- own my own building.

Goal: Maximize My Marketing

Recognizing that image and public relations are a large part of marketing, I will

- create the best recital I've ever had;
- go into that waiting room and get to know my students' parents better;
- offer community performances;
- create professional-looking brochures, literature, and newsletters;
- get together regularly with other dance educators to share ideas.

Monitor Your Progress

Keep a journal of your goals and look back periodically. Once you've put them in writing and they're firmly embedded in your subconscious mind, you will start to move in the direction you have set for yourself.

Continue to

- set goals. Do it every week.
- look back at your goals. You will be surprised at how many of them you have actually achieved.
- believe that you can accomplish even the hardest goals that you have set for yourself. It will be a great journey and in the end you may get more than you expected.

Identifying needs and setting goals helps to relieve stress and depression by giving you direction and putting you in charge.

HOW DO YOU MEASURE SUCCESS?

Going after your dreams is not always pleasant. Learn from the setbacks as well as the victories. Don't judge yourself or deny yourself the opportunity to grow.

You may find yourself defining success by the myths our society perpetrates, including "bigger is better," or that we must endure punishment to be a success. Is it true that if you don't have the guts to suffer you won't be a success? It's easy to brand yourself a failure because of one attempt that backfired. Talented people think they're not worthy because they couldn't make it through some college program that didn't spark their interest. Others have to face the reality that their own training was not as good as they thought. This doesn't mean you can't be a success. Look at it as an opportunity to seek more education, allowing you to give more to your students.

Success is always right in front of us, but we have to have the ability to see it! Life gives us many opportunities to learn, especially when we experience diversity. Sometimes the best kind of education comes from life's dilemmas.

"When one door closes another door opens;
but we so often look so long and so regretfully upon
the closed door, that we do not see the ones
which open for us." —Alexander Graham Bell

Keeping Perspective

Sometimes we lose sight of the reasons that we became a dance educator in the first place. We forget we started with nothing but the dream of someday having 100 students. Now, 10 years later, we may have 400 students, but we're still not satisfied. Why? Because we compare our success to that of others.

If the studio up the street has 1,000 students and a huge facility, do you assume you should, too? Are you convinced that the owner of that studio is happier than you are?

Maybe not. Perhaps he puts in 20 hours a day, living under more pressure than you could withstand. Imagine dealing with 1,000 sets of parents, week in and week out! And that is only one aspect of the everyday strains of operating a dance studio that size. Sometimes we are pressured by others (parents, partners, and friends) to be what *they* would consider a success. Forget about them; be what you want and do what makes you happy!

When I first started producing dance events, I dreamed of being the biggest. I wanted to go to more cities and attract more participants than all the others did. I did reach my goal a couple of times, but I couldn't see straight and my company's service suffered. The stress on my employees was more than they deserved, and I found myself not appreciating what I did for a living. There wasn't time to enjoy the achievement; there was barely time to keep up with the responsibility. The pressure to produce was overwhelming. The goal had been reached, but was it the right one?

My mother, who was my first dance teacher, used to say,

"Your biggest dream could turn into your worst nightmare!" I used to laugh and wonder why she would say such a thing, but now, many years later, I know exactly what she meant.

I realize that being happy about what I do and having the time to appreciate it is the greatest success. Being the biggest doesn't necessarily mean being the best. I had changed my goal to producing events that were about quality. I did everything I could to make my company unique, and more important, to reflect integrity and respect for the art of dance. I stopped worrying about the finances as much, because the focus on quality seemed to be appreciated and the money followed.

If you have 200 students—or 100, or 50—who are happy and receiving the best training possible, you are a success! Sometimes it is better to have fewer dancers attending class more often than it is to have 1,000 students attending once a week; you don't appear to be a "factory" without the time to offer personal service. Two hundred students taking more classes will give you greater satisfaction if your goal is to produce the best dancers. Another huge benefit: It's your opportunity to personally get to know your clientele. You will probably have less turnover than a large studio would, because when parents and kids feel like they know you, they become loyal to the school and its philosophies. When that happens, you gain an element that's critical to running a successful dance teaching business: positive word of mouth.

SEVEN

The Politics of Parent Relations

"The ultimate measure of a man is not where he stands in moments of comfort and convenience, but where he stands at times of challenge and controversy." —Martin Luther King Jr.

Positive word of mouth is a remarkably powerful advertising tool—and it can't be bought. It's the result of a studio that runs on the basic tenets of respect, communication, and professionalism. Project Motivate has shown that the number-one issue on the minds of today's dance educators is "handling the parents." Any activity involving children means dealing with parents and their concerns—*guaranteed!*

THE IMPACT OF NEGATIVITY

Every school has "problem" parents who present unique challenges to a professionally run school. These parents do not see the same child you see. More often than not, they see much more talent than you do, and think their child should be offered every advantage appropriate to that talent.

Here are some of the challenges parents can present:

- The same parents who consider their children extremely talented and want them to have every advantage usually don't want to pay for it.
- Some watch the other students in an attempt to make sure their child doesn't miss out on something that someone else's child is getting.
- They think you're not giving their child enough attention. Sometimes they sit in the waiting room counting the number of times you say their child's name during class.
- They question the placement of their child in classes and choreography.
- They take their time paying class tuition, costume payments, entry fees, and convention fees.
- They gossip in the waiting room or on the ride home with a car full of kids.
- They want to speak to you at the worst times, usually between classes.
- They think they know more about a good dance education than you and your faculty do.
- They go to the recital expecting to see their child front and center at all times.
- They think their child should do a solo many years before you believe the child is ready.
- They go to every competition expecting that every entry their child is in will win a gold medal. After all, that's what they are paying you for.
- They think they have to applaud only for their own children.

Ironically, often dance teachers will act the same way when it comes to their own child's activities! It's human nature to be biased toward your child, and it's something we have to learn how to deal with.

Those parents who have a normal, healthy concern for their children and their dance training will respond positively when communication is a priority and mutual respect between teachers, parents, and students is evident. Remember:

- *Most* parents want to be part of their child's education.
- *Most* parents do not go out of their way to give you a hard time.
- *Most* parents become concerned when they don't understand. (And in the world we live in, a concerned parent is a healthy thing.)

TIPS | **Communication Is Key**

Most parents' concerns can be mitigated through good communication. There are various ways to ensure that parents and students are well informed and feel valued, such as

- newsletters,
- rap sessions (for parents or students, or both),
- posting and distributing copies of studio policies,
- posting important information on the school Web site,
- parent/teacher conferences,
- a suggestion box in the waiting room.

Communication means listening, too. Parents and dancers often appreciate the opportunity to express their opinions, and you may learn a few things by hearing what they have to say. Being open to ideas is good for business!

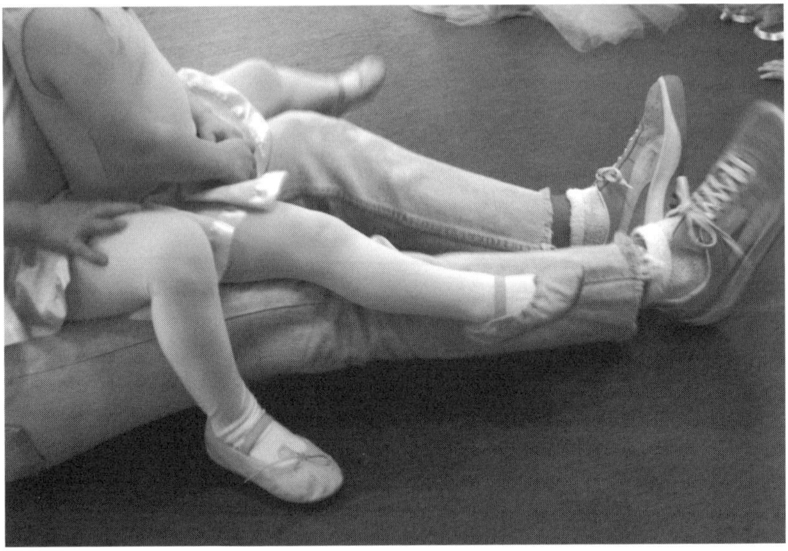

Know what you're talking about—then put it in writing.

By putting studio policies, philosophy, and rationales in writing, you can forestall many communication problems. A studio handbook is the perfect way to make sure that everyone who becomes a part of your school's family dances to the same beat. Just make sure that your materials are well thought out, succinct, clear, and an accurate reflection of your practices. If you don't adhere to your own policies, consistently and fairly, then parents and students will not respect and trust you.

The following topics are best addressed in a handbook and/or in separate handouts (which you might want to make available in a display rack in the school lobby).

- How student placement levels are determined
- Factors determining when a dancer can go on pointe
- Criteria for which students get solos. Include the reasons

why participating in a duo, trio, or small group may be more advantageous than a solo.

- Casting decisions, particularly Clara or other coveted roles in the annual *Nutcracker*
- Tuition and other payments (such as costumes, entry fees, master classes)
- How to contact a teacher with a concern
- Why the school presents a recital
- The importance of attending dress rehearsal
- Your philosophy about why you participate in competitions and how your studio works as a team. Include policies concerning behavior, arrival time, commitment, and any other competition issues.

The key to communication is to be ready with an answer that is well thought out and followed without exception.

Most teachers have the ability to sense when they have a disgruntled parent and if they don't know it firsthand, they have heard it from someone involved. If you hide from conflict you might end up with a situation that is out of control. One unhappy parent in the waiting room can turn the entire school upside down. Confront the situation rather than avoiding it. You may be surprised to find that many parents become your best supporters when you take the time to address their concerns. Be patient and calm, and hold your conversations in private. Always remember that you are a professional; if you're angry, give yourself a cool-down period before addressing the situation.

If a parent continues to contribute to a bad atmosphere, becomes a distraction, or emotionally batters you despite your efforts to communicate, it's time to ask her to leave. Never be afraid to give disgruntled parents a list of all the dance studios in your area. In most cases, they will not want to leave and will back down. Some may leave and come back in two weeks. Others will be long gone, and you will be better off without them. You must have the confidence in yourself to know you are doing the best you can.

Sometimes the best dancers' parents are the hardest to please; some think that you should be honored to have their children in your studio. Remember: *You need no one!*

TIPS | **Parent–Teacher Conferences**

Approaching parents can be difficult and uncomfortable. They may be in denial about their child's true abilities as a dancer or reluctant to admit that their child has a discipline problem.

Some tactics to consider:

- Make all conferences private. Never discuss the problem in the classroom, in the waiting room, or on the telephone. Set up an appointment to meet in your office.
- Sit behind your desk. A desk between you and the person you are speaking with represents authority and gives you the upper hand.
- Always direct concerns about the child to the parents in the form of a question, such as: "How is Mary doing in school?" "Have her teachers made any reference to her behavior?" Try to get the parent talking about the issue you want to bring up.

Choose your words carefully, emphasizing the positive. Key phrases could include:

- *His/her capabilities are* . . . rather than *He/she is not capable of* . . .

- *He/she is better suited for such-and-such a class,* rather than *He/she can't handle this class.*
- *This age level is better for him/her socially*, rather than *He/she is a little immature for this class.*

The Irate Parent

You must hold your ground and handle confrontation in a very professional way, and most important, with your self-esteem intact.

If a conversation becomes an argument, find a way to turn it in another direction by pointing out something positive or changing the subject. The biggest mistake is responding to a personal attack or unfair criticism. This shows adversaries that they have hit a nerve and that's probably exactly what they wanted to accomplish. Now you could be in for a real battle.

Instead of becoming defensive, ask an open-ended question such as, "I'm not sure what you mean," or "Can you explain what you mean by that?" Try not to respond to the attack with an attack, no matter how tempting. A cool demeanor will show the aggressive parent that you are not going to fall into an argumentative trap. By being strong the first time an irate parent approaches you, you may avoid years of negative interaction with this person.

Keeping your cool gives you the advantage in any confrontation.

When you are getting nowhere, find a way to end the conversation, perhaps by saying something like, "I think we should talk about this at another time, when we both have had an opportunity to think about it a little more."

When debating emotionally charged issues, you may find that your philosophy and the parent's simply don't jibe. However, you can show the parent that you do understand their point while clearly exercising your right to disagree. Example: "I know you feel strongly about what you are saying and we disagree on the way I want to handle it, but I can't think of a fairer way of doing this. It's always worked so well in the past."

To avoid saying something you will regret, try this (in a firm voice): "Since we obviously are not going to change each other's mind, why don't we just agree to disagree?" Then try to redirect the conversation to a more positive subject, such as a recent performance.

Enforce your right to privacy. The following are some techniques to evade personal or business-related questions you don't want to answer, especially between classes or in a waiting room full of people.

- Provide a vague answer and ask a question. This will deflect unwanted questions and provide little if any information. Asking a question in return throws the conversation ball into their court. Example: "Wow! You had so many people register you must be making a fortune!" The reply could be: "I'm very pleased; how are you doing financially?" That should end the conversation quickly!
- Refuse to answer and change the subject. This lets the parent know you don't want to answer and serves as a diplomatic way out of a sensitive subject.
- If a parent persists in asking for information you're not ready to disclose or asks questions about another student or family, you could reply, "Please don't ask. It's our policy to post that information for everyone to see at once," or

"Please don't ask me that. My policy is never to discuss my clients or students with anyone." If they're smart they will respect you; they know you wouldn't talk about them.

Confrontations or toxic conversations with parents are not easy. Pushy parents can push us over the edge. When it happens, take a deep breath and try to say nothing. They will not know how to react to your silence because it defused them. Always respond in a way that maintains your integrity, self-respect, and composure.

Maximize Your Satisfaction

Discontent can filter down from parents to the students. Often, we hear about the disappointed teacher whose prized dancer left the studio. Don't let talent be the sole criteria for where you focus your energy. Be sure to invest your extra time and effort in those who clearly appreciate it, regardless of their skill level. There is no better satisfaction than receiving a letter 10 years after a student has left your studio, thanking you for the positive impact you had on his life!

ON REFLECTION

Standing Up to the Disgruntled Parent

As I travel the country presenting my seminars, I always ask each group, "What do you find is the hardest issue to deal with as a dance educator?" It never fails that a huge majority of responses have to do with parents.

Most dance teachers believe that parents should watch classes periodically and make an effort to educate themselves about dance enough to know that their child is safe and receiving proper instruction. But when do loving attentiveness and parental pride become unjustified meddling or a demand for attention? And when should a studio owner take action?

Ms. Waite (all names are fictitious) is the mom of 10-year-old Rachel, who has been training at Mary Jane's School of Dance for two years. Before that, Rachel had studied at three other schools. Ms. Waite, who has no background in dance, was not satisfied with the teachers, policies, or training at the previous schools, although she admitted that Rachel seemed happy at each. Ms. Waite made a point of watching all classes and rehearsals.

When Mary Jane decided to enter Rachel's intermediate-level class in a competition, she called a parent meeting to describe the experience and outline the time and financial commitments. At the end of the meeting, several parents thanked Mary Jane for including their children. Ms. Waite, however, wanted to know which students would get to be in the front of the group, and then she singled out two other students, asking if they were good enough to compete. Mary Jane explained that she had confidence in all the students and felt they were all ready for the experience.

At the first rehearsal, Rachel was 10 minutes late. Ms. Waite did not apologize, seeming not to comprehend that a late arrival compromises her daughter's training and wastes the time of the teacher and the other students.

Ms. Waite became unhappy as she watched rehearsals. She thought the choreography was too simple and that Rachel was better than most of the other dancers. She wondered why her daughter wasn't being used to her full potential. She complained to the other parents (and in front of Rachel and her classmates) about the choreography and the structure of the rehearsals. She seemed unaware that making such negative comments sets an example of disrespect.

On the day of the performance, Rachel was late again, arriving 15 minutes before the performance. The students, parents, and Mary Jane were very stressed, wondering whether Rachel would make it in time. Rachel was a mess; she knew she should have been there earlier, and she had had no chance to warm up. Once again, Ms. Waite made no apology.

The performance was not as good as it could have been. The dancers seemed to lack confidence, and when Rachel was "front and center," she forgot the choreography. Still, the group received a bronze medal.

Several of the parents thanked Mary Jane for the time and effort she had put into the competition. But Ms. Waite was livid about the bronze medal. In front of Rachel and several parents, she criticized the choreography and some of the dancers, embarrassing her daughter and infuriating the other parents.

Mary Jane felt terrible. Had she let the children down, or was she a bad choreographer? After a sleepless night, Mary Jane realized she had done the best she could. Her real problem was Ms. Waite. She enjoyed having Rachel as a student, but it was time to have a talk with her mom.

Ms. Waite arrived late to the meeting. She started the conversation with more criticism, saying that if the dancers had done more tricks, they would have scored better at the competition.

Mary Jane listened, then asked, "Do you think the group might have been more successful if you and Rachel had arrived on time?" She told Ms. Waite how stressed everyone in the group had become by Rachel's tardiness. Ms. Waite responded with excuses and blame, finally threatening to pull Rachel from the school. Mary Jane answered, "I enjoy having Rachel in my classes and I will miss her, but I will not put up with your continued negativity." Ms. Waite left without saying a word, as though she had been through this before.

So what's a teacher—or a parent—to do? Communication is essential. Studio owners need to set clear parameters about expected and acceptable behavior, from both students and their parents. And parents should have the grace and consideration to voice their concerns through appropriate channels. They have the right, even the responsibility, to be involved in their children's activities and to inquire when something doesn't seem right. But at the same time, they must trust the professionals to do what they do best.

—Rhee Gold, January 2003
from *Dance Magazine*

COMMUNICATION 101: NEWSLETTERS

I can't say it often enough: Keeping parents and students informed is a major component of a successful studio. Good communication leads to happy customers, which leads to *more* happy customers. One of the best ways to keep everyone informed and project a professional image for your studio at the same time is to create a monthly or every-other-month newsletter (see appendix 2). Use it as a reminder about important dates for the season, including recitals, dress rehearsals, special performances, ticket sale day, costume payment deadlines, etc. Post it on your Web site as well as mailing or distributing hard copies. Remember, it's also a marketing tool, so consider some of the following:

- Include a "spotlight" on a different faculty member or student in each issue. Not only does it remind your clients how outstanding the faculty is and help them get to know the students, it makes the featured person feel great!

- Create a "Happy Birthday" column that includes birth dates (no years!) of your dancers and faculty. If you decide to do this, be organized and add each new student's name to your master calendar immediately—if you forget a dancer, you could find yourself with an unhappy child or parent.
- Write about performances the studio has given in the community; send the story to the local newspapers as well.
- Brag about the competitions you have participated in. Take a group picture at each competition and include it with the article.
- Create a "Did You Know?" column and include historical facts and other tidbits about the studio. Did your building have a former life as a gin mill during Prohibition? Write about it! Did a now-famous dancer train at your school? Name names! Include facts about you, your staff, and alumni, and jazz it up with some old photographs.
- Vary the format with "ads" that provide information about recitals, summer programs, team auditions, and other activities.

Proofread your final document carefully, and give it to someone else on your staff who can look at it with a fresh eye. A wrong date or misinformation could create confusion or problems and makes you appear less professional.

Consider making a separate in-studio newsletter for the recital, competitive teams, or summer program. If possible, send out recital newsletters in January, and don't forget to make extra copies for those families with multiple households or for those who lose theirs. Otherwise, send it to everyone on your mailing lists, including people who have called and asked for a brochure in the past three years. Your newsletter may be just the impetus they need to try a class. Keep former customers on your mailing list for three years; they may have younger children, relatives, or neighbors who want to take dance. Consider adding a note asking them to pass the newsletter on to anyone who might be interested.

TIPS | **Make Your Newsletters Work for You**

For recitals include:

- Rehearsal schedule
- Dates of each event and times to arrive
- Cast lists for each performance
- Which students will be included in the finale
- Location and directions
- Time of performance
- Auditorium rules (such as no eating or drinking)
- Admission policy
- Dressing room locations and which dancers are where. Draw a diagram of the facility and give it to each family.
- Policy for costume distribution
- Which tights are required for each number
- Which shoes will be needed for each number and what color
- Hairstyles for each number
- Camera and/or video policy
- Photo shoot information—where, when, what's needed, how to purchase photos
- Date that tickets go on sale and how to purchase them

For summer programs include:

- Dates and times
- Program description (include the details that make your program unique, such as master teachers, trips to dance concerts, or music and acting classes)
- Age level for participation
- Registration deadlines
- Registration form
- Dress code, if any
- Who's teaching and their bios

For competitions include:

- Your competition philosophy
- Competition etiquette, including expected behavior onstage, backstage, and in the audience, for participants and their parents, and how to interact with dancers from other schools
- Basic rehearsal schedule
- All scheduled competitions and their locations, including summer events such as national competitions and workshops. Include dates, fees, and other pertinent details.
- The preferred arrival time for dancers
- Expenses, including entry fees, convention fees, extra shoes or costumes, etc.
- List of nearby hotels for out-of-town events (including rates)
- Does your school have competition team uniforms? If so, remind students to wear them to the events. (Also remind parents to wear school jackets, sweatshirts, or T-shirts if they have them).

There are several desktop publishing programs on the market (I've found Microsoft® Publisher to be user-friendly) that make creating newsletters, business cards, stationery, and flyers a snap. But if you're intimidated by such programs, you can stick with a word-processing program like Microsoft Word for simpler documents. If you plan to include photos in your newsletters and brochures or on your Web site, you will need to purchase a scanner or a digital camera.

Newsletters are great communication tools, but they also help keep school owners organized by providing essential information at a glance. Plus, they make excellent references for the future.

BUILDING TRUST

Building trust, like good communication, goes a long way toward minimizing conflict with parents. Parents should feel welcome in your school, and the best way to accomplish this is to create a relaxed, open atmosphere. How? By making parents feel at home the minute they set foot in the door and by showing you have nothing to hide.

Waiting Room Ambience

I have often heard teachers say they that have small waiting rooms so that parents won't hang out at the studio. This may not be the best idea. A friendly, inviting waiting room allows parents to feel comfortable and become informed. It may also make a big impression on your existing or potential clients, so it should be comfortable, clean, and a selling point for the school.

Class Observation

There was a time when many school owners considered class observation something to avoid. In today's society, I wouldn't recommend this approach. Hundreds of parenting books state that if a school of any kind doesn't allow parents to observe what's going on in the classroom, it's not the right place for their children. Many parents have a desire to be a part of their child's education; encourage them.

You may argue that class observation is a distraction for both the dancers and the teacher. The solution is to come up with a balance that allows parents access within reason. Many parents just want to *know* they can observe; often they don't take advantage of the opportunity. They simply want to know that you have nothing to hide. The older the child, the less likely a parent is to come in and observe.

How Much Is Enough?

There are various factors to consider when determining the appropriate amount of observation for your school. One is the need for privacy for your students. Dance class is not only a place to learn technique—the students are also learning about who they are and how to relate to one another. It's a social network for many of them. If you think about it, how comfortable would your child be if you could observe him at his academic school any time you wanted to? These students need to feel safe in the classroom, not as if they're on display. Another argument for limiting observation to less frequent intervals is that parents can see their child's progress more readily if they're not in there watching constantly. Because the development of technique is incremental much of the time, parents may complain that their child isn't learning because they don't see huge changes from week to week. They're more likely to be impressed with their child's dancing if the improvement is obvious.

Some schools have an open-door policy that allows observation at all times; others limit it to twice a year. Then there's everything in between. Offering class viewing once a month is a reasonable policy. If you collect tuition on a monthly basis, coordinate observation with tuition-collection week. Or you may want to allow observation for the entire first month of the season. New students and their parents will have the opportunity to view class and develop a trust that you have nothing to hide. After the first month, you may never see the parents again.

See Without Being Seen

The observation window is the most common way to allow parents to view their child's classes. Remind the parents not to tap on the windows or try to gain their child's attention. Constructing an observation window with one-way glass is a smart option. Parents can observe but the students can't see them, so there's less distraction for everyone involved.

Closed-circuit TV offers another option. Inexpensive systems are sold at many office supply stores. Strategically placed cameras in each classroom can provide a video feed to monitors in the waiting room. This technique offers no distractions and may impress your clientele, but your students may be uncomfortable knowing the monitors can be turned on at any time.

If you offer in-studio observation, remind parents not to distract the students by talking to each other or their children. Set up chairs for the visitors in the most inconspicuous place possible, preferably the back or side of the room.

EIGHT

The Recital: A Reflection of You

"We do onstage things that are supposed to happen off. Which is a kind of integrity, if you look on every exit as being an entrance somewhere else."

—*Tom Stoppard*, Rosencrantz and Guildenstern Are Dead

That annual staple of the dance school, the recital, conjures up images of childhood and Americana for many. It's a rite of passage for thousands of youngsters, a chance to shine in front of family and friends that they anticipate with nervous excitement. As a dance school owner, you'll have a slightly different perspective: The recital (or revue, or concert, or festival) is one of your best marketing tools. Take full advantage of it by making the best possible impression on your current students and parents and those potential new clients out there in the audience. The next year's enrollment will be only as good as your last show.

BE PROFESSIONAL IN EVERY WAY

As a professional, you'll want your school recital to be as organized as you are. School directors and faculty members should appear calm, cool, and collected. No matter how pressured you feel, you want to create the appearance of being efficient and in control. You have been through this so many times that your show runs like clockwork—and it's apparent to everyone. Your clientele appreciates your professionalism and spreads the word to family and friends, giving you that most valuable advertising tool: positive word of mouth.

It's not only you and your staff who create that air of competence; every aspect of your recital should be planned and orchestrated to produce a professional production that reflects the high standards of your studio. No detail is too small; it's the combination of all those little particulars that add up to one impressive show.

Even if you're producing your first recital, make it look like you're a veteran. If your show runs like clockwork it'll be apparent to everyone that you know what you're doing.

Front of House

Whether or not you charge admission, make sure your audience feels valued. Hire or enlist volunteer ushers who are friendly and knowledgeable to guide audience members to their seats. Present each ticket holder with a well-designed, tasteful program. And start the show on time. If you have a hard time getting the audience seated, flash the house lights or play an overture; this will usually ensure that your audience is seated and ready for a great performance.

Before the show begins, make an announcement that because this is a professional production, you ask that audiences remain in their seats for the entire performance. Emphasize that if anyone must leave during the show, they will be reseated only at the discretion of the ushers.

Make sure your audience feels valued: Present a well-run, professional production.

Also announce that the use of video cameras or flash photography is not permitted. There is nothing more distracting or unprofessional than flashes going off throughout the show. It's a hazard to the dancers and destroys the quality of your video. Consider allowing video and photography at the dress rehearsal. You may want to hire a professional photographer to shoot candid shots at the dress rehearsal, who can then sell photos to the dancers and their families. Plus, you may end up with some terrific shots that will spice up your advertisements, newsletters, and brochures.

Onstage

Scenery can help make a show. It also shows your clientele you are willing to go the extra step to make their children look good. Creating a sense of place or atmosphere onstage is also helpful when presenting dancers who may not be your strongest or who lack confidence in performance. If you feel that sets and props take too much time, consider asking parents to volunteer as set and prop builders, scenery painters, and backstage crew. You may be surprised at how many will step forward—and volunteering has the added benefit of building camaraderie among the parents.

Specialty lighting is very effective. Rent extra lighting equipment if the auditorium you use is inadequate. Effective lighting can enhance your best dancers and offer kind camouflage to those who are less technically proficient. You might be surprised to find how much a simple black light can cover up! Well-designed lighting enhances the entire production and contributes dramatically to the audience's overall impression.

Make It Flow

Most recitals have two acts. Some have a different theme for each act; others carry the same theme through both acts (see appendix 3 for sample themes and programs). If your show is too long, you will start to lose your audience. If a longer show is unavoidable, consider breaking it into two performances, and use your best dancers in both.

A recital should never exceed 2 ½ hours, and the second act should be shorter than the first.

Keep the pace moving briskly. Blackouts are an effective way to end a number, but don't overdo it—have one set of students exit dancing while the next group dances onstage. Limit intermissions to 10 or 15 minutes. If the show length is kept to a minimum, consider not having an intermission at all; this guarantees that some audience members won't leave before the end of the show.

By using all the dancers in the finale, you're guaranteed to have your audience stay for the entire show.

Make awards presentations or introductions of faculty as brief as possible. (You can facilitate this by rehearsing them at the dress rehearsal, so that they're smooth and well orchestrated.) Many schools honor their 5-, 10-, and 15-year students; those who show the most potential or the best teamwork; those with perfect attendance; the most helpful parent(s); and graduating students.

Although recognizing the achievements of your dancers is important, this part of the evening is exciting only to the parents of the award recipients. Brainstorm a bit to determine the best time and venue for your presentation. Some options:

- Present the awards at the school or at a cast party following the show.
- Make the presentations at the end of the first act, immediately before intermission.
- Introduce the award recipients throughout the show. Close the traveler and present the awards in front of the curtain while the set change, prop placement, or acro mat set-up goes on behind it. This method allows you to avoid tedious blackouts while getting the awards over with at the same time. At the first break, introduce the 5-year dancers; at the next, the 10-year dancers, and so on.

ANTICIPATE, ORGANIZE, PREPARE

For a recital that runs smoothly, preparations begin months in advance, long before work starts on the choreography. Anticipating problems will minimize their actual occurrence, and knowing you're organized and well prepared will decrease your anxiety. Plus, there are simple organizational steps you can take to minimize everyone's stress level. Here are some suggestions to make life easier during the big event:

- Don't wait until the end of the dress rehearsal to run through your finale. Either do it at the beginning of the rehearsal (when all the dancers will be there) or after Act I. Those parents whose children are in only the first act will appreciate your thoughtfulness.

- Create an "Extras Box." In it, you keep everything your dancers could possibly forget: extra tights, hats, canes, props, bobby pins, hair elastics, safety pins, a sewing kit, pointe shoe elastic and ribbons, and anything else you can think of.
- Keep preschoolers and other young children in their own dressing room. Stock it with coloring books, games, and other activities, along with a couple of people who love kids.
- Consider having video monitors in your dressing rooms. This allows the dancers to watch the performance without having to be in the auditorium. It's also a helpful way for those dancers who have a long wait between their numbers to keep track of the performance.
- Create a system for parents to pick up their children after the show. Do not allow them to go backstage until the performance is completed. Give them the confidence that their child is well taken care of. If you want to appear professional in your presentation, no dancers should be in the audience in costumes.
- If you have a large facility with extra seats, consider having a section in the back of the house for the kids who have danced or are waiting to dance. Make sure you have adult monitors in this area so that the children remain seated and quiet. If they must remain backstage during the performance, be specific and firm about where they are allowed to be. Crowds of dancers in the wings can be noisy and distracting to those performing and may get in the way of set changes or exits and entrances.
- If there are several dressing rooms, make a chart of the

facility and list which children are assigned to each room. Distribute this information ahead of time, in class and in the recital newsletter. Post copies of the chart in several locations backstage, and keep a copy on your clipboard. You will have less confusion when trying to gather your dancers and you will look extremely organized.

- If the dancers' shoes have been dyed or colored, stock the "extras box" with dye or paint for those who somehow couldn't do it themselves or for touch-ups. Inevitably, one or two dancers will show up for a dress rehearsal with their shoes the wrong color. The best way to avoid this problem is to have each class turn in their shoes well before the performance date; have someone from the studio color the shoes for the entire class. This also eliminates the variations in color that result when each dancer dyes her own shoes. Charge a small fee to cover the cost of the dye or paint.

Keeping Your Cool

Preparations like the suggestions just mentioned make studio directors and teachers less likely to lose their cool when things do go wrong. But even when trying situations arise, it's important to handle them in a professional manner.

Consider this: You have informed a particular class that their tap shoes need to be dyed tan for the recital. At dress rehearsal two dancers enter the stage with white tap shoes. You feel like you have told this class and their parents the shoes needed to be tan a hundred times, yet they still didn't do it. You're under stress to begin with, so you pick up the microphone and blast the dancers.

However justified your anger might be, you just lost control in front of your entire clientele—which does *not* create a good impression! Perhaps you could have handled the situation differently. For example, if you had shoe dye ready and waiting backstage, you could simply pick up the microphone and, in a kind way, let the dancers know the dye is available and that their parents should see you right away. The result? No stress for anyone involved. And the impression you leave is that you have been at this for so long that you've anticipated any problems. That's fine fodder for positive word of mouth.

Keeping in control during times of stress is one way to create a good impression on your clientele.

LAYING THE GROUNDWORK

Many recital preparations should take place months ahead of time, including planning the theme, choosing and ordering costumes, and designing a program.

Decision #1: Choose a Format

There's no law that says you have to stick with the format of a traditional recital. Think of performances as opportunities to demonstrate your creativity, not only as a choreographer but as a producer of well-designed ways to show off your dancers and the caliber and scope of training offered at your school.

"Anyone who has never made a mistake has never tried anything new." —Albert Einstein

Several suggestions follow, but don't hesitate to come up with ideas of your own.

- Consider a separate showcase for solos, duos, and small groups, held in a dinner club or smaller auditorium. Give it a different name, such as Dance Festival, and present it a month or two before the annual recital. Watching solo after solo in the general recital can become boring to the audience; present soloists only if they are title winners or graduating seniors (see appendix 4 for a sample participation form).
- Another interesting concept is a special show for only the preschool dancers. Some studios present it in the afternoon prior to the full recital. This format has the advantage of not having overwhelmed or exhausted preschoolers in the main recital. However, the negative side to it is that the preschoolers and their parents don't have the opportunity to watch and be inspired by the older or more experienced dancers unless they choose to attend the primary recital as well.
- Do a special number for the parents. A fathers' number is always a big hit, or consider a father/daughter dance. It may not be your strongest technical performance of the evening, but it certainly is an audience favorite and will create lasting memories for the participants and the audience.

There's no law that says you have to stick with the format of a traditional recital

More About Showcases

By eliminating solos and smaller groups from the recital you offer a second performance opportunity to students who show potential or are at a more advanced level. During the performance, introduce each piece with a few words about the dancers. This gives the presentation a more personal flair than a regular recital and creates a more intimate atmosphere.

I suggest using duos, trios, and small-group pieces with six to eight dancers as the backbone of the performance. Limit solos to the most advanced students who have proved their dedication and have solid technique. It is financially better for the studio and choreographers (who typically split the fees 50/50) to have more group works than solos in the showcase, but there's an even better reason for doing so (which you may find yourself explaining to the parent who desperately wants her child to dance a solo): Often young dancers will learn a solo only to hit the stage and forget their dance in the middle. It's a devastating experience, and one that can discourage a child from continuing with dance training. By working in a duo or a group, the children feel safer and more self-confident. Also, they have the rewarding experience of working together to accomplish a goal. And audiences usually enjoy the dynamism of multiple bodies onstage at once.

Decision #3: Costumes

Costume catalogs are sent out much earlier than in the past, so if possible, complete your orders by the first of December. (The Thanksgiving break is a perfect time to do this.) Start measuring students in mid-October (adjusting for growth) and be ready to order before Thanksgiving. If you haven't received some of the catalogs you want, don't wait; call the company to request one right away. In some cases an order placed in November or by the first of December will be delivered within a few weeks or less. Orders placed in January could take a couple of months; ordering later than that for a late spring or early summer performance puts pressure on the costume company (and you) and could result in a late delivery.

Choosing costumes that fit your budget and then placing the orders can be a monstrous job for one person. Consider assembling your faculty for a "costume party" to help you with the process. Also, include one of the office staff to fill out the order forms. Pre-order lunch and make it fun.

Most studios add to the wholesale cost of the costumes to defray the cost of staff time spent measuring and ordering. If you do a markup, make sure your students' parents feel like they're getting what they paid for. After the costumes arrive, remove them from the small plastic bags they're packaged in for shipping and present them to your clientele in a professional manner by placing them on hangers in a protective dry-cleaning bag. Attach an additional plastic bag to the hanger for accessories such as tights, gloves, and hats. Presentation *is* important!

The secret to a no-stress costume experience is simple: Order early!

TIPS | **Costume Practicalities**

- If you order the bulk of your costumes from one company, ask them to send you a run of their basics. Instead of doing all the measuring, try the basics on each dancer to determine the appropriate size without having to go through the sizing charts.
- When the costumes arrive, hang them in view in the waiting area or a section of the classroom. The children will want to take them home, encouraging their parents or guardians to take care of the final payment much sooner!

Making a Profit

When you go to Macy's to purchase a blouse for $40, you can count on the fact that the store's cost was $20 or less. Most retailers sell their stock at a 100 percent markup. In most cases, dance school owners can't go for the 100 percent markup; however, it is not inappropriate to make a profit. The time and effort put into sizing, choosing, preparing and distributing costumes, and filling out order forms, as well as the cost of postage, should be factored into costume cost. A good goal is 25 to 35 percent per costume. This could be an average, with the percentage varying on some costumes. At the minimum, you should make a profit of $10 to $15 per costume.

It's OK *to make a profit on costumes*!

Payments and Deposits

The average retail cost of a recital costume seems to be $55 to $65 for children and $65 to $75 for adults. Consider offering your clientele an installment payment option as an alternative to paying the full amount up front; for example, two or three payments in September, October, and November. Ideally, all payments should be made by mid-November so that studio owners have the funds on hand to order the costumes by the first of the year.

TIPS | **Sample Installment Plans**

Child costume @ $65		**Adult costume** @ $75	
September 15	$25	September 15	$30
October 15	$25	October 15	$30
November 15	$15	November 15	$15

State Your Policies

Prepare a handout about costume costs and policies so that there are no surprises, and make sure each family gets one. Post one on the studio bulletin board and your Web site as well. Although you may still encounter the occasional parent who claims she didn't know the policies, putting them in writing can forestall many problems. You may want to include some of the following:

- No costumes will be given out to those students whose families have a balance due to the studio, whether for costumes or tuition. Explain to the parents that your accountant will be closing the books within seven days after the show, which cannot be done unless there are no balances due.
- Accounts must be paid in full in order to purchase recital tickets.
- During the last 30 days before the recital, only cash payments are accepted.

PROGRAMS WITH PIZZAZZ

Now that decisions about theme and costumes are behind you, it's time to move on to designing a program. Don't make the mistake of thinking that a program is just a list of dance numbers and dancers' names—it's much more than that. You've got an audience full of potential clients out there, and the program that's thrust into their hands when they enter the auditorium is the first impression many of them will have of you. Make it professional, something that will enhance the school's image. It's also a free marketing tool. Promote your school, summer programs, the philosophy of the school, the faculty, registration dates, and anything else you want to advertise.

Too time consuming, you say? If you think of the program

as an opportunity to generate extra income, you may find it easier to squeeze in the time to make it a standout. Chances are you've got a graphic designer on your school roster who might be willing to donate his services. Let someone else do the layout and production; all you need to do then is provide the copy and photos. Don't forget to encourage parents or extended families to buy a congratulatory ad for their dancers. Consider soliciting ads from local merchants and your program may pay for itself or even turn a profit (see appendix 5 for a sample program ad form).

PHOTO SHOOTS

Photo shoots are an opportunity for parents to obtain professional-quality portraits and group shots of their children, in costume. They can also provide the school owner with high-quality images to use on Web sites and in studio brochures and all kinds of advertising.

Again, planning and organization are key components of a successful photo shoot. Make sure to schedule the shoot early enough that the photos will be ready for use in the program. Post notices of the upcoming event on the studio bulletin board, include the information in your newsletter, and send a flyer home with each child well in advance. The sample flyer in appendix 6 will give you an idea of which details are essential.

TENSION-FREE TICKETING

Order tickets early so you can make them available for purchase two months before the show. If you have reserved seating, be prepared with a seating chart of the facility. That way, the purchasers know exactly where their seats are so that there are no surprises or hassles at the show. The reserved seating option has enough advantages to make it worth serious consideration:

- It gives more credibility to the process, since most professional performances do offer reserved seating.
- It minimizes conflict at the show—no more parents fighting over seats!
- It eliminates that mad rush when the doors open and those desperate for front-row seats start running or even trampling others to get there!
- Audience members may appreciate not having to get to the performance an hour or so early in order to be guaranteed a good seat.

- If you have a large auditorium but a small audience, you have control of where people are going to sit. For example, you can sell only the orchestra seats to keep everyone at the front of the auditorium.
- It conveys a message of overall professionalism and organization to your existing and potential clientele.

If you expect many people to show up for the first day of ticket sales, be prepared to hand out numbers as they arrive so that there are no disputes about whose turn it is. Handle each order as quickly as possible—and with a smile! You might consider offering coffee while your customers wait.

Rather than selling tickets to school families, some schools charge a flat recital fee. In some cases, the fee includes a costume and a designated number of tickets; others simply include tickets and a program. If you choose to go with a recital fee, be sure to limit the number of tickets included. Allowing each family an unlimited number of tickets could result in a lot of empty seats if they take more than they need—and unhappy people who were unable to buy tickets because there were none left.

Let's say you include five tickets per family with the recital fee. You could charge for any additional tickets above five or allow those who want more to wait until all tickets have been distributed, then make the remaining ones available on a first-come, first-served basis.

Luck of the Draw

If you do plan to sell tickets, using a lottery system eliminates the first-day rush. There are several ways to do this:

- When families pre-register for the following year, give

them a number based on the order in which their registration (see appendices 7 and 8 for sample registration and medical release forms) was received. A couple of months before the recital, send out a letter reminding parents of their numbers and ask them to return a form with the number of tickets they will need for the recital. You process and mail or distribute the tickets from the studio office. This method encourages pre-registration and gives you a better idea of who is coming back in the fall.
- A great way to encourage payment of the season's final bill is to base the order in which people can purchase tickets on who is paid in full. The first person to pay in full receives number one, and so on. Again, you could do the processing by mail or have a ticket sale day.
- Have the students draw a number during class.

Make it a policy that you cannot sell recital tickets to anyone who has an overdue balance with the studio.

NOW—ON WITH THE SHOW!

You've made the months leading up to the recital smooth sailing by planning, organizing, and delegating. Plus, you've bought yourself peace of mind, knowing that you're presenting a professional image to your dancers, their families, and potential new clientele. There's no question that putting on a recital is a huge commitment of time and energy, but by minimizing the potential for stress, you've made it a more enjoyable process for everyone involved. Hopefully it's left you with reserves of creative energy, allowing you to make dynamic, high-caliber dances that you'll be proud to present.

NINE

Marketing Demystified

"You can't build a reputation on what you are going to do."—Henry Ford

A good marketing strategy is one of the major keys to success, and positive word of mouth is the key to good marketing. Studio owners spend many hours planning classes and choreography; marketing techniques are just as important.

ETHICS

The people whom you have the most in common with are the dance teachers within your community, who share your profession and love of dance; your clients may attend the same schools or participate in other activities together. If you show respect for your fellow educators, you stand a chance of having a good relationship with them. Instead of regarding each other as competition, you could get together to discuss music, locations for recitals, themes for shows, and maybe even work together to promote dance in your community.

Your marketing campaign directly reflects your attitudes about other schools in the area; make sure your spoken words match up with what you say in print.

- Don't create ads or literature that are obvious slams against other studios in your area.
- Develop your own clientele; don't let it be your objective to attract dancers from other schools. You will have fewer headaches as a result, plus you'll have a better relationship with other studios.
- Never make negative comments about other educators or their schools in front of your students or their parents. If you do, it could backfire. The more you talk about a competitor, the more curiosity you will develop among the people with whom you are gossiping. If that person happens to become disgruntled with you or the studio, they will know where to go—and you gave them the information! Some will choose to go to the studio you spoke about disparagingly because they know it will bother you!

Keep Your Ego Out of It

If you like to see your name in full-page ads, but those ads don't bring in more students, you are wasting your hard-earned profit simply to stroke your own ego. Sometimes the smaller ads with only the essential information are more effective. Also, beware of using 30-year-old dance photos or head shots of yourself—new clients will come to the studio expecting to see you look just like your photos! Don't give them any reason to question your motivations or trustworthiness.

KNOW YOUR TARGET AUDIENCE

The average dance studio's target audience is the parents of 4- to 12-year-olds. This is the population that has the most potential to bring you years of income. Snag a child in preschool, and she may dance at your studio until she leaves for college. However, it's important to take a careful look at the demographics of your community. Is there a big kindergarten population or are more of the children high-school age? If it's kindergarten, then you need to offer a lot of preschool classes with different time options. Your ads, brochures, and other literature should show that your school is just the place to meet the needs of parents with young children. Don't waste money trying to attract a high school population if it doesn't exist in large enough numbers to make it worth your while.

Where should you advertise? The newspaper is where the majority of dance studios market their businesses. You are going to spend a lot of money, so make sure your ads are effective. Do your research. Look for publications that include news pertaining to your local school system and print the school menus or bus routes, or those that target the parents of young children. Placing your ads in the newspapers that these parents read guarantees that they'll be reading about you. Still not sure where to advertise? Test different newspapers, and try different days and different sections of each paper. This will help you determine which locations work best for your business.

Keep It Professional

Make your ads distinctive, with a professionally designed logo (see samples in appendix 9). Your ads should stand out because they—and your studio—look nothing like the ads for other dance studios in your area. A logo is a critical marketing tool, establishing your identity in the mind of a reader with only a glance. Give it time; often it takes repeated exposure to your ad or logo before a parent will pick up the phone. It can take up to 13 viewings before a person will recognize your logo. Never send out a piece of literature or place an ad without including this marketing essential, including all studio correspondence, which should be written on letterhead that incorporates your logo.

Consider including testimonials from happy parents in your newspaper ads. These are especially effective if the families travel a long distance to study with you (list the town they are from). A testimonial used in an ad should be short and to the point. A couple of lines telling why the parent loves your studio are enough. Gather several endorsements so that you can vary them from time to time.

Make the studio look fun, fun, and fun! Use photographs of children having a good time in class in your ads and brochures. Gather a group of younger dancers (preschoolers work well for your market) for a photo shoot. Take pictures of them at the ballet barres or in costumes—always with great big smiles!

Utilizing pictures of your competition award winners is OK, but they may not appeal to the market group you are trying to attract. If you appear to be too much into competition or to cater only to the career-minded dancer, you may scare off potential customers who simply want a fun, recreational activity for their children. You may offer a great deal more, but you need to get these families into the studio first.

Sometimes less is more. Run focus ads, which are one- or two-square-inch ads that market a specific class or group of classes. These ads work best with adult and preschool programs or if you need to fill a particular age level class.

TRACK YOUR ADVERTISING

If you don't know whether your ads are bringing in business, you don't know if your money is well spent. There are many ways to determine if your advertising is effective.

- When you receive phone inquiries, always ask the callers how they heard about your studio. Newspaper? Yellow Pages? Friends? Saw your sign? Went to your recital?
- If a caller tells you she saw your ad in the newspaper, ask for specifics: which ad, in which paper?

In order for the methods just mentioned to be successful, everyone who answers the phone at your school must participate. Consider the following foolproof techniques:

- Place a different extension number in each newspaper ad. When the callers ask for a certain extension, you'll know which ad motivated them to call.
- If you utilize coupons, place a different tracking number on each. When they are turned in, you will know which coupon served you best.
- If you have more than one phone line, designate certain lines to specific ads. When that line rings, you'll know it is coming from a certain ad.

ARE YOU INTERNET SAVVY?

Do the words "Internet" and "Web site" terrify you? I hope not, because in the new millennium, studio owners must be able to utilize the Internet as a marketing tool. You may not spend a lot of time surfing the Web, but according to the Corporation for Public Broadcasting's report "Connected to the Future," as of 2002, 78 percent of America's children lived in homes in which they or their parents used the Internet. And it's only going to increase: That number is a 70 percent increase from 2000. Children love to see pictures of themselves and their friends on your site, and they'll tell everyone they know to check it out!

A school Web site is not only a great marketing tool, it's a convenient way to help keep your dancers and their parents well informed. Use it as an adjunct to your school's bulletin board, newsletter, and handbook. The more ways you can get your information out there, the more likely your attempts to communicate will be successful. Include your Web site and email addresses in all newspaper advertising, brochures, and other literature. Give potential clients as many ways to reach you as possible.

Web site design has become a very competitive industry, making it much less expensive than it used to be to produce a quality site. You could check with local colleges or universities to find a student to design your site. Often students are less expensive than a professional because they need the credits for school or want the experience on their resumes. Let your clients know you're looking for a designer; you may have a parent in your school who would volunteer her services or design a site for you in exchange for tuition. If you're a do-it-yourselfer, search "Web design" on the Internet for tips on how to get started, or use a program such as Microsoft Front Page.

If you have someone design your site for you, make sure that you can maintain and update it once it's up and running. The designer may not always be available to do it for you.

Tailor your site to meet your needs and reflect the personality of your studio. You may want to include the history of the school, bios of you and your staff, alumni news, and upcoming events. You might consider placing your entire brochure and a registration form on the site, but don't include tuition; let people call you for that info. Also, if you've created unique literature, such as handbooks, don't post them on the site where they're easy for others to duplicate. Be sure prospective customers can email you with their questions, and include an easy-to-find phone number.

MORE MARKETING METHODS

When you think of marketing, do you think only of ads and brochures? The fact is, any form of communication can be a marketing tool.

Email

Collecting email addresses provides you with an instant mailing list. When potential clients call, ask for their email address, and include a space for email addresses on registration forms. Once a month, send an "e-newsletter" to your students and all those who've made inquiries about the school. It's free and usually gets a good response. (Make sure to include an "unsubscribe" option.)

Email lists are most useful if you create sub-lists, such as preschool clients or competition participants, so that you can target separate audiences with pertinent information. Use the master list for press releases, school-wide topics, and timely tips; for example, you may want to remind your clients that school merchandise makes a great gift at the holidays.

Telephone Trials and Triumphs

Do you have good intentions but never get around to returning calls? Do you let uninformed students, volunteers, or staff members answer the phone? The phone is a major communication tool, and often it's the first experience a potential client has with your studio. Make sure that first impression is a positive one. Return your phone calls—every one—in a timely fashion, even at the busiest times in the season. During registration is the most critical time because many potential customers are calling several studios for information. If you don't call them back right away, the teacher up the street probably will, and that client will more than likely register with the first one who actually talks to them. Set aside particular hours you will be available to talk or return your calls, and make sure that all phone answerers have the information they need at their fingertips and have been coached in proper phone etiquette. Consider creating scripted answers to the most common questions, and give them to your office manager, receptionist, and anyone else who is likely to field questions. That way, you will be sure everyone is getting the same information and that it's being presented the way you want it to be.

Keep your telephone working for you during off hours by including your Web site address on your answering machine. It's like giving potential clients an instant brochure!

TIPS | **Telephone Etiquette**

- Identify yourself immediately.
- Ask if you are calling at a convenient time. If the person is busy, ask when is a good time to call back.
- Avoid screening your telephone calls. If you always screen your calls, it gives the impression you are unavailable. You may want to set a specific time when customers can reach and speak to you personally.
- Don't keep two people on the line. Call waiting allows you not to miss important calls, but you don't want to upset the first caller or demean their importance. A good rule to follow is to put the first call on hold for no more than 45 seconds. Tell the second caller that you're on

the other line and you'll call them back in a few minutes. However, if it is important for you to take the other call (avoid this if possible), quickly go back to the first caller and tell them you need to take the call and will call them back shortly. Then do so!

- If the call is about a problem, be sure to listen and don't monopolize the conversation. Always try to come up with something positive, especially at the end of the conversation. Hang up giving the caller the impression that you appreciate their input and concerns.
- Avoid offering advice unless they ask for it. Present your "words of wisdom" with tact and keep it short. Instead, ask a question like "What are your options?" or something similar that can lead to problem solving.
- Phone calls are your chance to "telebond"! Find something about the conversation you felt was positive and repeat it. End with a warm and enthusiastic phrase, such as "It was

great talking to you!" or "I'm really glad we had a chance to discuss this."

Your Captive Audience

The waiting room is a great place to market. You never know who is coming in to drop off one of your students. It could be a neighbor or relative whom you can sell your studio to. A few suggestions:

- Be sure there are plenty of brochures on hand.
- Post notices about new programs such as adult or hip-hop classes.
- Hang head shots of the faculty along with their bios.
- Display all credentials and membership certificates attained by you and your faculty.
- Post press releases and newspaper articles about community performances.

Pay close attention to what visitors (and returning families) see when they enter the school. The personality and philosophy of your school should be apparent at all times, but be especially careful about the image you present during heavy-traffic periods such as registration and ticket-sale days. Have experienced and friendly people greet your potential customers; there is nothing more irritating to a parent than asking questions of someone who does not know the answers. Make sure the studio is spotless. (I know of one woman who went to all the local dance schools and then enrolled her child in the one with the cleanest bathroom!) Play videos of your recitals, local performances, and competitions in the waiting area, have faculty available to talk to parents, and take the time to walk potential clients through the facility.

Some schools offer a demonstration or open house at registration time. If you do, include all levels of dancers (including preschool) in demonstrations or performances so that parents can see that your studio offers a terrific education to every dancer regardless of skill. If you make the mistake of using only your advanced dancers, some parents with young children or teens who have never danced before may be intimidated and go elsewhere.

Create an Orientation Kit

At registration time, create a little studio kit for each dancer. Include a warm welcome letter, last season's recital program, copies of the studio history, policies, letters from satisfied customers, and a gift (such as pens, keychains, mini calendars, bumper stickers, etc.) with the studio logo and telephone number on it.

Referral Rewards

Offer incentives to current clients who refer new students to your school, such as a discount on classes or a studio T-shirt.

Bring-a-Friend Week

Allow your dancers to bring a friend to class, either to observe or participate. Offer a discount or some sort of incentive to new students who enroll because of this promotion. Be aware that some of your students' friends may dance at another studio; be very cautious of your sales pitch and don't try to solicit students from other schools.

Sell Team Uniforms or School T-Shirts

Your dancers and their parents will wear items with the studio name on them proudly. The kids will probably wear them to school and other places where young people who might want to dance hang out. Sell studio T-shirts, jackets, and/or sweatshirts with your logo on them. Carry adult as well as children's sizes; you want those parents to wear them too!

More Research

At mid-point or the end of the season, whichever is more advantageous to you, create a survey to find out how you're doing in your customers' eyes. Not only will it help you understand your clients' needs better, it will offer you some testimonials that can be utilized in future brochures and advertising. (Make sure you state clearly that any comments they make may be used for publicity purposes.) A survey can help with preemptive damage control if the responses enlighten you about issues that could turn into problems. Some suggestions:

- Utilize user-friendly multiple-choice questions. Leave space for additional comments and for issues or ideas not covered in the survey.
- Include questions about particular teachers and the office staff.
- Allow for anonymous responses.
- If you mail the survey, include a self-addressed stamped envelope for the reply.

A survey (see appendix 10 for a sample) gives you the opportunity to check up on your product, services, and employees. It also lets your clients know that you care about their opinions. Be prepared, though—some clients will use it to vent about things they're not happy with. Don't be offended; you may even find it valuable.

MARKET YOUR IMAGE

We've already discussed how portraying your studio as a training ground for professional dancers or the one that wins the most awards may make you feel good but could deter potential customers. Sit down with your staff and brainstorm ways to show that you're a committed and vital part of the community. Make your school as visible as possible:

- Participate in local parades.
- Do benefit performances, even if you have to produce them yourself.
- Provide entertainment at assemblies for candidates who are up for election.
- Perform at the shopping malls in your area.
- Get involved in the local school district's parent-teacher organizations.
- Produce an event for National Dance Week.
- Go to the local cable television station and offer your dancers for a show, even if you produce it yourself.
- Dance at the Fourth of July celebration in your community.
- Offer your dancers for community theater productions.
- Offer to choreograph community theater productions or high school musicals.
- Arrange teaching exchanges with schools that provide other activities, such as music or martial arts.

When your school does community performances, be sure to include younger dancers and preschoolers along with the advanced kids.

The Recital as a Marketing Tool? You Bet!

Recital time is the busiest time of the season for most dance studios, but it is important to take the time to produce an eye-catching ad for it. People who are considering dance lessons for their child could decide that the recital is the perfect way to check out your studio. You may want to design an ad that will serve for the recital, any holiday performances, or special shows throughout the season—just change the dates and name of the event, and you're good to go!

Give potential customers the opportunity to register at the recital, and offer a discount on the first month's tuition for registering at that time. You may choose to waive or discount the registration fee as well. If you have a summer program, promote it by including a flyer about it in the recital program. If the next season's brochure is ready, have a stack of them at your registration table.

Press Releases

Press releases are a great way to get free publicity (see appendix 11). Send them to your local newspaper as well as your mailing lists ("snail mail" and email) and post them on your Web site. Newspapers are more likely to run your item if you include a dynamic photo with it. The following are good subjects for press releases:

- Master classes
- Summer programs
- News about educational seminars that you and your students attended
- New programs being offered
- News about successful school alumni (academic or professional)
- Competition results

A press release is a statement of the facts, so keep to the point. Don't worry about perfect journalism techniques; virtually all media rewrite what you submit to fit their own needs for style, length, or time. Your biggest concern should be to make sure all the facts are there. A left-out key fact is more likely to get your release tossed than not having perfect writing skills. But following certain guidelines will minimize the chance that your release will end up in the "round file."

- Each release should be typed and double-spaced, never handwritten. Utilize wide margins on both sides of the release, as well as top and bottom (an inch to an inch and a half is good).
- The name and address of the company or person sending the release should be prominently displayed at the top of the release. A letterhead works well.
- Always include the name and telephone number of a specific person to be contacted in case more information is needed. Make sure you put both a home number and a studio number. If you are not the contact person, make sure the person who is can answer questions quickly and correctly. It's better to use your name on a release.
- Include a release date and time. If you want it to run on a specific date, include it at the top of the release, e.g. "For release July 19, 2004." If the date isn't essential, you can say "For immediate release"or "Release at will."
- Include a suggested headline. Think creatively and put only a few words describing the most important part of the story.
- Always make your lead, or first paragraph, the most important part of the article. Don't save the best for last;

make your opening a good sales pitch so that readers will want to know more.

- Follow up with the facts of your story in descending order of importance.
- If the text goes on to a second page, write "More" or "Continued" at the bottom of the page to indicate that this is not the end. It's better to send a one-page press release and let the editor call you for more information than to make your original release too long. Editors will not take the time to determine your most important facts; they will toss the release first.
- Write "End" at the end of the text.

The School Brochure

One of the keys to success is the way you present yourself to potential customers. For those who haven't had the opportunity to see your performances or visit the studio, the brochure is an important reflection of your school. Collect brochures from other studios and take note of what works well and what doesn't—then design yours so that it'll make the best impression possible. Be sure to include photographs—not of only the competition winners or intensive dancers but of preschoolers and young dancers having a great time in the classroom. In addition to being attractive, the brochure should be easy to understand. Price charts, class schedules, program descriptions, and so on can be confusing to those who aren't "dance studio smart," so they need to be easy to decipher. Otherwise, the parents of your potential new student will send their child where they completely understand what they are getting into.

Have brochures available at all of your community performances. Drop them off at locations throughout the community, especially where kids hang out, such as libraries, community centers, preschools and kindergartens, convenience stores, and pediatricians' and dentists' offices. Perhaps the local chamber of commerce will display some for you. Ask local real estate companies if they will distribute your brochure to new homeowners in the area. Consider purchasing a mailing list from your town hall or the school system. Some towns make available a list of families with children. Also, contact other organizations that cater to children to see if they're willing to exchange mailing lists with you. Possibilities include preschools and kindergartens; music, art, martial arts, and gymnastics schools; and community or recreation centers.

The better known you are in your community, the easier it is to network. By sharing brochures and mailing lists, you extend your school's reach into the community and tap into other markets.

TEN

Money Matters

> *"Money is better than poverty, if only for financial reasons."* —Woody Allen

Dance training can be expensive; there's no getting around it. Classes, costumes, class attire and warm-ups, pointe shoes, medical costs, travel expenses, master classes and workshops—the list goes on and on. No wonder some already-burdened parents regard class registration fees, competition entry fees, and related costs as tantamount to extortion. Once again, good communication skills—in this case, how you present the rationale for such charges to the parents—make all the difference. And make sure they have all the information well ahead of time so that there are no surprises.

FEE-ING FRENZY

Registration

Some parents argue the need for a registration fee, so it's best to be prepared with your rationale for charging one. Once they understand that the money covers insurance, newsletters, flyers, postage, special events, costs associated with extra rehearsals (utilities, extra pay for the staff), and in some cases, teacher bonuses, their arguments usually disappear. Registration fees range from $20–$35 per child in the schools represented at my seminars; some charge $30 for an individual registration but offer a family fee of $40 for those with more than one child in the school.

Tuition

Most schools collect tuition on a monthly basis. Others require or offer the option of semester tuition, or two to four payments over a season. (To determine the amount of each payment, divide the total fee for the season by the number of payments.) This system eliminates having to process tuition on a monthly basis, but a drawback is that it seems more expensive to the client than when tuition is paid on a monthly basis. A yearly tuition payment is the easiest to manage for the studio, but is usually the least favorite option for the clients. Schools usually offer a 5–10 percent discount to those who pay for the entire season up front.

The average hourly tuition, paid monthly, is approximately $36–$42 ($9–$10.50 per hour), and private lessons range from $35 to $50 per hour.

Discounts for more than one class per week should be well thought out. It is important to understand that your faculty, electric company, office staff, etc. are not offering you a discount to operate additional classes. The cost of operating a second, third, or fourth class for a particular dancer costs you the same as the first class did. However, many studios do offer discounts.

- Discounted rates for multiple classes per week:
  First hour: $42/month
  Second hour: $38/month
  Third hour: $34/month
  Fourth hour: $30/month

(This represents a $1 discount for the second hour, a $2 discount for the third hour, and a $3 discount for the fourth class hour.)

- For dancers who train more than four hours per week, an unlimited intensive program with a flat fee allows them to take as many hours as they would like during any given month.
  7–9 years of age: $150/month (5–7 classes weekly)
  10–12 years of age: $175/month (6–8 classes weekly)
  13+ years of age: $200/month (7–9 classes weekly)
- Family discounts of 10–25 percent (on the lower tuition) for additional family members (applies only to those living under one roof; no cousins, etc.). A family unlimited program, where a flat fee (for example, $150 per month) covers the tuition for an entire family, is another option.

TIPS | **Tuition Collection Options**

- Tuition envelopes or payment books (similar to a car or mortgage payment; see appendix 13): Each month's tuition is preprinted on a payment slip or an envelope. The payments are mailed or dropped off at the school office on preappointed payment days.
- Automatic debit payment: The parent signs a form authorizing you to deduct a set amount from his or her bank account each month. It's a convenient option for both school (no need for repeated billing and trips to the bank to deposit checks) and parent (no check writing or remembering tuition due dates).
- Credit card payments: It's an extra expense for the school

but a major convenience for the client, particularly when the balance due is large and cash on hand is tight.

- Prepayment discounts: Establish a deadline for payment; if the payment is made before that date, there is a $5 discount. (So that you don't lose money by offering this incentive, raise the tuition payment by $5. This provides a better incentive to pay by the due date than charging a late fee if payments are not made by the deadline.)
- Collection of first and last tuition payment in September: This decreases end-of-season stress for your clients. At a time when recital tickets, shoes, tights, etc. could be expensive, they will not have to worry about their final tuition payment.

Students' Use of Studios

Another potentially sticky issue is whether to charge for studio time when the students want to rehearse on their own. On one hand, it's important to appreciate that the dancers are motivated enough to put in extra time. On the other hand, the heat, lights, and wear-and-tear on the sound equipment are expenses for the studio owner.

TIPS | **Studio Time—To Fee or Not to Fee?**

- Charge a minimal fee.
- Work on a barter system; ask the dancers to help you keep the studio clean. Give them some cleaning supplies and ask them to wash the mirrors.

When you're feeling put upon, remember that dancers who have the drive to put in extra time are good for your business.

When they perform or compete, their polished performances will make you and the studio look good. Plus, they may motivate other students to work harder.

THE HIGH COST OF COMPETITION

If you participate in competitions, you know how much work goes into them—and what they cost you in dollars as well as time and energy. Let the parents know what it takes to keep their kids competing. If you'd rather avoid surcharges altogether, it's time to start asking for parent volunteers to do some of the work.

How Much Does Competing Really Cost?

From the parents' point of view, they're already paying a sizeable amount for lessons, costumes, shoes, extra fees for solos, and hotel and transportation costs. If you let them know, without playing the martyr, what your costs are, they are more likely to accept the expense of dance training.

Time: The cost of spending hours

- Planning the season.
- Researching and purchasing the right music for the competition dancers.
- Recording and editing music for each of the competition entries.
- Making long-distance phone calls to find appropriate competitions, hotels, and transportation.
- Meeting with faculty to place the competition dancers on the correct teams.
- Designing or selecting the costumes.
- Scheduling rehearsals and classes.

- Collecting entry fees.
- Running to Federal Express with last-minute entries.
- Brainstorming new ways to motivate the kids to do their best.
- Planning for the next season.

Money: You're paying for

- Office staff to fill out entry forms, make reservations, order costumes, etc.
- Long-distance phone calls.
- Fronting entry fees for parents who are late with their payments.
- Extra postage to send the entry forms and payments by FedEx before the deadline. (They're late because the parents didn't pay the fees on time and you didn't have the money to pay up front for them.)
- Personal transportation and hotel costs at the competitions (possibly for the faculty too).
- Faculty to cover classes at the studio during competitions.
- Music rights from ASCAP or BMI.
- Tapes and/or CDs and any recording costs.

Personal wear-and-tear:

- The stress of late-arriving costumes.
- Trying to accommodate each parent's special requests.
- Fatigue because the competition ended late on Sunday and the studio must be open on Monday morning.
- Consoling the dancers who didn't score as well as they had hoped.
- Dealing with the parents who aren't happy with the way

their children scored at the competition.
- The thought that there is another competition next weekend!

FUND-RAISING

When expenses seem to be getting out of hand and the parental grumbling is reaching a crescendo, it time to play on the team atmosphere and get everyone involved through fund-raising. You may choose to distribute funds based on each student's or parent's effort or use them to defray total costs so that everyone benefits equally; either way, fund-raising can raise enthusiasm as well as money.

Fund-Raising Ideas

- Spaghetti dinner (sometimes with celebrity hosts and waiters)
- Dance-a-thon
- A benefit evening at a local restaurant, where a percentage of the evening's intake goes to the school. Make sure you fill the restaurant that evening.
- Rummage sales
- Car washes
- Raffles, including 50/50 prizes (where cash is the prize, and half the amount goes to the raffle ticket holder and half to the school)
- Auctions (live or silent)
- Candy sales, including the ever-popular candy bar (one of the best fund-raisers of them all. Kids and parents take them to school or work—everyone wants a candy bar!)
- Tupperware parties
- Avon sales

- Christmas or holiday gifts
- Carnivals

The possibilities are endless! One studio went to a local office building and took orders for lunches for the week. They delivered each day and the profit was tremendous.

Consider running a studio competition—a closed event open only to students at your school. Charge a nominal fee (around $5), with all proceeds going into the competition team fund. Let the students work with other dancers or create solos for themselves. You will be surprised at what your dancers will come up with. Offer the winners the opportunity to perform in your recital or include their work in the next performance or competition. Hire outside judges (perhaps friends of yours who are in the business). Give special awards as well as first, second, and third places, and make sure everyone goes home with something. This event can raise team spirit as well as money!

GENERATING EXTRA INCOME

If your studio is like most, it's a hive of activity in the afternoon and early evenings—and some mornings, if you have a preschool program. But the rest of the time the space is empty, and it costs you money to have it sit there unused. Explore the various ways that the space could be utilized outside of your regular class offerings, and you just might find that there's an upswing in your bottom line at the end of the month.

Adult Programs

September and January are the best times to start and promote adult programs. Often we start off with a hefty enrollment; however, by the time the holidays arrive, many students have stopped coming. Try offering adult programs in six- or eight-week sessions, either in the mornings or evenings—or both, if there's enough interest. Charging for the entire program in advance gives the students more incentive to show up for class and gurantees you enough income to staff the session. You might offer a special rate to parents who have a child registered at your studio. Adults are looking for fun and exercise, so make sure you promote this program that way!

Studio Rentals

Renting one or more of your classrooms during "dead times" will not only generate direct income to you, but it's also a great way to open your doors to potential customers. Renting your space is not difficult; all you have to do is make sure the studio is open and be

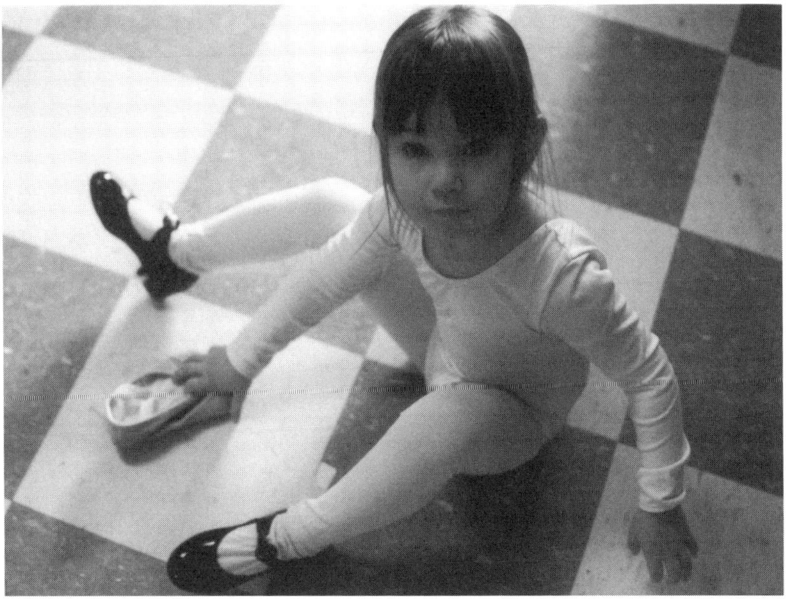

clear about what the rental includes. (For example, you may choose to make your sound system off limits.) Your tenant (if you trust them) or office manager could do it. Dance studios are excellent spaces for karate, aerobics, preschool programs, birthday parties, ballroom or line dance classes, drama or voice lessons, yoga, and meditation. If your renter uses the studio for a physical activity, be sure your insurance covers them, or ask the renter if their policy covers them at your location. You could also offer the space for meetings of such activities as book clubs, writers' groups, and new mothers' groups (with the added bonus that these new moms may soon have budding dancers on their hands!). Set clear rules about eating and drinking in the classrooms or you may find that a major cleanup is needed before the floors are safe for dancers.

A Terrific Twos Class

This special class for parent and child is perfect for those morning hours and can provide a much-needed activity to children who are not in preschool or day care. Promote it as an introduction to dance and offer the program in six- or eight-week increments. Many of these students will end up being at your studio for life! Make it fun for both the kids and their parents. One teacher told me about a program at her school for children up to age 4, called First Steps. She had 300 preschool-age children registered!

Dancewear Sales

Make buying dress-code items easier for your students and parents by offering them for sale, along with warm-ups, hair accessories, and T-shirts and sweats with the school name and logo on them.

Try selling healthy snacks and drinks along with dancewear and accessories—they can be a huge hit!

Master Classes

Take out an ad in the newspaper or send notices to other studios inviting them to participate. Build goodwill and maybe make money in the process! Allow teachers who bring five or more paying students to take the class at no charge.

Summer Programs

Summer intensives are a great way to keep your school producing year-round. Try to include guest faculty, not just the same teachers your students have had all season, and supplement your school-year offerings with classes in drama, voice, auditioning, fencing, dance history, musicality, or dance on film, to name a few ideas. Give them a different curriculum than they would get during the season.

Promote the program in your local newspapers and do a mailing to all those who have inquired about your school over the past three years. Consider working with other teachers in your area to produce a joint program. You will be guaranteed more students, plus you will share the expenses.

In my travels around the country with Project Motivate, I've encountered participants who have shared with me their unique concepts for summer programs or camps. But before you use the word "camp" to describe your summer activities, check with your insurance company to be sure you are actually covered to produce a camp at your school. Some states require camps to have a nurse on site during activities. If that's the case for you and you don't want the added expense, call your program something else. If you do want to offer a camp, consider renting an actual campground for your summer program. You then could include other activities such as swimming, hiking, and evenings by the campfire.

Your Target Market

Since the majority of the market for dance schools is made up of the parents of 4- to 12-year-old children, create programs that will appeal to those age groups. But you want your intensive dancers to participate, you say? Many schools do; some even make it mandatory. But consider the following: By making it a requirement, you might be putting financial stress on those parents who have spent the most money at your school. It can also create a personal burden for the whole family, since summer might be the only time that they have the chance to go on a vacation together, because of the dance commitments of the regular season. Those dancers might also like to broaden their experience by attending summer programs offered by other schools around the country. Remember, your job is to offer them the best education possible—and that means allowing them to benefit from exposure to other teachers or styles of dance.

Many studio owners rely on summer programs to cover their school's costs during those lean months. That's totally understandable. But don't limit your thinking; there may be even better options out there that allow you to minimize the financial stress on your intensive families, attract new students, keep the recreational students interested in dance so that they'll re-register in the fall, and possibly generate more income than an intensive dancer program would. Here are a few ideas:

- ***Kinder-Camp***

  Offered to the preschool age level. The curriculum could include dance, singing, tumbling, arts and crafts, and games. Three days a week for up to four or five hours (it could be less, but not more) a day is perfect.

- ***Theme Camps***

  Broadway Camp: A program that focuses on teaching dancers about the realities of a Broadway career. Include voice lessons, dance, acting, auditioning, and resume preparation. Center each day's activities on a different Broadway show—teach the students the history of the show and utilize its music in your classes or combinations. Bring in a master teacher who has Broadway experience, not only to teach class but to lead a rap session about life "on the boards." You could produce a Broadway-type show for parents and friends of the camp participants at the end of the week. If you're close to a big city, book a block of tickets for a touring musical and see if you can arrange a backstage tour for the students.

  Video Camp: Dancers learn how to perform for the camera and go home with a video they've created during the camp. Offer classes and choreography that lead to a filming day during which participants perform the dances they've learned for the camera. Tape the video in a variety of locations: in the classroom, a parking lot, a stairwell, or at a park or beach. Bring in a master teacher who has experience performing in music videos.

  Ballet Camp: Each day of the camp focuses on famous ballets such as *The Nutcracker* or *Coppélia.* Teach the history and story of the ballet along with variations from each, and conclude with a performance. Bring in a master teacher who dances with a professional ballet company (or used to) to offer the inside scoop on the ballet world.

Fantasy Camp: Each day follows a different fairy tale theme; if you have boys enrolled in this program, be sure to plan something special for them. They might enjoy re-creating themselves as princes, knights in shining armor, or hideous monsters. Or you may want to expand the concept to include fantasy themes with a higher testosterone quotient, such as Harry Potter, Spiderman, *Star Wars*, or *Lord of the Rings.*

Can I Afford It?

If you're not sure that a summer program makes financial sense for your school, or if you're just nervous about launching one, consider collaborating with other schools in your area; that way, you'll share the marketing expenses and ensure enough students to make the program a success. After a year or two, you and your collaborators may find that there's enough interest for you to go your separate ways and offer programs that are unique to each school.

Marketing the Program

By planning your summer programs well in advance, you'll be able to take advantage of months of marketing. Many parents start looking for summer activities for their children in January or February; you'll want to be advertising along with the rest in order to maximize your enrollment. Continue marketing it in various ways, right up until the camp begins—unless, of course, you've been so successful that your programs are fully booked!

- Create a brochure specific to the camp.
- When people inquire about the school's programs, send them the camp brochure along with the school brochure.
- Tuck the camp brochure into the recital program or include information about it on a page of the program.
- Send a press release about summer offerings to your email list, and post it on your Web site.
- Include a press release or ad in the school newsletters.
- Place an ad in the local newspapers in January or February, and run the ad periodically up until a few weeks prior to the camp.
- Inquire about placing an ad or including a press release in public school newsletters.
- Market your program through other community organizations that offer children's programs, including kindergartens, preschools, music schools, and gymnastics clubs. Make it reciprocal—offer to carry their brochures in your waiting room or include ads for their programs in your newsletters or on your Web site.
- Offer an early registration discount.

Take plenty of photos of your happy camp attendees for next year's brochures and marketing—now *that's* thinking ahead!

ELEVEN

It's Not a Business—It's Your Life

"Go confidently in the direction of your dreams. Live the life you have imagined." —Henry David Thoreau

Dance educators tend to work at two speeds—fast and faster. Many teachers have what others view as the ultimate success: an exciting career (most of the time), a comfortable home, a nice car, perhaps a family. It's what many would call the American dream! The "dance life" appears to be the epitome of nonstressful living to those outside of it. What they don't know is that school owners are always at the studio teaching; very rarely do they spend more than a few hours in that comfortable home (which, by the way, carries a huge mortgage), and the nice car looks like hell from transporting students to and from dance events.

But those who choose our profession are doing far more than dancing their lives away, and often, they're not doing it within the confines of a nine-to-five workday. In what I used to refer to as the "normal world" (as I get older I realize *normal* is a matter of interpretation), there's little understanding of the challenges, stresses, and joys that face those who center their world around dance.

NOT SUCH A SIMPLE LIFE

The dance educator may not start teaching until 4 PM, but her workday begins long before then. Many teachers spend most of their waking hours preoccupied with the responsibilities of being the best dance educators and businesspeople they can be. "Complicated" is the best way to describe it. I once read *Living the Simple Life: A Guide to Scaling Down and Enjoying More* by Elaine St. James. Chapter 6, "The Things That Complicate Our Lives," was extremely revealing to me. I have taken many of Ms. St. James's points, added a few of my own, and related them all to our profession.

So what complicates the life of a dance school owner? How about big studios with huge mortgages or rents? Property taxes. Studio upkeep. Multiple credit cards. Not having time to spend with our partners. Not having time to spend with our children. Difficult in-laws, always asking when you are going to get a "real job." Family expectations. Our own expectations. Seventy-five-hour work weeks. Holding down a second job to keep the school going. Car payments. Obstinate employees. Long commutes. Traffic jams. Grudging competitors. Demanding clients. Silent partners who don't remain silent. Staff meetings.

Not having time to spend with our friends. Not having time to spend alone. Organization meetings. Neighbors who complain about the music. Attorneys. Accountants. Insurance people. Taxes. Costume companies that deliver late. Repair people who show up late. Contractors we wish had never shown up. Telephone solicitors. Cheap gadgets that don't work. Expensive equipment that does not work.

Worrying. Not winning at a competition. Fear of losing students. Getting students from other schools who create turmoil in your school. Parents who aren't happy with the class placement of their children. Parents who question your decisions. Kids who show up late. Kids who are not dedicated, in the same class with kids who are.

Those who choose our profession are doing far more than dancing their lives away.

The dance profession can be very challenging, but those of us who love what we do take the issues in stride and learn through experience. Part of the feeling of success comes when we realize we are good at dealing with the things that have nothing to do with the classroom.

THE BURNOUT BLUES

When burnout strikes, we suddenly become good at dealing with nothing—not studio business, not teaching, not our personal lives. A common misperception is that if we just keep muddling along, things will get better. Somehow, we tell ourselves, our stress will magically disappear. Wrong. The best remedy—in fact, the only remedy, is to slow down.

So here's a shocker: Taking personal time is good for business. "What?" you exclaim. "I don't have time!" Does this scenario sound familiar?

It's mid-November; you've been at the studio five or six days a week for two months. Parents have scolded you because they believe their kids should be in a higher-level class, yet you know their children are where they belong. One of your newer teachers doesn't seem to be the professional she made herself out to be. The studio secretary is always late because her kids seem to be sick every day. And your own kids are laying guilt trips on you because you're always at the studio when they get home from school.

It's OK to stop! When you're burned out but just keep going, you're doing an injustice to yourself and your students. Your health and mental well-being suffer, and your feelings could encourage a negative atmosphere in the studio, affecting your employees and clientele.

A person can only take so much pressure before their decisions and judgment become irrational. Suddenly things that were minor issues seem like monstrous problems without easy solutions. Continuing to operate under these conditions for an extended period of time can take quite a toll on you—and your business.

When a mother walks up to you to ask a simple question and you snap at her, it's not good for business. You may say to yourself, "I have been answering the same question for the past 20 years and I'm sick of it," but remember, to the person asking the question, it's the first time, and she deserves a friendly response. The more questions you encounter, the more you know people are interested in your product. Look at these inquiries as opportunities to invest your clients more fully in what your studio has to offer.

If you desperately need a break and exhibit your stress in front of your employees or faculty, they will want out, too! In most cases, employees understand your feelings better than anyone else. A good faculty will do their best to alleviate or cover up the problem, but if you treat your employees irrationally or unkindly, they too will become the enemy. Then you will be dealing with much more than your own negative feelings—you will have created an atmosphere that is not conducive to education, retaining your current clientele, or attracting new students for the future.

Don't blame others for the way you feel. And don't assume the solution is to just "plow through"— it will only enhance the fatigue, anger, and confusion. Give yourself the opportunity to clear your mind—take a break. It will help you make decisions with a rational mind-set. Treat yourself to the time off you deserve, and do it with no guilt!

For workaholics, guilt is a big issue. They think about stopping, but there is a sense of falling behind or someone else getting ahead of them if they don't work or think about their profession 24 hours a day. That guilt can even override their attention to their own health. Often they fantasize about what they'd like to do (for a moment), then wipe it out of their minds and get back to work.

Working more hours will not eliminate the feeling of being overwhelmed. Take it from a workaholic: It's time to take a day off—or maybe three!

Take it from a fellow workaholic—it's time to call someone to cover your classes and time to forget about all those parents, your faculty, and the secretary's kids. Take a day off—or maybe three! Spend time doing things for yourself. The "dance department of your mind" is closed—no question. Do something that you have been putting off because you've been too busy. Maybe a massage! Or go shopping (someplace far away from the studio). Go to the museum that you've never had time to enjoy. Take your kids to the movies and spend the day just loving them. Surprise your partner with a couple of days away at a resort.

At this point you may be thinking, *I can't afford to go to a hotel or do something so frivolous with my money.* You can't afford *not* to! What's funny about dance people is that spending the money wouldn't be a question if we had another conference, convention, or competition to attend. Why is our personal well-being not as important as those dance-related commitments? Clarity of mind and a calm soul is more important to your business than another dance event.

When you do return to the studio, you, your employees, and your dancers will feel a fresh, new energy. Then you can tell those parents what you really think (in a kind way) or you can sit down with that "professional teacher" and let her know how amateurish she really is (also in a kind way), and you can buy your secretary a big bottle of children's aspirin!

'No' Is a Beautiful Word

OK, so you absolutely can't take time off. There are other ways to lighten your stress load. For starters, learn to say no.

To be creative, whether it's choreography, laying out a newsletter, planning a recital, or setting goals, you have to take the time to think and figure it out. Digging deep into your creative energy can't be rushed or done at the last minute. Yes, you might get the job done, but will you be able to pat yourself on the back, knowing you did the best you could? Or will you always know in the back of your mind that you could have done more? Will knowing you could have done better bother you? These kinds of thoughts or questions sap our creative energy.

Where to begin? Start by eliminating the things that are not necessary. If you spend every day trying to catch up, burnout is imminent. It will leave you feeling overwhelmed, and you may even begin to wonder why you became a dance educator in the first place!

Don't spend your life rushing through responsibilities. The outcomes will never be as good as they could have been.

Sometimes you need to say no! Many of us don't have the ability—we like to be good people, so when somebody wants us to do something, we say yes without thinking about how it will affect us. Sometimes we sacrifice our own success or happiness.

In their book *The Awakened Heart: Finding Harmony in a Changing World,* John Robbins and Ann Mortifee write about the ability to say no:

No can be a beautiful word, every bit as beautiful as yes. Whenever we deny our need to say no, our self-respect diminishes.

It is not only our right at certain times to say no, it is our responsibility. For it is a gift to ourselves when we say no to those habits that dissipate our energy, no to what robs us of our joy, no to what distracts us from our purpose. And, it is a gift to others to say no when their expectations do not ring true for us, for in so doing we free them to discover more fully the truth of their own path. Saying no can be liberating when it expresses out commitment to take a stand for what we truly need.

If we find ourselves being inauthentically "nice," saying yes when we mean no, this can be an opportunity to bring an unwanted fear in ourselves to the light. Through such self-honesty, we can reclaim our source of personal power, inner joy, and self-esteem.

Saying No at the Studio

Say NO to the dancer who wants to do a solo—or a second one. Students need to realize that a solo is an honor that they must work to achieve. When they ask for a second solo, explain that they need to be focused on the one they already have to make it the best it can be. If you encourage four dancers who want a solo to come together as a group, it will be one lesson per week and not four. You may have just saved yourself three valuable hours per week. Plus, with fewer pieces to choreograph, you may find that the overall quality of your dance-making improves.

Say NO to 12 *Nutcracker* performances; cut it down to 4. You will sell out the house and may even have time to spend the holidays with your family and friends.

Say NO to participating in four or five competitions per season. Instead, choose a couple of events that will offer your dancers the best education. The extra stress of doing several competitions per season takes a toll on you, your staff, students, and their parents. Go back to making competition a fun thing, not a pressure thing. Replace some of the competitions with lower-stress options, such as local performances for charities or at shopping malls, which require less preparation and fewer individual numbers. They're an excellent way to provide your students with performance opportunities and promote your studio at the same time.

Say NO to dancers participating in 15 competition numbers. Working as a team to create four to five excellent pieces of choreography will make you and your faculty more creative, and you will probably score higher as a result. Parents will spend less money on costumes, entry fees, and transportation, and you and the parents will enjoy the experience more!

Say NO to the parent who pressures you to give their child something you know he's not ready for. You know in your gut whether or not a child is ready for something. If not, you must be able to give the child's parents a well-thought-out explanation, in a friendly and positive way. If we present legitimate reasons in an objective way, more than likely the parent will understand—and maybe even appreciate the fact that you won't allow a child to perform before he's ready simply so that you can make money.

Say NO to being at the studio six or seven days a week. Once you have built a studio that is operating six or seven days a week, be proud. However, understand that the size of this business means you must let go and let others assume some of the responsibility. Constantly work with your team of employees to create a clear understanding of the way you need things done. Then allow them to do it and make time for you to do what's important to you and your family.

GETTING YOUR PRIORITIES STRAIGHT

Managing the studio and making time for your family, partner, or friends is a difficult balancing act. Nonetheless, it's one of the most important components to a successful career. Through all of life's ups and downs, your family and friends are the people who will always be with you. They need to be part of your "big picture" at all times. Some dance educators find themselves with regrets many years down the road, most of them based on how their children felt about growing up at the studio or having a parent that was at the studio most of their lives.

Taking time for yourself and your family is one of the smartest business moves you can make.

When I was little, my mother's most common answer to a request was "After the recital." I understood because I grew up in the studio; I learned at a very young age that dance was about commitment and dedication. However, I had an older brother who wasn't interested in dance. He wanted to play baseball and other sports. But my mother, a single parent who was running a business by herself, couldn't always be there for his games or to recognize his accomplishments. As he reached his teen years, he became rebellious and ended up in trouble a lot of the time.

I believe his difficulties were a direct result of a mother who was doing the best she could to keep up with all of her responsibilities but couldn't find the time to make her son's non-dance ambitions a priority. Today, he is proud of what he has accomplished, and he has his own family to nourish. However, I wonder if life would have been easier for him if our mother had had more time to spend with him, sharing the things he loved to do.

Make the time to share in your children's hopes and dreams. They may be different from yours, but they are just as important to them as dance is to you. If you have time to travel to and attend conventions, competitions, or continuing education programs, you can certainly take a weekend or two to spend with your family. They will remember and appreciate it for a long time.

Do all that you can to share dance with your family—make

them feel like they're a part of that world—but don't forget to take time to listen to what's important in their lives.

Don't Take It Home With You

Taking time off, learning to say no, and making your family or friends a priority aren't the whole answer when it comes to your well-being. It's difficult not to become emotionally involved with your students and their problems. However, you must remember that you can't change the person or situation you're dealing with. But you can change your attitude toward them. Don't let it have a negative effect on your personal life. Train yourself not to take it home with you; come up with a phrase or a word you can repeat to yourself as a self-hypnotic suggestion. "I won't go there" works well.

"Experience is not what happens to you. It is what you do with what happens to you." —Aldous Huxley

Remember your right to privacy. You are a celebrity to your dancers and parents. They want to know all about you and love being around you, but they need to know that your home and especially your home phone are off limits. If someone invades your privacy, be sure to let them know that they have crossed the line. Situations like these can be very difficult, especially for the teacher who has been in business for a long time and has made some great friends along the way. But it's important to keep those friendships separate from the relationships you have with them at the studio.

When you are in a social setting with parents or dancers from the studio, avoid discussing your business or your teaching. Of course the subject of dance will come up, because that is who you are and everyone thinks you love to talk about it. Never discuss your business policies or teaching philosophies. Speak in general terms and discourage any personal questions. Never discuss other clients or students with anyone; if you practice this policy at all times, soon parents will learn that you will not discuss their child with others.

Make it a policy: Your studio office is the place where you discuss business-related concerns—and leave them there when you go home. You'll be a better teacher for it, and a better businessperson, even a better parent. Make looking out for number one—you—a top priority, and you'll find yourself well on the way to personal and professional success.

Appendices

Appendix 1
SAMPLE FACULTY CONTRACT

Please Note: This is a sample and not intended for official use. Please consult with an attorney to create a contract that is legally binding in your state.

ABC School of Dance
10 South Your Street
Anytown, St 00000
555-555-5555
Email: ABCSchool@url.com

NONDISCLOSURE AGREEMENT AND RESTRICTIVE COVENANT
The ABC Studio of Dance (hereinafter referred to as the "EMPLOYER") and
____,
residing at ____,
in the town of ____________________ in the state of _________________,
and is identified by the social security number of ____________________
(hereinafter referred to as the "EMPLOYEE").

As a condition of employment and/or continued employment by the ABC Studio of Dance, the undersigned hereby consents to the following terms and conditions of employment.

It is acknowledged that the names and identities of the students, their parents, their addresses, their telephone numbers, and their email addresses are to be kept confidential and are not to be revealed to any third party without the express written consent of the employer.

The names, addresses and telephone numbers of the students and parents are not to be copied or otherwise recorded for the personal use of employees without the express written consent of the employer. All correspondence and/or telephone communications with such students and/or parents are to be made by the secretaries unless any other employee is expressly permitted to make direct communications with such students and/or parents by express written consent of the employer.

Upon the termination of employment for any reason whatsoever, the undersigned will not engage in any similar business, either directly or indirectly, as a share holder, officer, or director of any corporation, or as a partner in any general or limited partnership or individually as a sole proprietorship engaged in a similar business within a five (5) mile radius from the ABC Studio of Dance, for a period of not less than five (5) years from the date of written termination of employment from the ABC Studio of Dance.

It is further agreed, that as a condition of employment and/or continued employment by the ABC Studio of Dance, the undersigned will not solicit or do business with any of the students and/or parents of the students of the ABC Studio of Dance, during the two (2) years prior to the termination of employment and for a period of not less than three (3) years from the date of termination of employment, for whatever reason, notwithstanding that the undersigned may be engaged, either directly or indirectly in a similar business beyond the five (5) mile limitation described above.

This agreement shall be binding upon the undersigned, his or her personal representatives, successors and assignees, and shall insure to the benefit of the ABC Studio of Dance, or its successors and assignees.

The undersigned hereby agrees that in the event of any breach of this agreement, in addition to any other rights or remedies that the ABC Studio of Dance may be entitled to receive as damages for such a breach, the ABC Studio of Dance shall also be entitled to preliminary and permanent injunctive relief as well as an equitable accounting of all profits and benefits arising out of such breach.

DATED: ___________
EMPLOYEE SIGNATURE: ______________________________
EMPLOYER SIGNATURE: ______________________________
WITNESS SIGNATURE: ______________________________

Appendix 2
SAMPLE SCHOOL NEWSLETTER

Newsletter Date
Volume 1, Issue 1

ABC's Dancin' News

10 South Your Street, Anytown, ST 00000
555/555-5555

"The essence of all art is to have pleasure in giving pleasure."

--Mikhail Baryshnikov

Dancers to Perform at Bally Nursing Home

The ABC School of Dance will present a special holiday performance on December 5 at 6:30 PM at the Bally Nursing Home in Reeddale. This is the second year our dancers have entertained the home's residents during the holidays.

This season we are proud to present the junior dancers performing their new production number, "Over the Rainbow." Fifty dancers will participate.

The performance is open to the dancers' parents at no charge. Performers must arrive at the nursing home, at 12 Lowell Street, Reeddale by 5:30 PM. Directions are posted on the bulletin board in the school waiting room.

Participating dancers include: Sandra B., Jane B., Kim C., Cassidy C., Tim D., Helen E., Tony F., Jim F., Taylor G., Lisa G., Sondra G., Kim H., Mary H., Kristen I., Tammy J., Tommy J., Elizabeth K., Joyce L., Angel L., Andrea M., Tonya M., Gloria N., Katie O., Ann P., Belinda P., Ashley R., Kim R., Timmy R., Ruth S., Sandy S., Ryan T., Tammy T., Pam U., Roger V., Victoria Y., and Paulette P.

We wish the best of luck to all the ABC dancers and we look forward to a great performance!

Tim Ward to Teach Master Classes December 12

The ABC School will present open master classes with Tim Ward, who is currently starring in the Broadway hit *Fosse*. Don't miss out on this great opportunity!

Classes will be offered for three age levels. Each class costs $10 and preregistration is a must. Please call the studio at 555-5555 by December 5.

Add photo here

Class schedule (1 hour each):

10 AM: 7-9 tap

11 AM: 7-9 jazz

1 PM: 10-12 tap

2 PM: 10-12 jazz

3:30 PM: 13-15 tap

4:30 PM: 13-15 jazz

6 PM: rap session for all students and parents. Join us for a chance to get the inside scoop on dancing on Broadway!

Contents

SAMPLE SCHOOL NEWSLETTER (CONTINUED)

HAPPY BIRTHDAY!

To Jenny S., Paula W., Tammy T., Rebecca J, and Timmy B.

You deserve the best birthday on Earth . . . not to mention the moon, the stars, and the universe!

Reminder!
Holiday raffle tickets are available from the team dancers or in the office. Great prizes, including a color TV! Drawing on 12/11!

We're on the Web!
See us at:
www.webaddress.com

ABC School's All-New, All-Ages Summer Camp

Due to the overwhelming response to last year's summer camp, this summer we will offer two full weeks of classes. Both weeks will include three age levels: 7-9, 10-12, and 13 and over. Classes will include ballet, tap, jazz, lyric, musical theater, acrobatics, and more. There will also be a special drama and voice workshop taught by Broadway performer Nancy Paige, which will be open to all camp participants. Other guest faculty will be announced in upcoming newsletters.

The camp will run July 10-14 and August 3-7. Students may enroll in one or both sessions. Fees are $150 for one session and $250 for both. Each session will offer more than 20 classes per age level. Preregistration is required by June 1; classes will be limited to 25 dancers.

For more information, please call 555-5555.

Faculty Spotlight: Tanya Ticherovya

Ms. Ticherovya began her dance training at age 8 in St. Petersburg, Russia. She joined the Russian National Ballet at age 17 and was promoted to the rank of prima ballerina assoluta at 21. She is best known for her ravishing portrayals of Giselle and Juliet, but her favorite role was Kitri in *Don Quixote*.

During a tour to the United States in 1983, Ms. Ticherovya fell in love with New York City. She moved there the following year and began teaching at schools throughout the city. Her students now dance with many major companies worldwide.

Ms. Ticherovya joined the ABC faculty in 1995. She and her cat, Pirouette, are well loved at the school. We're lucky to have her!

Dear Parents...

When it seems like dance is taking up too much time or costing too much money, remember that it gives your children much more than another costume or trophy. They are learning what hard work and determination can accomplish. They're learning life skills that will help them succeed, whether it's getting into the college of their choice or landing the perfect job. Kudos to all of you!

The ABC School of Dance Artistic Staff

Appendix 3

SAMPLE RECITAL THEMES AND PROGRAMS

Theme: **Imagine That!**

TITLE	MUSIC	CLASS DESCRIPTION
Opening	Imagine/Pure Imagination	Dance Company Members
Pink Elephants	Pink Elephants on Parade	Preschool Ballet
I'm Surfin'	Surfin' USA	7–9 Jazz
Karate Black Belt	Mortal Combat	13+ Advanced Tap
We Made Friends!	You've Got a Friend in Me	10–12 Beg./Intermediate Ballet
Nascar Driver	Speed Racer	10–12 Int./Advanced Tap
Undercover Agents	Mission Impossible	13+ Advanced Jazz
Walking in Paradise	Stairway to Paradise	7–9 Tap
Prima Ballerina	*Nutcracker* medley	Advanced Ballet Production
2000 B.C.	Roll Back the Rock	10–12 Beg./Intermediate Jazz
Dream Come True	Whatever You Imagine	1st Act Closing
	INTERMISSION	
Walk on the Moon	2001: A Space Odyssey	Gymnastics/Acro Production
Animals Talk?	Talk to the Animals	Preschool Tap
I'm a Star!	On Broadway	10–12 Int./Advanced Jazz
Back in the '50s	We Go Together	Father/Daughter
I'm a Mermaid	Part of Your World	7–9 Ballet
On a Safari	Welcome to the Jungle	Teen Hip-Hop
Join the Circus	Send in the Clowns	10–12 Beg./Int. Ballet
The Pearly Gates	Heaven Hop	10–12 Beg./Intermediate Tap
A Carousel Ride	Carousel Waltz	13+ Advanced Ballet
Time Goes By	When I'm 64	Adult Beginner Tap
Finale	Figment of Your Imagination	Entire Cast

Theme: **Don't Touch That Dial!**

TITLE	MUSIC	CLASS DESCRIPTION
Opening	Medley of TV hits	Dance Company
Cartoon Channel	Scooby-Doo	Preschool Ballet
a. Josie and the Pussycats	Josie and the Pussycats	7–9 Jazz
Survivor	I'm a Survivor	13+ Advanced Tap
Arts & Entertainment	Theme from *The Red Shoes*	10–12 Beg./Int. Ballet
Good Morning America	Good Morning	10–12 Int./Advanced Tap
American Idol	On the Wings of Love	13+ Advanced Jazz
Nickelodeon	Music, Music, Music	7–9 Tap
Travel Channel	Disney medley	Advanced Ballet Production
a. Caribbean	Hot Hot Hot	10–12 Beg./Int. Jazz
The Learning Channel	School Days	1st Act Closing
	INTERMISSION	
Animal Planet	Welcome to the Jungle	Gymnastics/Acro Prod.
a. Lions	Just Can't Wait to Be King	Preschool Tap
Home Improvement	You Better Work	10–12 Int./Adv. Jazz
ESPN	Sweet Georgia Brown	Father/Daughter
Sesame Street	Rainbow Connection	7–9 Ballet
MTV	Bye, Bye, Bye	Teen Hip-Hop
The Movie Channel	*Mary Poppins* medley	10–12 Int./Adv. Ballet
a. The Mask	Cuban Pete	10–12 Beg./Int. Tap
Disney Channel	*Fantasia* medley	13+ Advanced Ballet
Home Shopping Club	What Girls Want	Adult Beginner Tap
Finale	Sleeping With the Television On	Entire Cast

Theme: **From Sea to Shining Sea**

TITLE	MUSIC	CLASS DESCRIPTION
Opening	Coming to America	Dance Company Members
Kids in America	Kids in America	Preschool Ballet
a. At the Playground	Girls Just Wanna Have Fun	7–9 Jazz
Favorite Pastimes	Saturday Night's Alright	13+ Advanced Tap
a. Concerts	Sing a Song	10–12 Beg./Int. Ballet
b. Sports	Take Me Out to the Ballgame	10–12 Int./Advanced Tap
Vacation Spots	Echa Palante	13+ Advanced Jazz
a. Grand Ole Opry	Cotton Eye Joe	7–9 Tap
b. Disney World	Disney medley	Advanced Ballet Prod.
The Armed Forces	Captain Jack	10–12 Beg./Int. Jazz
Our Nation's Capital	Proud to Be an American	1st Act Closing
	INTERMISSION	
New York Tribute	On the Town	Gymnastics/Acro. Prod.
a. Broadway	Broadway Baby	Preschool Tap
b. Radio City Music Hall	I Wanna Be a Rockette	10–12 Int./Advanced Jazz
Blast From the Past	American Bandstand	Father/Daughter
a. '60s	Little Bitty Pretty One	7–9 Tap
America's Favorites	Like I Love You	Teen Hip-Hop
a. Academy Awards	Circle of Life	10–12 Int./Adv.Ballet
b. People's Choice Awards	The Big Time	10–12 Beg./Int. Tap
c. Grammy Awards	I Believe	13+ Advanced Ballet
d. Entertainment Tonight	Le Jazz Hot	Adult Beginner Tap
Finale	Living in America	Entire Cast

Theme: **Shop Till You Drop**

TITLE	MUSIC	CLASS DESCRIPTION
Opening	Money, Money	Dance Company Members
Pet Store	Parakeets in Tap Shoes	Preschool Ballet
a. Puppies for Sale	Who Let the Dogs Out?	7–9 Jazz
Music Store	Sing Sing Sing	13+ Advanced Tap
Toys R Us	The Doll Dance	10–12 Beg./Int. Ballet
Beauty Supplies	Hairspray	10–12 Int./Advanced Tap
Old Navy	Feelin' Good	13+ Advanced Jazz
Fine China	Be Our Guest	7–9 Tap
Christmas Tree Shop	Christmas medley	Advanced Ballet Production
Sports Authority	Are You Ready for This?	10–12 Beg./Int. Jazz
Window Shopping	Pretty Woman/Simply Irresistible	1st Act Closing
	INTERMISSION	
Comp USA	2000 Watts	Gymnastics/Acro.
Baby Gap	Baby Face	Preschool Tap
School Supplies	School Days	10–12 Int./Advanced Jazz
Bridal Shop	Butterfly Kisses	Father/Daughter
The Disney Store	Beauty and the Beast	7–9 Ballet
Video Store	AM to PM	Teen Hip-Hop
Flower Shop	Waltz of the Flowers	10–12 Int./Adv. Ballet
Barnes & Noble	The Book of Love	10–12 Beg./Int. Tap
Jewelry Store	Music from *Jewels*	13+ Advanced Ballet
Shoe Store	Hot Shoe Shuffle	Adult Beginner Tap
Finale	Medley from the show	Entire Cast

Theme: **Legends in Music**

TITLE	MUSIC	CLASS DESCRIPTION
Opening	Listen to the Music	Dance Company Members
Shirley Temple	Animal Crackers in My Soup	Preschool Ballet
Billy Joel	Uptown Girl	7–9 Jazz
Liza Minnelli	Shine It On	13+ Advanced Tap
Michael Feinstein	Pure Imagination	10–12 Beg./Int. Ballet
Elton John	Honky Cat	10–12 Int./Advanced Tap
Manhattan Transfer	Twilight Zone	13+ Advanced Jazz
Harry Connick, Jr.	Old Macdonald	7–9 Tap
George Gershwin	Rhapsody in Blue	Advanced Ballet Production
Sonny & Cher	The Beat Goes On	10–12 Beg./Int. Jazz
Neil Diamond	America	1st Act Closing
	INTERMISSION	
Bruce Springsteen	Born in the USA	Gymnastics/Acro. Prod.
Carly Simon	Itsy Bitsy Spider	Preschool Tap
Bobby Darrin	Mack the Knife	10–12 Int./Advanced Jazz
Frank Sinatra	High Hopes	Father/Daughter
Janet Jackson	Rhythm Nation	Teen Hip-Hop
Lee Ann Rimes	Amazing Grace	10–12 Int./Advanced Ballet
Judy Garland	Get Happy	10–12 Beg./Int.Tap
Celine Dion	My Heart Will Go On	13+ Advanced Ballet
Andrews Sisters	Boogie Woogie Bugle Boy	Adult Beginner Tap
Finale	That's Entertainment	Entire Cast

Theme: **Come Sail Away**

TITLE	**MUSIC**	**CLASS DESCRIPTION**
Opening	Sea Cruise	Dance Company Members
Bon Voyage	Bye, Bye Baby	Preschool Ballet
Leaving From Miami	Hot Hot Hot	7–9 Jazz
Port of Call	Mexican Mambo	13+ Advanced Tap
Sea Breeze	Sail Away	10–12 Beg./Int. Ballet
Anchors Aweigh	Anchors Aweigh	10–12 Int./Advanced Tap
Let's Celebrate	Celebration	13+ Advanced Jazz
Confetti & Streamers	Let the Good Times Roll	7–9 Tap
Captain's Ball	Masquerade from *Phantom*	Advanced Ballet Production
Game Room	Pinball Wizard	10–12 Beg./Int. Jazz
The Nightclub	Rhythm of the Night	1st Act Closing
	INTERMISSION	
Skin Diving	Under the Sea	Gymnastics/Acro Prod.
The Ship's Pool	Yellow Polka-Dot Bikini	Preschool Tap
Floor Show	I'm the Greatest Star	10–12 Int./Advanced Jazz
Casino	Luck Be a Lady	Father/Daughter
The Crew	Whistle While You Work	7–9 Ballet
Watch Out for Sharks	Scream	Teen Hip-Hop
Island Sunset	Sunrise, Sunset	10–12 Int./Adv. Ballet
Dinner With the Captain	Be Our Guest	10–12 Beg./Intermediate Tap
The Gift Shop	Waltz from *Coppélia*	13+ Advanced Ballet
Last Stop	Margaritaville	Adult Beginner Tap
Finale	Sea Cruise	Entire Cast

Theme: **On the Newsstand**

TITLE	MUSIC	CLASS DESCRIPTION
Opening	Medley from *Newsies*	Dance Company
Glamour	You're Adorable	Preschool Ballet
Consumer Reports	Shop Around	7–9 Jazz
Fortune	More	13+ Advanced Tap
Vanity Fair	True Colors	10–12 Beg./Int. Ballet
Field & Stream	A Reef With a View	10–12 Int./Advanced Tap
Teen	Funk Soul Brother	13+ Advanced Jazz
Bride Magazine	Get Me to the Church on Time	7–9 Tap
Dance Magazine	*Swan Lake* excerpt	Advanced Ballet Prod.
Shape	I'm in Shape	10–12 Beg./Int. Jazz
Variety	Broadway medley	1st Act Closing
	INTERMISSION	
Sports Illustrated	Olympic Games theme	Gymnastics/Acro Prod.
Good Housekeeping	Whistle While You Work	Preschool Tap
Wall Street Journal	Money Money	10–12 Int./Advanced Jazz
Parenting	Butterfly Kisses	Father/Daughter
Home & Garden	Wouldn't It Be Loverly?	7–9 Ballet
Seventeen	Get This Party Started	Teen Hip-Hop
National Geographic	What a Wonderful World	10–12 Int./Adv. Ballet
USA Today	Kids in America	10–12 Beg./Int. Tap
Travel & Leisure	American in Paris	13+ Advanced Ballet
The New York Times	New York, New York	Adult Beginner Tap
Finale	Extra	Entire Cast

Theme: **Chapter and Verse**

TITLE	MUSIC	CLASS DESCRIPTION
Opening	Book of Love	Dance Company
Children's Books	Charlotte's Web	Preschool Ballet
a. Mother Goose	Rappin' Rhymes	7–9 Jazz
Business & Investing	9 to 5	13+ Advanced Tap
Outdoors & Nature	Somewhere Out There	10–12 Beg./Int. Ballet
Photography	Freeze Frame	10–12 Int./Advanced Tap
History	History Repeating	13+ Advanced Jazz
Biographies	Elegance	7–9 Tap
The Classics	Excerpt from *Romeo and Juliet*	Advanced Ballet Production
Mysteries & Thrillers	Thriller	10–12 Beg./Int. Jazz
Almanac	Tornado	1st Act Closing
	INTERMISSION	
Health, Mind & Body	Time of Your Life	Gymnastics/Acro Prod.
Science Fiction	Galaxy Girls	Preschool Tap
Nonfiction	Future So Bright	10–12 Int./Advanced Jazz
Parenting	Side By Side	Father/Daughter
Arts	Ballerina Girl	7–9 Ballet
Computers & Internet	2000 Watts	Teen Hip-Hop
Literature	Excerpt from *Les Sylphides*	10–12 Int./Advanced Ballet
Travel	Choo Choo Cha Boogie	10–12 Beg./Int. Tap
Romance Novels	Somewhere in Time	13+ Advanced Ballet
Cooking, Food & Wine	I Can Cook Too	Adult Beginner Tap
Finale	Medley from the show	Entire Cast

Theme: **Leaving on a Jet Plane**

TITLE	MUSIC	CLASS DESCRIPTION
Opening	Take Off With Us	Dance Company
Hawaii	My Little Grass Shack	Preschool Ballet
Caribbean	Going' Bananas	7–9 Jazz
Paris	Diamonds	13+ Advanced Tap
Siam	March of the Siamese Children	10–12 Beg./Intermediate Ballet
Aspen	Baby, It's Cold Outside	10–12 Int./Advanced Tap
Japan	Kodo	13+ Advanced Jazz
New York	Broadway Baby	7–9 Tap
a. Theater	Music of the Night	Advanced Ballet Prod.
Rio de Janeiro	Welcome to Rio	10–12 Beg./Int. Jazz
California	Hooray for Hollywood	1st Act Closing
	INTERMISSION	
Washington, DC	Armed Forces medley	Gymnastics/Acro Prod.
The North Pole	Santa Baby	Preschool Tap
Dallas, Texas	5, 6, 7, 8	10–12 Int./Advanced Jazz
Nashville	Elvis medley	Father/Daughter
Alaska	Let It Show	7–9 Ballet
France	We Can (*Moulin Rouge*)	Teen Hip-Hop
London	Feed the Birds	10–12 Int./Adv. Ballet
Florida	Walkin' on Sunshine	10–12 Beg./Int. Tap
Egypt	Excerpt from Cirque du Soleil	13+ Advanced Ballet
Las Vegas	Luck Be a Lady	Adult Beginner Tap
Finale	Medley of upbeat songs from the show	Entire Cast

Theme: **Magic of Dance**

TITLE	MUSIC	CLASS DESCRIPTION
Opening	Magic to Do	Dance Company
Out of a Hat	Bunny Rabbit Blues	Preschool Ballet
Off to See the Wizard	We're Off to See the Wizard	7–9 Jazz
Magic Wands	Have Fun, Go Mad	13+ Advanced Tap
Bedknobs and Broomsticks	Bedknobs and Broomsticks	10–12 Beg./Int. Ballet
Peter Pan	We Can Fly	10–12 Int./Advanced Tap
Eclipse	Excerpt from Cirque du Soliel	13+ Advanced Jazz
I Dream of Jeannie	*I Dream of Jeannie* theme	7–9 Tap
Harry Potter	Medley of music from the films	Advanced Ballet Production
Sabrina the Teenage Witch	Theme from the show	10–12 Beg./Intermediate Jazz
Master Magicians	Tornado from *The Wiz*	1st Act Closing
	INTERMISSION	
Merlin	The Sorcerer's Apprentice	Gymnastics/Acro Production
Black Cats	Stray Cat Strut	Preschool Tap
Genie in a Bottle	A Friend Like Me	10–12 Int./Advanced Jazz
Voodoo Daddy	Voodoo Daddy	Father/Daughter
Puff the Magic Dragon	Puff the Magic Dragon	7–9 Ballet
Buffy the Vampire Slayer	Scream	Teen Hip-Hop
The Last Unicorn	The Last Unicorn	10–12 Int./Adv. Ballet
Shooting Stars	Swing on a Star	10–12 Beg./Int. Tap
Phantom of the Opera	Music of the Night/Think of Me	13+ Advanced Ballet
Black Magic	That Old Black Magic	Adult Beginner Tap
Finale	Do You Believe in Magic?	Entire Cast

Appendix 4
SAMPLE SHOWCASE ANNOUNCEMENT LETTER

ABC School of Dance
10 South Your Street, Anytown, ST 00000
www.webaddress.com 555/555-5555

Dear Parents,
The ABC School of Dance is proud to present its 7th Annual Dance Showcase, featuring some of the school's finest talent. This opportunity is offered to students who are recommended by their teachers and are willing to work to their highest potential. Your child has been chosen to participate in the performance, which will take place on May 19 at the Mountain View Theatre.

Showcase choreography will be scheduled over six (6) one-hour lessons between November and February. We will attempt to schedule these sessions on a day that your child is already at the studio. However, your child must be available to attend rehearsals at times other than regular class days should the need arise.

Many Showcase participants will be entered into competitions and participate in community performances in the spring. Please note that the decision regarding participation in competition is strictly up to your child's choreographer.

Your child has been chosen to perform in the following pieces:

TYPE OF DANCE	CHOREOGRAPHER	DAY/TIME	START DATE
Ballet Solo	Tom Jeté	Wed./4:00 pm	11/15
Jazz Trio	Mary Jane Chainé	Wed./5:00 pm	11/15
Tap Group	Mary Jane Chainé	Sat./1:00 pm	1/21

Participation in the ABC School Showcase requires a commitment from the student, parent, and teacher/choreographer. Studio time will be set aside to ensure that your child has adequate opportunity to learn the choreography and feel comfortable performing it. We discourage missed sessions; your child will be excused from rehearsals for emergencies only. A 48-hour advance notification is required to receive credit for the session. Please remember: Duos through small groups require a team effort, and a missed lesson affects all involved.

Choreography Fees: (not including costumes, which average $50–$100 each)

Solo	$250
Duo/Trio	$150 per dancer
Small group (4–8 dancers)	$100 per dancer

Payments for Showcase choreography are made in two installments: 50% is due on the first lesson and the balance is due on the fourth lesson.

Appendix 5
SAMPLE RECITAL PROGRAM AD FORM

ABC SCHOOL OF DANCE
Program Ad Info & Order Form

AD DEADLINE: APRIL 10 **NO LATE SUBMISSIONS**

TEXT-ONLY ADS		
Booster	$10	Up to 10 words
Booster Box (2.5 x 1.5)	$30	Text only; no photo or artwork

PHOTO ADS		
1/6 Page (2.5 x 5)	$65	Text and one photo
1/4 Page (4 x 5)	$85	Text and one photo*
1/2 Page (8 x 5)	$150	Text and one photo*
Full Page (8 x 10.5)	$275	Text and one photo*
* additional photos $10 each		

The printer will professionally design each ad to insure consistency. Please use the back of this form to lay out your ad (one form per ad). The ABC School of Dance and/or the printer are not responsible for errors. You will have the opportunity to approve your ad at the school office during the week of May 1.

<table>
<tr><td colspan="6">Student Name:</td></tr>
<tr><td colspan="6">Parent Signature:</td></tr>
<tr><td colspan="3">Telephone:</td><td colspan="3">Email:</td></tr>
<tr><td colspan="6">Ad Size (circle one)</td></tr>
<tr><td>Booster</td><td>Booster
Box</td><td>1/6</td><td>1/4</td><td>1/2</td><td>FULL</td></tr>
<tr><td colspan="3"># of photos _____</td><td colspan="3">Amount Enclosed ________________</td></tr>
</table>

Return this form with photo(s) and full payment to the school office by April 10. Please make your ad reservations early; space is limited.

Appendix 6
SAMPLE PHOTO SHOOT ANNOUNCEMENT

ABC SCHOOL OF DANCE PICTURE NOTICE

Student Name: ______________________________

PLEASE BE PROMPT; WE ALWAYS START ON TIME.

Date	Time Slot	Costume	Tights	Shoes
March 12	2:30 pm	Jazz	Capezio 101	Black Oxford

Students who train in more than one style will be photographed in the costume specified above. All gymnastics classes will also be photographed. Each student also has the option to have a solo portrait done.

Fee: $8 per dancer for class pictures. (Covers the cost of placing group photos in the program. No photo included; prints may be ordered.) Fee must be paid in advance.

Photo packages start at $11. Information on package options, pricing, and ordering will be available at the school the week before the recital.

Required tights and shoes are listed above. Other required accessories are listed on the chart posted on the school bulletin board. ONLY THE TIGHTS LISTED ABOVE MAY BE USED (to insure that all students have the same shade and weight).

All ankle socks must be plain white with no lace or trim.

All students should wear light makeup, and girls must wear their hair in a French braid or bun for class pictures. Students may wear their hair any style for solo pictures.

Tights, shoes, gloves, shoe paint, and accessories are available at the studio at discount prices.

Appendix 7
SAMPLE REGISTRATION FORM

ABC SCHOOL OF DANCE REGISTRATION FORM		
Student Name		
Address		
City	State	Zip Code
Tel #1	Tel #2	
Email:	Would you like to receive the school newsletter via email? Yes No	
Name: Parent Guardian #1 Occupation:		
Name: Parent/Guardian #2 Occupation:		
In case of emergency, please notify		
Emergency Telephone		
Student's Age (as of 9/1)	Birth Date	

Programs or curriculum choices: Creative Movement (ages 3-4) ❑ Kinder-Movement 1 (ages 5-6) ❑ Ballet ❑ Pointe ❑ Tap ❑ Jazz ❑ Hip-Hop ❑ Acrobatics ❑ Adult Program ❑ Intensive Program ❑ Boys Class ❑ Apprentice Teacher Program (14+) ❑		
Previous training? Please list past experience in dance (include styles of dance and number of years) Name of previous dance school:		
Any health or physical restrictions?		
Which days would you prefer that your child attend classes?		
Weekday ❑	Saturday ❑	Either ❑
How did you hear about our school?		
Newspaper ❑	Phone Book ❑	Web site ❑
Performance ❑	Word of Mouth ❑	Other ❑
Please note: We have a dress code! Please pick up the dress code information sheet at the front desk.		

Appendix 8
SAMPLE MEDICAL RELEASE FORM

ABC SCHOOL OF DANCE
Medical Release Form

I, ______________________________ (parent/guardian's name) hereby give permission for any and all medical attention to be administered to my child __________________________ (child's name) in the event of accident, injury, sickness, etc., under the direction of the physician(s) listed below or at any necessary emergency facility, until such time as I may be contacted. I also assume the responsibility for the payment of any such treatment. This release is effective for the period of one year from the date given below.

ADDRESS: ____
____
____

HOME PHONE: ____

INSURANCE COMPANY: ____________________________________

POLICY NUMBER: ____

CHILD'S PHYSICIAN: _____________________________________

ADDRESS: ____

PHONE: ____

KNOWN ALLERGIES: ______________________________________

SIGNATURE (PARENT/GUARDIAN) ___________________________

DATE ________________

Appendix 9

SAMPLE ADS

ABC School of Dance

A 20-year tradition!

Age 3 through adult
Preschool Programs, Ballet, Tap, Jazz,
Hip-Hop, Modern, Tumbling,
Boys Classes, Adult Programs

Step #1...HAPPY CHILDREN

Step #2...Motivating young minds to be the best they can be!

Register this week Mon.- Sat.
12 noon to 7:00 PM
Classes begin Sept. 7
FREE BROCHURE 555-555-5555

100 Any Street
Anytown, USA
www.abcdance.com
555-555-5555

Let your spirit soar...

Dance!

www.abcdance.com

100 Any Street, Anytown, USA
555-555-5555

ABC School of Dance

Register this week
12 noon to 7:00 PM

FREE
BROCHURE
555-555-5555

Making dreams come true for 20 years!

ABC
School of Dance

Register this week
Mon.-Sat.
12 noon to 7:00 PM
Classes begin Sept. 7
FREE BROCHURE
555-555-5555
www.abcdance.com

100 Any Street, Anytown, USA
555-555-5555

WWW.ABCDANCE.COM
555-555-5555

HIP-HOP CLASSES
WWW.ABCDANCE.COM
555-555-5555

PRESCHOOL DANCE
WWW.ABCDANCE.COM
555-555-5555

ADULT TAP & JAZZ DANCE
WWW.ABCDANCE.COM
555-555-5555

Appendix 10
SAMPLE PARENT SURVEY

ABC School of Dance
10 South Your Street, Anytown, ST 00000
www.webaddress.com 555/555-5555

May 2003

Dear Friends:

We would like to thank you for having your child participate in our dance program and annual recital. It is our goal to provide your child with a positive, nurturing learning environment along with the best dance training we can offer. With your support, we have been able to do so for the past 15 years.

It is also our goal to offer parents a supportive environment conducive to open communication. Your input is important to us; many of the changes we have made in our operations and policies over the years have come from listening to the needs of parents and students. As we prepare for the next season, we'd like to hear from you. Attached is a survey that we at ABC Studio of Dance consider a valuable tool. Please take a few minutes to fill it out, and feel free to add any other comments.

We look forward to seeing you and your child in the fall.

Sincerely,

Director,
ABC School of Dance

ABC School of Dance
Parent Survey

Student's name (optional): ____________________________________

Please rate the following:	Excellent	Good	Fair	Poor
Quality of instruction				
Convenience of class scheduling				
Courteous, helpful service				
Tuition rates				
Convenience of location				
Appearance of studio				
Timeliness and clarity of newsletters, bulletins, flyers, etc.				
Quality of dancewear sold				
Prices of dancewear sold				

Has your child enjoyed his/her classes this season?

Do you feel that your child/children learned a great deal about dance and/or progressed technically?

Please rank the following in order of importance (1 being most important):

__ Location or schedule
__ Quality of instruction and/or instructor's background
__ Teacher's rapport with children
__ Cost of tuition or costumes
__ Recital

Please rate the following recital issues:	Excellent	Good	Fair	Poor
General policies and procedures				
Photo packages and quality				
Quality and prices of costumes/access				
Video quality and price				
Flower-ordering procedure and prices				
Rehearsal schedule				
Ticket policy				
Backstage policies				
Quality of recital				

If your child will not be returning to ABC School of Dance, please select the reason that applies best:

__ My child lost interest in dance.
__ Dissatisfaction with school policies or instructor
__ Dance lessons became too expensive
__ Time schedule became too demanding or involved
__ Unhappy with quality of instruction
__ Other (please explain)

If you could change one thing about ABC School of Dance, what would it be?

Comments and suggestions:

Thank you!

Appendix 11
SAMPLE PRESS RELEASES

Note: Sample below should be double-spaced.

ABC School of Dance
10 South Your Street, Anytown, ST 00000
www.webaddress.com 555/555-5555

FOR IMMEDIATE RELEASE

CONTACT: Mary Jane Cambré, Artistic Director
10 South Your Street, Anytown, ST 00000
Studio: 555-555-5555
Home: 555-555-5555

Anytown, ST, July 10, 2003

ABC SCHOOL OF DANCE TO HOST OPEN HOUSE

The ABC School of Dance, located in the Center Shopping Complex in Anytown, under the artistic direction of Mary Jane Cambré, announces an open house for young people interested in dance. The event will take place Saturday, August 28 at 4:00 p.m. It will feature a performance by the school's competition teams and a tour of the newly renovated studios.

Other activities will include an open preschool class for boys and girls ages 3 through 6 at 3:00 p.m. This special class will be taught by faculty member Tammy Tombé, who has a degree in dance and preschool education and has been on the school's staff for 12 years.

The ABC School was founded in 1981 by Ms. Cambré and has attracted thousands of young dancers from throughout the South Shore area for 22 years. The facility offers four classrooms with state-of-the-art equipment, ballet barres, and hardwood floors. The curriculum includes ballet, tap, jazz, acrobatics, and preschool and adult programs for beginner through professional levels. Fall classes begin September 6. For more information contact the studio between 10:00 a.m. and 4:00 p.m. weekdays at 555/555-5555.

END

ABC School of Dance
10 South Your Street, Anytown, ST 00000
www.webaddress.com 555/555-5555

FOR IMMEDIATE RELEASE

CONTACT: Mary Jane Cambré, Artistic Director
10 South Your Street, Anytown, ST 00000
Studio: 555-555-5555
Home: 555-555-5555

Anytown, ST, July 10, 2003

ABC SCHOOL DANCER WINS BIG HONOR

The ABC School of Dance is proud to announce that 17-year-old Tina Chassé, of Anytown, recently won the title of Northeast Miss Dance. The competition, held in Boston, featured 35 contestants from throughout New England and New York. The Dance Teachers Association of America, Northeast Chapter, presented the award.

The three-day event features several categories of competition, including interview, classes, and talent. Contestants have the opportunity to work with a professional choreographer on a special opening number for the competition. Each participant presents a three-minute performance in the genre of their choice.

Ms. Chassé, a junior at Taunton High School and a member of the honor society, has trained in ballet, tap, and jazz for the past 12 years at the ABC School, located at the Center Shopping Complex in Anytown. Her performance, *Wind Beneath My Wings,* was choreographed by Ms. Cambré and received rave reviews from the audience and judges. Ms. Chassé will represent the Northeast Chapter of the Dance Teachers Association at the America's Miss Dance Scholarship Competition in Los Angeles. At the national level there will be 25 chapter representatives from across the United States and Canada vying for the title of America's Miss Dance. More than $10,000 in scholarships will be presented, and the winners will appear at special engagements throughout the United States and Canada representing their titles.

END

ABC School of Dance
10 South Your Street, Anytown, ST 00000
www.webaddress.com 555/555-5555

FOR IMMEDIATE RELEASE

CONTACT: Mary Jane Cambré, Artistic Director
10 South Your Street, Anytown, ST 00000
Studio: 555-555-5555
Home: 555-555-5555

Anytown, ST, May 18, 2003

AMERICAN DANCE COMPANY'S BETTY SUE FONDU JOINS ABC SCHOOL FACULTY

The ABC School of Dance is proud to introduce its newest faculty member, Betty Sue Fondu. Ms. Fondu has danced with the world-famous American Dance Company for the past five years. With the company, she has traveled the world, both as a dancer and assistant choreographer.

Ms. Fondu was born and raised in Boston, where she studied with the Boston Ballet and several modern studios in Massachusetts, Connecticut, and New York. She has a bachelor's degree in dance from the Boston Conservatory and received a contract with the American Dance Company upon graduation.

She has taught at New York's Broadway Dance Center and Steps on Broadway studios. At the ABC School, Ms. Fondu will offer classes in both modern and jazz to dancers ages 8 and over. For more information or to receive a school brochure, call 555/555-5555 today. Classes start September 6.

END

Appendix 12
SAMPLE FINANCIAL REPORTS #1

Detailed reports showing income, expenses, and per-class profit (recreational and intensive dancer programs) for a moderate-size dance school

Report #1:
SCHOOL FINANCIAL STATISTICS FOR REGULAR (NON-INTENSIVE) CLASSES ONLY

Enrollment:	250 students
Faculty:	4 teachers, including owner
Staff:	1 office person
Number of classes:	30 classes (hours) per week

Tuition rates:	
1 hour tuition:	$44/month
2nd hour tuition:	$40/month (total $84/month)
Intensive dancers:	$125/month (5 classes/week)

Teaching wages: 2@ $17/ hour; 1 @ $25/hour; owner @ $30/hour

The following does not include private lessons, costumes, recital, summer program, or in-house merchandise sales. This report also does not reflect dropouts. Two reports should be prepared annually: approximately one month after opening for the season and one month before closing the season.

CLASS INCOME

CLASS INCOME (9 MOS)		MONTHLY	ANNUAL
100 students (preschool & recreational)	@ $44/mo.	$4,400	$39,600
75 students (recreational)	@ $84/mo.	$6,300	$56,700
75 students (Intensive)	@ $125	$9,375	$84,375
TOTAL		**$20,075**	**$180,675**

CLASS EXPENSES
Note: We separate general expenses from payroll, for the purpose of preparing report #2.

This is a simple report demonstrating a procedure you may utilize to determine the profitability of your school, based on classes. Your report may include additional or other expenses not indicated below, such as snow removal, trash removal, post office box rental, indoor and outdoor maintenance, cleaning, etc. Your accountant can tell you your various expense categories and the totals, or if you utilize Quick Books or another accounting program, the categories and figures will be available.

GENERAL EXPENSES (12 MONTHS)		**MONTHLY**	**ANNUAL**
Rent		$3,500	$42,000
Utilities		$700	$8,400
Telephone		$125	$1,500
Insurance			$5,000
Brochure/Ads			$3,500
Newsletter	$0.50 x 300 x 4		$600
Brochure Mail	$0.37 x 350		$129.50
Newsletter Mail	$0.37 x 300 x 4		$444
Office Supplies		$125	$1,500
Equipment			$2,500
Accounting		$125	$1,500
Health insurance (owner)		$400	$4,800
Office help @ $10/hr	x 30 hours wk.=120/month	$1,200 (9 mos.)	$10,800
Extra office help @ $10/hr	x 100 hours annually		$1,000
Payroll taxes, workers' comp.		$1,500 (9 mos.)	$13,500
TOTAL			**$97,173.50**

PAYROLL/9 MO. SEASON		MONTHLY	ANNUAL
Teacher @ $17	x 8 classes/wk. =32/month	$544	$4,896
Teacher @ $25	x 17 classes/wk. =68/month	$1,700	$15,300
Teacher @ $30	x 5 classes/wk. =20/month	$600	$5,400
TOTAL			**$25,596**

GRAND TOTAL CLASS PROFIT

INCOME VS. EXPENSES		MONTHLY	ANNUAL
Gross Class Income			$180,675
Gross Class Expense			$122,769.50 ($97,173.50 + $25,596)
Profit			**$57,905.50**

PER-CLASS PROFIT BREAKDOWN

COST PER CLASS				
30 classes/ wk.	120 classes/ mo.	1080 classes annual (9 mos.)	Divided by expense $122,769.50	**$113.68 per class**

GROSS PER CLASS				
30 classes/ wk.	120 classes/ mo.	1080 classes annual (9 mos.)	Divided by income $180,675	**$167.29 per class**

PROFIT PER CLASS	
Gross per class minus cost per class	**$53.61 per class**

Financial Report #2

FINANCIAL STATISTICS FOR THE INTENSIVE DIVISION

INTENSIVE DIVISION TEACHER EXPENSE BREAKDOWN
When determining the profit for an individual division of your school, there may be various wages paid to different teachers.

INTENSIVE DIVISION TEACHER EXPENSE				
14 classes/wk. =56 hours/mo.				
	Rate #1 36 classes @ $25/hr.= $900/mo.	Rate #2 20 classes @ $30/hr. = $600/mo.	Monthly total: 56 classes @ both rates = $1,500	Annual total: 504 classes @ both rates $13,500

TAKE THE GENERAL EXPENSE FROM REPORT #1:

GENERAL EXPENSE FROM REPORT #1	
General class expense total ($97,173.50) from report #1 (not including payroll), divided by 1,080 (grand total of all classes annually) from report #1	$89.98 per class

Continued on next page

INTENSIVE DIVISION PROFIT PER CLASS

ANNUAL INTENSIVE DIVISION INCOME	
75 students @ $125 (total $9,375/month x 9 mos.)	**$84,375**

INTENSIVE DIVISION EXPENSE	
Multiply $89.98 x 504 classes annually	$45,349.92
Add to that Intensive Division teacher expense	$13,500
TOTAL EXPENSE	**$58,849.92**

INTENSIVE DIVISION PROFIT	**$25,525.08**

PER-CLASS PROFIT	
504 Intensive Division classes annually, divided into the annual profit ($25,530.12)	**$50.65 per class**

Appendix 13
SAMPLE TUITION PAYMENT ENVELOPE AND COUPON BOOK

The ABC School of Dance Tuition Payment Envelope

Please discount your total by $5 if payment is made prior to the 7th of the month.

Student Name:		
Date:	Amount Paid:	
Payment description: If you choose "other," please indicate the account on back.		
❏ Tuition	❏ Costume	❏ Other
Amt. $	Amt. $	Amt. $
Please check one:		
❏ Check	❏ Cash	❏ Credit Card
Note: Do not put your credit information on the front of this envelope. We have your information on file. However, please sign the credit authorization below.		

I authorize the full payment listed above to be charged to my credit card on file at the school.

Authorized Signature: ______________________________

The ABC School of Dance Tuition Payment Coupon

Payment No.	Account Number	Amount Due	Due Date
49	123456789	$175	12/01/03
		Amount Due	If Received After
		$180	12/07/03

Sally Arabesque
123 Jete Street
Anytown, USA

Amount Enclosed ____________

DISCLAIMER

This text is intended as a guide to educate, entertain, and motivate the reader, and does not guarantee specific results by following its recommendations. It is not intended as the ultimate source of information on teaching dance and/or operating a dance school; it represents the opinions and experiences of the author, his associates, and participants in Project Motivate seminars. As such, the author and Gold Standard Press shall have neither liability nor responsibility to any person or entity with respect to any loss or damage caused, or alleged to have been caused, directly or indirectly, by the information contained in this book.

The monetary amounts specified in this book are intended as guidelines only and are current only up to the date of publication.

The documents included in the appendices and on the accompanying compact disc are intended for use as customizable templates. The information therein is provided as an example or sample; the author and publisher are not engaged in rendering legal, accounting, or other services. If legal or other expert services are required, the services of a competent professional should be retained.

If you do not wish to be bound by the above, you may return this book to the publisher for a full refund.

INDEX

I

K

L

M

N

P

R

WOULD YOU LIKE MORE COPIES OF THIS BOOK?

Fax: Send this page to 508/285-3179.

Telephone: Call 508/285-6650. Have your credit card information ready.

Email: rhee@rheegold.com

Internet: Go to www.rheegold.com and click on "Products."

Mail: Gold Standard Press, P.O. Box 2150, Norton, MA 02766

Please send information on: Project Motivate: the Teacher Edition ❑
Project Motivate: the Student Edition ❑
Individual Consultation ❑

Name:_______________________________________
Address:_____________________________________
City: ____________________ State: ______Zip: _______
Telephone: ___________________________
Email address: ______________________________
Number of books ordered: ____________ @ $39.99 each

I would like to receive the *Goldrush* newsletter. Yes ____ No _____

Sales tax: Please add 5% for products shipped to Massachusetts addresses.

Shipping by air:
U.S.: $4.00 for first book and $2.00 for each additional book
International: $9.00 for first book and $5.00 for each additional book (estimate)

Payment method: Check _____ Credit card _____
Visa __ MasterCard __ AmEx ___ Discover __
Card number:_________________________________
Name on card: _______________________________
Expiration date: ________________